MODERN TRACTI

CLASSES 24 - 27

edited by
PAUL CHANCELLOR

RCTS PUBLICATIONS

rcts.org.uk

ISBN 978-1-0683883-3-0

Published by
The Railway Correspondence and Travel Society
16 Welby Close
Maidenhead SL6 3PY
United Kingdom

Printed by Spellman Walker of Bradford.

Typesetting and page layout by RCTS Members

FRONTISPIECE

ABOVE

Class 26 26037 awaits the arrival of Class 25, 25064, at Invergordon on 6th August 1976.

(D. L. Dott/Colour-Rail.com

FRONT COVER

Class 24 5077 in blue livery with full yellow ends passes Weston Rhyn with a train of track panels in April 1974. *(Colour-Rail.com*

REAR COVER

Blue and green Class 24s and Class 25s gather around the turntable in Leeds Holbeck Roundhouse on 19th May 1968.

(E. J. Gulash/Colour-Rail.com

FOREWORD

The whys and wherefores of locomotive histories and allocations have intrigued enthusiasts for almost as long as there have been engines to record. For well over a century such information was hard to come by requiring much research as the owning companies did not make it public. Whilst Societies such as the RCTS started to publish limited allocation data between the two World Wars it took the arrival of the Ian Allan abc series of books to popularise the spotting hobby and formalise loco information. This was enhanced by the later addition of the Locoshed series of books giving the allocation of each engine. However, such books only gave the details of the current fleet and its location.

Fast forward into the 21st century, but before the widespread use of the internet, and we had a new series of books compiled by Roger Harris that purported show the operational history of every modern traction locomotive that had been used on the network. Roger stopped updating that information in 2015 but history building rolled on! At the same time many internet sites blossomed, mostly concentrating on individual classes and varying in the quantity and quality of the information provided. It appeared that no single source covered every locomotive from cradle to grave.

With its track record of accurate and comprehensive record keeping the RCTS has taken on the task of providing this complete listing via the development of its locodata.org.uk website, but while many enthusiasts like its instant access capability, we know that others like to have a 'book on the shelf', hence the production of this, the second of many volumes, that will make all of that data available in book form.

Thanks are extended to Andrew Lait for assistance in presenting the data for this title.

INTRODUCTION

USER NOTES

In the following pages you will find the complete listing of numbering and renumbering, allocations, namings, withdrawal and subsequent history for all the Class 24-27 Type 2 locomotives. The events are listed in date order for each engine. Stock change data is followed in the text by a date that has a suffix as follows:

E denotes an exact date, M a month and Y just a year, this latter signifying that the event took place and possibly in that year. For month dates we have to point out that these are generally based on BR advice and the regions employed different systems with some giving a week of movement, some a calendar month, whilst others used 'four week' periods which overlapped a month end. In the case of the latter the month quoted for a move has been taken as the month in which the period ended.

Sectorisation saw locomotives allocated to depots operated by their relevant sector which were often a considerable distance from where the locomotive was actually in use and this trend increased with privatisation and the gradual closure of many of the remaining depots. It should also be noted that information such as loco allocation and use became 'commercially sensitive' and a number of post-privatisation entries relate to 'personal sightings' rather than being based on information from the operators.

CONTENTS

RCTS Modern Traction Loco Data - Part 2 - Classes 24 - 27

Allocation History Class 24 1
Allocation History Class 25 33
Allocation History Class 26 111
Allocation History Class 27 129
Names Carried in BR Use 150
Class Renumberings 151
Specimen Allocations 152

CLASS 24

The first order for what was to become Class 24 under the TOPS scheme was placed as part of the BR Modernisation plan in 1955 which called for small orders of a number of locomotive designs in each power classification to enable evaluation prior to a decision on the best designs to take forward.

There was a plethora of Type 2 offerings but mass orders were placed before much, if any, information had been gained about performance in service and the BR-built Type 2 was selected alongside what later became Class 31. They were Bo-Bo diesel-electrics fitted with an 1,160 hp Sulzer 6LDA28A engine with British Thomson Houston traction motors. The first of the class was delivered in 1958 with the first 30 being constructed at Derby Works as were D5066-75 and D5149-50. Crewe Works was responsible for D5030-D5065 and D5076-D5093 whilst D5094 to D5148 came from Darlington, this batch being the first diesel locomotives to be built there. Given the three sources it is hardly surprising that deliveries were not in numerical order but all were in service by 1961.

The first arrivals were for operation in the Crewe and Derby areas, but fifteen were soon moved to the Southern Region to cover for delays in the Kent Coast Electrification scheme. Here the heavy weight was not acceptable and the locomotives in question had to have their boilers removed before they were accepted. The LMR examples in the London area found employment on some secondary passenger duties but empty stock movements at Euston and freight services were the main duties allocated.

The Eastern Region was the beneficiary of the next tranche with March and Ipswich sheds being favoured with the aim of the complete elimination steam from the area. These were primarily intended for freight duties but, in due course, they were ousted from the area by the arrival of many Brush Type 2s, also the decline in freight work and they gravitated to LMR work in the north west and north Wales. The North Eastern Region was the recipient of D5096 to D5113 initially at both Leeds and Newcastle but in due course the batch became associated with the working of Tyne Dock to Consett iron ore services, being fitted with equipment to work the air-operated wagon discharge doors.

D5114-32 were allocated to Inverness and became synonymous with rail operations in the Scottish Highlands both passenger and freight. D5114 was the first of the class to have the four digit reporting number panels. The final batch of Class 24s were allocated to the London Midland Region for use on the 'Western Lines' which included duties on the Cambrian lines in due course but not until the mid 1960s when the class, along with the Class 25s became the only regular power on the line, other than DMUs. The ever evolving motive power scene eventually saw the class working primarily in the northwest of England and southern Scotland with many former England-based examples moving north of the border.

For what was considered a 'standard' type the Class 24s had a relatively short life as once the various non-standard Type 2 classes had been eliminated the 24s were next in line for condemnation as BR motive power requirements shrunk. That said, a number did not even make it to the TOPS renumbering as the class seemed to be particularly prone to accident damage. The final member of the class was condemned in 1980. Most were cut up at BR works including Swindon. However, three were selected for Departmental use which in due course enabled them to be rescued for preservation along with D5032 which had been acquired from a scrap yard for use on the North Yorkshire Moors Railway.

Both TOPS renumbering and livery application were fairly simple for the Class 24s with all except D5000 receiving a TOPS number directly relatable to the one originally carried whilst the class went through the standard progression of liveries of green, then green with yellow panels or full yellow ends to BR blue with full yellow ends.

D5000
Allocated to Derby Works 07/58, possibly for evaluation trials.
5B Crewe South 05/09/1958 E
17A Derby 09/1958 M
73C Hither Green 27/01/1959 E
1A Willesden 06/1962 M
73C Hither Green 06/1962 M
1A Willesden 07/1962 M
5A Crewe North 08/1963 M
1A Willesden 09/1963 M
1B Camden 01/1965 M
1A Willesden 02/1965 M
1E Bletchley 09/1965 M
D01 London Division (WCML) 18/04/1966 E
D05 Stoke Division 04/1967 M
Store 01/1969 M
Withdrawn 04/01/1969 E
55A Leeds Holbeck 05/10/1969 E
Reinstated 05/10/1969 E
66A Polmadie 10/1971 M
65A Eastfield 03/1972 M
Renumbered 24005 11/1973 M
LO Longsight 01/1975 M
Store 06/07/1975 E
Stored at Reddish 06/07/75
Withdrawn 31/01/1976 E
Remained stored at Reddish, then moved to ZL Swindon Works 15/02/77 and cut up by 18/04/77.

D5001
Allocated to Derby Works 08/58, possibly for evaluation trials.
5B Crewe South 29/10/1958 E
17A Derby 01/11/1958 E
73C Hither Green 04/02/1959 E
1A Willesden 06/1962 M
73C Hither Green 06/1962 M
1A Willesden 07/1962 M
1C Watford 09/1962 M
1A Willesden 02/1963 M
5A Crewe North 08/1963 M
1A Willesden 09/1963 M
1B Camden 01/1965 M
1A Willesden 02/1965 M
1F Rugby 09/1965 M
2F Bescot 03/1966 M
D02 Birmingham Division 18/04/1966 E
D01 London Division (WCML) 09/1966 M
D05 Stoke Division 04/1967 M
Withdrawn 01/1969 M
55A Leeds Holbeck 10/1969 M

D5001 contd.
Reinstated 10/1969 M
66A Polmadie 10/1971 M
65A Eastfield 03/1972 M
Renumbered 24001 16/04/1974 E
LO Longsight 01/1975 M
ED Eastfield 02/1975 M
Store 07/07/1975 E
Stored at Carlisle Kingmoor 07/07/75
Withdrawn 05/10/1975 E
Remained stored at Carlisle Kingmoor, then moved to ZF Doncaster Works for scrap 26/10/77 and cut up by 25/11/77.

D5002
5B Crewe South 03/12/1958 E
17A Derby 12/1958 M
73C Hither Green 20/01/1959 E
5B Crewe South 05/1962 M
1A Willesden 05/1962 M
5B Crewe South 06/1962 M
2A Rugby 06/1962 M
Allocation recoded 2A to 1F 09/1963 M
1E Bletchley 06/1965 M
1F Rugby 03/1966 M
D01 London Division (WCML) 18/04/1966 E
D05 Stoke Division 04/1967 M
Store 01/1969 M
D05 Stoke Division 03/1969 M
Returned to Service 03/1969 M
65A Eastfield 03/1971 M
Allocation recoded 65A to ED 05/1973 M
Renumbered 24002 04/1974 M
Store 07/07/1975 E
Stored at Carlisle 07/07/75
Withdrawn 05/10/1975 E
Remained stored at Carlisle, then moved to ZH Glasgow Works 15/3/76 and cut up by 07/77, leaving only the cab remains, disposed of in 07/78.

D5003
5B Crewe South 12/12/1958 E
17A Derby 12/1958 M
73C Hither Green 24/01/1959 E
5B Crewe South 04/1960 M
73C Hither Green 05/1960 M
5B Crewe South 03/1962 M
1A Willesden 03/1962 M
5B Crewe South 06/1962 M
2A Rugby 06/1962 M
Allocation recoded 2A to 1F 09/1963 M
1E Bletchley 06/1965 M
D01 London Division (WCML) 18/04/1966 E

D5003 contd.

D05 Stoke Division 04/1967 M
65A Eastfield 03/1971 M
Allocation recoded 65A to ED 05/1973 M
Renumbered 24003 04/1974 M
Store 07/07/1975 E
Withdrawn 16/08/1975 E
Stored at Polmadie 16/08/75, moved to Carlisle later the same month and then to ZH Glasgow Works 10/75, both for further storage. Moved to ZF Doncaster Works 23/01/76 and broken up 07/76.

D5004

5B Crewe South 22/12/1958 E
17A Derby 01/1959 M
73C Hither Green 27/01/1959 E
5B Crewe South 01/1960 M
73C Hither Green 03/1960 M
1A Willesden 06/1962 M
73C Hither Green 06/1962 M
1A Willesden 09/1962 M
1B Camden 01/1965 M
1A Willesden 02/1965 M
1F Rugby 09/1965 M
D01 London Division (WCML) 18/04/1966 E
D05 Stoke Division 04/1967 M
65A Eastfield 03/1971 M
Allocation recoded 65A to ED 05/1973 M
Renumbered 24004 03/1974 M
LO Longsight 01/1975 M
ED Eastfield 02/1975 M
Store 07/07/1975 E
Stored at Carlisle 07/07/75
Withdrawn 05/10/1975 E
Remained stored at Carlisle, then moved to ZH Glasgow Works 15/03/76 and cut up 05/77, leaving the cabs only on 04/06/77. These were still on site on 27/05/84 and are believed disposed of by 12/84.

D5005

5B Crewe South 03/01/1959 E
17A Derby 01/1959 M
73C Hither Green 25/01/1959 E
5B Crewe South 06/1960 M
73C Hither Green 08/1960 M
5B Crewe South 05/1962 M
5A Crewe North 05/1962 M
5B Crewe South 06/1962 M
2A Rugby 06/1962 M
Allocation recoded 2A to 1F 09/1963 M
1E Bletchley 06/1965 M
D01 London Division (WCML) 18/04/1966 E

D5005 contd.

D05 Stoke Division 04/1967 M
Withdrawn 25/01/1969 E
During 1969 both D5005 and D5025 were involved in incidents. This appears to have resulted in the body shell of D5005 being used to create a rebuilt D5025.
Moved to ZE Derby Works, noted there 15/06/69 minus cabs and was broken up 12/69.

D5006

5B Crewe South 03/01/1959 E
17A Derby 01/1959 M
73C Hither Green 30/01/1959 E
5B Crewe South 03/1960 M
73C Hither Green 04/1960 M
5B Crewe South 03/1962 M
5A Crewe North 05/1962 M
1F Rugby 09/1963 M
5A Crewe Diesel 07/1965 M
1F Rugby 09/1965 M
D01 London Division (WCML) 18/04/1966 E
D05 Stoke Division 04/1967 M
65A Eastfield 03/1971 M
Allocation recoded 65A to ED 05/1973 M
Renumbered 24006 04/1974 M
Store 07/07/1975 E
Stored at Eastfield 07/07/75
Withdrawn 16/08/1975 E
Remained stored at Eastfield, then moved to ZH Glasgow Works 09/80 and cut up 12/80, with bogies only left on 01/02/81.

D5007

5B Crewe South 07/02/1959 E
17A Derby 02/1959 M
73C Hither Green 16/03/1959 E
1A Willesden 06/1962 M
73C Hither Green 06/1962 M
1A Willesden 11/1962 M
1B Camden 01/1965 M
1E Bletchley 12/1965 M
D01 London Division (WCML) 18/04/1966 E
D05 Stoke Division 04/1967 M
Store 01/1969 M
D05 Stoke Division 13/08/1969 E
Returned to Service 13/08/1969 E
65A Eastfield 03/1971 M
Allocation recoded 65A to ED 05/1973 M
Renumbered 24007 04/1974 M
Store 07/07/1975 E
Stored at Carlisle 07/07/75
Withdrawn 05/10/1975 E

D5007 contd.

Remained stored at Carlisle, then moved to ZF Doncaster Works 08/12/77 and scrapped 01/78.

D5008

5B Crewe South 28/02/1959 E
17A Derby 03/1959 M
73C Hither Green 16/03/1959 E
5B Crewe South 05/1959 M
18A Toton 05/1959 M
17A Derby 09/1959 M
5B Crewe South 10/1959 M
1B Camden 10/1959 M
73C Hither Green 01/1960 M
1B Camden 07/1962 M
1C Watford 09/1962 M
Allocation to Watford unconfirmed, not shown in BR official returns 09/1962 M
12B Upperby 10/1962 M
1B Camden 12/1962 M
5A Crewe North 01/1963 M
1A Willesden 09/1965 M
1F Rugby 01/1966 M
D01 London Division (WCML) 18/04/1966 E
D05 Stoke Division 04/1967 M
65A Eastfield 03/1971 M
Allocation recoded 65A to ED 05/1973 M
Store 03/1974 M
Stored at St. Rollox Works with fire damage 03/74
Renumbered 24008 07/1974 M
Renumbered to 24008 while at St. Rollox Works, then moved to Cadder Yard, Glasgow 07/75 for further storage
Withdrawn 16/08/1975 E
Remained stored at Cadder Yard, Glasgow. Moved to ZH Glasgow Works 10/75, then to ZF Doncaster Works 18/02/76 and cut up there in 05/76.

D5009

5B Crewe South 14/03/1959 E
17A Derby 03/1959 M
73C Hither Green 25/03/1959 E
5B Crewe South 05/1962 M
5A Crewe North 05/1962 M
1A Willesden 11/1963 M
5A Crewe North 12/1964 M
1B Camden 01/1965 M
1E Bletchley 12/1965 M
D01 London Division (WCML) 18/04/1966 E
D05 Stoke Division 04/1967 M
65A Eastfield 03/1971 M

D5009 contd.

Allocation recoded 65A to ED 05/1973 M
Renumbered 24009 04/1974 M
Store 08/1975 M
HA Haymarket 08/09/1975 E
Returned to Service 08/09/1975 E
Store 05/1976 M
Stored at Carstairs 05/76
Withdrawn 18/07/1976 E
Remained stored at Carstairs, moved to ZF Doncaster Works 08/77 and broken up by 25/11/77.

D5010

5B Crewe South 21/03/1959 E
17A Derby 03/1959 M
73C Hither Green 06/04/1959 E
5B Crewe South 05/1962 M
21D Aston 05/1962 M
5B Crewe South 06/1962 M
2A Rugby 06/1962 M
Allocation recoded 2A to 1F 09/1963 M
1E Bletchley 06/1965 M
D01 London Division (WCML) 18/04/1966 E
D02 Birmingham Division 07/1966 M
D05 Stoke Division 05/1967 M
Store 01/1969 M
Withdrawn 25/01/1969 E
D05 Stoke Division 29/07/1969 E
Reinstated 29/07/1969 E
66A Polmadie 10/1971 M
65A Eastfield 03/1972 M
Allocation recoded 65A to ED 05/1973 M
Renumbered 24010 04/1974 M
Store 07/07/1975 E
Stored at Carlisle 07/07/75
Withdrawn 05/10/1975 E
Remained stored at Carlisle, moved ZH Glasgow Works 15/03/76 and then moved to Doncaster but was held at Doncaster shed until late 08/76 when it entered ZF Doncaster Works and was cut up 01/77.

D5011

5B Crewe South 28/03/1959 E
17A Derby 03/1959 M
73C Hither Green 10/04/1959 E
5B Crewe South 05/1962 M
1A Willesden 05/1962 M
5B Crewe South 06/1962 M
2A Rugby 06/1962 M
Allocation recoded 2A to 1F 09/1963 M
1E Bletchley 06/1965 M
D01 London Division (WCML) 18/04/1966 E

All Class 24 locomotives plus some early Class 25s were delivered in plain green with a white band at the bottom of the bodyside. D5020 shows this livery to good effect at Derby Works on 13th August 1959. *(David Swale/Colour-Rail.com*

D5011 contd.

D02 Birmingham Division 07/1966 M
D05 Stoke Division 05/1967 M
Store 01/1969 M
D05 Stoke Division 06/1969 M
Returned to Service 06/1969 M
66A Polmadie 10/1971 M
65A Eastfield 03/1972 M
Allocation recoded 65A to ED 05/1973 M
Renumbered 24011 11/1973 M
Store 07/07/1975 E
Stored at Carlisle 07/07/75
Withdrawn 05/10/1975 E
Remained stored at Carlisle, then moved to ZH Glasgow Works 15/03/76 and cut up in 04/77.

D5012

5B Crewe South 11/04/1959 E
17A Derby 04/1959 M
73C Hither Green 20/04/1959 E
5B Crewe South 05/1962 M
5A Crewe North 05/1962 M
1A Willesden 11/1963 M
5A Crewe North 12/1964 M
1F Rugby 01/1965 M
2F Bescot 03/1966 M
D02 Birmingham Division 18/04/1966 E
D05 Stoke Division 05/1967 M
Store 01/1969 M

D5012 contd.

Stored at Chester 01/69, then moved to Willesden 03/07/69 for further storage
D05 Stoke Division 28/10/1969 E
Returned to Service 28/10/1969 E
66A Polmadie 10/1971 M
65A Eastfield 03/1972 M
Allocation recoded 65A to ED 05/1973 M
Renumbered 24012 03/05/1974 E
Store 07/07/1975 E
Stored at Cadder Yard, Glasgow 07/07/75
Withdrawn 16/08/1975 E
Remained stored at Cadder Yard, Glasgow, moved to ZH Glasgow Works and stored, then moved to ZF Doncaster Works 23/01/76 and broken up in 02/76.

D5013

5B Crewe South 18/04/1959 E
17A Derby 04/1959 M
73C Hither Green 23/04/1959 E
2A Rugby 06/1962 M
73C Hither Green 06/1962 M
2A Rugby 07/1962 M
Allocation recoded 2A to 1F 09/1963 M
D01 London Division (WCML) 18/04/1966 E
D05 Stoke Division 04/1966 M
D02 Birmingham Division 09/1966 M
D05 Stoke Division 05/1967 M
Store 04/1969 M

D5013 contd.
55A Leeds Holbeck 10/1969 M
Returned to Service 10/1969 M
66A Polmadie 10/1971 M
65A Eastfield 03/1972 M
Allocation recoded 65A to ED 05/1973 M
Renumbered 24013 11/1973 M
Store 07/07/1975 E
Stored at Carlisle 07/07/75
Withdrawn 05/10/1975 E
Remained stored at Carlisle, then moved to ZF Doncaster Works 29/12/77 and cut up by 02/78.

D5014
5B Crewe South 09/05/1959 E
17A Derby 05/1959 M
73C Hither Green 14/05/1959 E
2A Rugby 06/1962 M
73C Hither Green 06/1962 M
2A Rugby 06/1962 M
Allocation recoded 2A to 1F 09/1963 M
9A Longsight 12/1964 M
1F Rugby 04/1965 M
9A Longsight 11/1965 M
D01 London Division (WCML) 04/1966 M
D02 Birmingham Division 07/1966 M
D05 Stoke Division 05/1967 M
66A Polmadie 10/1971 M
65A Eastfield 03/1972 M
Allocation recoded 65A to ED 05/1973 M
Renumbered 24014 03/1974 M
Store 07/07/1975 E
Stored at Carlisle 07/07/75
Withdrawn 05/10/1975 E
Remained stored at Carlisle, moved to Carstairs for further store 11/75, then to ZF Doncaster Works 08/12/77 and cut up 03/78.

D5015
5B Crewe South 30/05/1959 E
17A Derby 06/1959 M
5B Crewe South 06/1959 M
1B Camden 08/1959 M
1A Willesden 09/1959 M
1B Camden 10/1959 M
2F Bescot 12/1965 M
D02 Birmingham Division 18/04/1966 E
D05 Stoke Division 05/1967 M
66A Polmadie 10/1971 M
65A Eastfield 03/1972 M
Allocation recoded 65A to ED 05/1973 M
Renumbered 24015 04/1974 M
Store 07/07/1975 E

D5015 contd.
Stored at Eastfield 07/07/75
Withdrawn 16/08/1975 E
Remained stored at Eastfield, moved to ZH Glasgow Works 10/75 and held there until moved to ZF Doncaster Works on 02/05/76 and scrapped in 01/77.

D5016
5B Crewe South 30/05/1959 E
17A Derby 06/1959 M
5B Crewe South 06/1959 M
1A Willesden 09/1959 M
1B Camden 10/1959 M
73A Stewarts Lane 04/1960 M
Allocation to Stewarts Lane and return to Camden unconfirmed, not shown in BR official returns. 04/1960 M
1B Camden 13/05/1960 E
1E Bletchley 12/1965 M
D01 London Division (WCML) 18/04/1966 E
D02 Birmingham Division 07/1966 M
D05 Stoke Division 05/1967 M
Store 03/1969 M
D05 Stoke Division 06/1969 M
Returned to Service 06/1969 M
66A Polmadie 10/1971 M
65A Eastfield 03/1972 M
Allocation recoded 65A to ED 05/1973 M
Renumbered 24016 04/1974 M
Store 07/07/1975 E
Stored at Cadder Yard, Glasgow 07/07/75
Withdrawn 16/08/1975 E
Remained stored at Cadder Yard, Glasgow, moved to ZH Glasgow Works 5/76, then to ZF Doncaster Works 02/05/76 and dismantled in 01/77.

D5017
5B Crewe South 06/06/1959 E
17A Derby 06/1959 M
73C Hither Green 07/1959 M
5B Crewe South 05/1962 M
1A Willesden 05/1962 M
5B Crewe South 06/1962 M
2A Rugby 06/1962 M
5A Crewe North 01/1963 M
1A Willesden 09/1965 M
1F Rugby 01/1966 M
D01 London Division (WCML) 18/04/1966 E
D02 Birmingham Division 07/1966 M
D05 Stoke Division 05/1967 M
Store 01/1969 M
D05 Stoke Division 07/1969 M

D5017 contd.

Returned to Service 07/1969 M
66A Polmadie 10/1971 M
65A Eastfield 03/1972 M
Allocation recoded 65A to ED 05/1973 M
Renumbered 24017 17/04/1974 E
Store 07/07/1975 E
Stored at Carlisle 07/07/75
Withdrawn 05/10/1975 E
Remained stored at Carlisle, moved to ZH Glasgow Works 16/03/76, then to Doncaster shed until moved into ZF Doncaster Works in 08/76, and broken up in 01/77.

D5018

5B Crewe South 27/06/1959 E
17A Derby 07/1959 M
5B Crewe South 09/1959 M
1B Camden 10/1959 M
73A Stewarts Lane 04/1960 M
Allocation to Stewarts Lane and return to Camden unconfirmed, not shown in BR official returns 04/1960 M
1B Camden 13/05/1960 E
1E Bletchley 12/1965 M
5A Crewe Diesel 03/1966 M
D05 Stoke Division 18/04/1966 E
D02 Birmingham Division 09/1966 M
D05 Stoke Division 06/1967 M
66A Polmadie 10/1971 M
65A Eastfield 03/1972 M
Allocation recoded 65A to ED 05/1973 M
Renumbered 24018 16/04/1974 E
Store 07/07/1975 E
Stored at Carlisle 07/07/75
Withdrawn 16/08/1975 E
Remained stored at Carlisle, then moved to Cadder Yard, Glasgow for further storage 08/75, moved to ZH Glasgow Works 10/75, then to ZF Doncaster Works on 23/01/76 and cut up in 06/76.

D5019

5B Crewe South 11/07/1959 E
17A Derby 07/1959 M
5B Crewe South 09/1959 M
1B Camden 10/1959 M
1E Bletchley 12/1965 M
D01 London Division (WCML) 18/04/1966 E
D02 Birmingham Division 07/1966 M
D05 Stoke Division 06/1967 M
Store 01/1969 M
Withdrawn 25/01/1969 E
Stored at Chester 1/69

D5019 contd.

55A Leeds Holbeck 05/10/1969 E
Reinstated 05/10/1969 E
52A Gateshead 05/1971 M
66A Polmadie 10/1971 M
65A Eastfield 03/1972 M
Allocation recoded 65A to ED 05/1973 M
Renumbered 24019 03/05/1974 E
Store 07/07/1975 E
Stored at Carlisle 07/07/75
Withdrawn 05/10/1975 E
Remained stored at Carlisle, moved to ZF Doncaster Works 14/02/78 and broken up by 06/78.

D5020

32B Ipswich 20/08/1959 E
30A Stratford 03/1961 M
1A Willesden 05/1961 M
1B Camden 01/1965 M
2F Bescot 12/1965 M
D02 Birmingham Division 18/04/1966 E
D05 Stoke Division 06/1967 M
D09 Manchester Division 03/1972 M
LO Longsight 05/1973 M
Renumbered 24020 04/1974 M
Store 06/07/1975 E
Stored at Reddish 06/07/75
Withdrawn 10/08/1975 E
Remained stored at Reddish, moved to ZL Swindon Works 15/02/77 and cut up by 04/04/77.

D5021

32B Ipswich 20/08/1959 E
30A Stratford 03/1961 M
1A Willesden 04/1961 M
1B Camden 01/1965 M
2F Bescot 12/1965 M
D02 Birmingham Division 18/04/1966 E
D05 Stoke Division 06/1967 M
D09 Manchester Division 03/1972 M
LO Longsight 05/1973 M
Renumbered 24021 30/03/1974 E
Store 06/07/1975 E
Stored at Reddish 06/07/75
Withdrawn 10/08/1975 E
Remained stored at Reddish, moved to ZL Swindon Works 14/02/77 and scrapped by 29/03/77.

D5022

32B Ipswich 07/09/1959 E
32A Norwich 09/1959 M
32B Ipswich 11/1959 M

D5022 contd.

1B Camden 03/1961 M
2F Bescot 12/1965 M
D02 Birmingham Division 18/04/1966 E
D05 Stoke Division 06/1967 M
D09 Manchester Division 03/1972 M
LO Longsight 05/1973 M
Renumbered 24022 12/04/1974 E
Store 06/07/1975 E
Stored at Reddish 06/07/75
Withdrawn 31/01/1976 E
Remained stored at Reddish, moved to ZF Doncaster Works 21/07/78 and cut up 08/78.

D5023

32B Ipswich 25/09/1959 E
1C Watford 03/1961 M
1A Willesden 06/1962 M
1B Camden 01/1965 M
2F Bescot 12/1965 M
D02 Birmingham Division 18/04/1966 E
D05 Stoke Division 06/1967 M
D09 Manchester Division 03/1972 M
LO Longsight 05/1973 M
Renumbered 24023 30/03/1974 E
CD Crewe Diesel 08/1975 M
Store 02/11/1977 E
CD Crewe Diesel 03/11/1977 E

D5023 contd.

Returned to Service 03/11/1977 E
Withdrawn 03/09/1978 E
Moved to ZF Doncaster Works 23/10/78 and dismantled 12/78.

D5024

32B Ipswich 02/10/1959 E
30A Stratford 03/1961 M
1A Willesden 03/1961 M
2F Bescot 12/1965 M
D02 Birmingham Division 18/04/1966 E
D05 Stoke Division 08/1967 M
Store 02/1969 M
Stored at Chester 02/69
D05 Stoke Division 03/1969 M
Returned to Service 03/1969 M
D09 Manchester Division 03/1972 M
D05 Stoke Division 06/1972 M
D09 Manchester Division 10/1972 M
LO Longsight 05/1973 M
Renumbered 24024 23/02/1974 E
Store 06/07/1975 E
Stored at Reddish 06/07/75
Withdrawn 10/08/1975 E
Remained stored at Reddish, moved to ZL Swindon Works 15/02/77 and cut up by 20/04/77.

In due course all of the Class 24s delivered in plain green acquired yellow warning panels. Most Class 25s fitted with end doors were delivered with a yellow panel with those that arrived in plain green being dealt with soon after delivery. Later Cass 24s and all Class 25s had four character headcode boxes from new. Class 24 D5132 is at Thurso on 7th June 1967.

(Keith Guthrie/RCTS Photo Archive

D5025
32B Ipswich 16/10/1959 E
1A Willesden 07/1961 M
1E Bletchley 12/1965 M
D01 London Division (WCML) 18/04/1966 E
D02 Birmingham Division 07/1966 M
D05 Stoke Division 08/1967 M
During 1969 both D5005 and D5025 were involved in incidents. This appears to have resulted in the body shell of D5005 being used to create a rebuilt D5025.
CE Crewe Diesel 05/1973 M
LO Longsight 05/1973 M
Renumbered 24025 05/1974 M
CD Crewe Diesel 05/1975 M
Store 06/07/1975 E
Stored at Reddish 06/07/75
Withdrawn 31/01/1976 E
Moved to Crewe Diesel 01/76 for further storage, then moved to ZL Swindon Works on 10/01/77 and broken up by 28/07/77.

D5026
32B Ipswich 22/10/1959 E
30A Stratford 09/1960 M
1B Camden 11/1960 M
2F Bescot 12/1965 M
D02 Birmingham Division 18/04/1966 E
D05 Stoke Division 08/1967 M
CE Crewe Diesel 05/1973 M
LO Longsight 05/1973 M
Renumbered 24026 18/03/1974 E
CD Crewe Diesel 03/1974 M
LO Longsight 01/1975 M
CD Crewe Diesel 05/1975 M
Store 06/07/1975 E
Stored at Reddish 06/07/75
Withdrawn 10/08/1975 E
Moved to Crewe Diesel 01/76 for further storage, then moved to ZL Swindon Works on 20/10/76 and cut up by 05/01/77.

D5027
32B Ipswich 31/10/1959 E
30A Stratford 09/1960 M
1A Willesden 12/1960 M
1F Rugby 01/1966 M
D01 London Division (WCML) 18/04/1966 E
D02 Birmingham Division 07/1966 M
D05 Stoke Division 08/1967 M
CE Crewe Diesel 05/1973 M
LO Longsight 09/1973 M
Renumbered 24027 05/1974 M
Store 06/07/1975 E

D5027 contd.
CD Crewe Diesel 12/1975 M
Returned to Service 12/1975 M
Store 02/1976 M
Stored at Crewe 02/76
Withdrawn 17/07/1976 E
Remained stored at Crewe, then moved to ZL Swindon Works 21/03/77 and broken up by 11/05/77.

D5028
32B Ipswich 13/11/1959 E
30A Stratford 09/1960 M
1A Willesden 03/1961 M
1E Bletchley 01/1966 M
D01 London Division (WCML) 18/04/1966 E
D02 Birmingham Division 07/1966 M
D05 Stoke Division 08/1967 M
Derailed at Chester General station 08/05/72 while hauling a loaded oil train, one tank exploded and set fire to the locomotive, moved to Chester depot and covered with tarpaulins.
Withdrawn 04/06/1972 E
Moved to ZC Crewe Works on 14/08/72, was being cut up 27/08/72 with completion in early 09/72.

D5029
32B Ipswich 28/11/1959 E
30A Stratford 09/1960 M
1A Willesden 03/1961 M
2F Bescot 12/1965 M
D02 Birmingham Division 18/04/1966 E
D05 Stoke Division 08/1967 M
CE Crewe Diesel 05/1973 M
LO Longsight 05/1973 M
CE Crewe Diesel 09/1973 M
Allocation recoded CE to CD 12/1973 M
Renumbered 24029 30/03/1974 E
LO Longsight 01/1975 M
CD Crewe Diesel 03/1975 M
Store 06/07/1975 E
Stored at Crewe 06/07/75
Withdrawn 10/08/1975 E
Remained stored at Crewe, then moved to ZL Swindon Works 10/01/77 and was broken up by 09/03/77.

D5030
31B March 06/06/1959 E
30A Stratford 01/1960 M
1A Willesden 01/1961 M
1E Bletchley 01/1966 M
D01 London Division (WCML) 18/04/1966 E

D5030 contd.
D02 Birmingham Division 07/1966 M
D05 Stoke Division 08/1967 M
CE Crewe Diesel 05/1973 M
Allocation recoded CE to CD 12/1973 M
Renumbered 24030 22/06/1974 E
Store 02/1976 M
Stored at Crewe 02/76
Withdrawn 17/07/1976 E
Remained stored at Crewe, then moved to ZL Swindon Works 21/03/77 and cut up by 04/05/77.

D5031
31B March 25/06/1959 E
30A Stratford 08/1959 M
1A Willesden 01/1961 M
1C Watford 09/1961 M
1A Willesden 02/1963 M
D01 London Division (WCML) 18/04/1966 E
D02 Birmingham Division 11/1966 M
D05 Stoke Division 08/1967 M
CE Crewe Diesel 05/1973 M
Allocation recoded CE to CD 12/1973 M
Renumbered 24031 27/02/1974 E
Store 06/07/1975 E
Stored at Crewe Diesel 06/07/75
Withdrawn 04/10/1975 E
Remained stored at Crewe Diesel, then moved to ZL Swindon Works 20/10/76 and scrapped by 30/12/76.

D5032
31B March 29/07/1959 E
30A Stratford 01/1960 M
1A Willesden 12/1960 M
1E Bletchley 12/1965 M
D01 London Division (WCML) 18/04/1966 E
D02 Birmingham Division 11/1966 M
D05 Stoke Division 08/1967 M
CE Crewe Diesel 05/1973 M
Allocation recoded CE to CD 12/1973 M
Renumbered 24032 02/03/1974 E
Store 02/05/1976 E
Stored at Bescot 02/05/76
Withdrawn 17/07/1976 E
For preservation
Sold to T. J. Thompson, Millfield Works, Stockton-on-Tees and moved there 22/07/76 for scrap, but went on indefinite hire instead, to the North Yorkshire Moors Railway from 21/08/76. Repainted in non-authentic two-tone green livery by 09/77, then back to original BR livery after 07/82 but by 10/82.

D5032 contd.
The locomotive was named *Helen Turner* on 30/10/82 on the NYMR. Nameplates removed between 10/85 when it was still in service and 06/06 when stored out of use in Grosmont sidings, subsequently moved into the maintenance shed at Grosmont by 2013 as a long term restoration project.

D5033
31B March 05/08/1959 E
30A Stratford 10/1959 M
1A Willesden 03/1961 M
1E Bletchley 01/1966 M
D01 London Division (WCML) 18/04/1966 E
D02 Birmingham Division 11/1966 M
D05 Stoke Division 08/1967 M
CE Crewe Diesel 05/1973 M
Allocation recoded CE to CD 12/1973 M
Renumbered 24033 30/03/1974 E
Store 03/08/1975 E
Stored at Crewe 03/08/75
Withdrawn 04/10/1975 E
Remained stored at Crewe, then moved to ZL Swindon Works 10/01/77 and cut up by 16/03/77.

D5034
31B March 03/09/1959 E
30A Stratford 02/1960 M
1A Willesden 03/1961 M
Allocation to Willesden was recorded as a loan in 03/61 but was made permanent in 04/61. 04/1961 M
1E Bletchley 01/1966 M
D01 London Division (WCML) 18/04/1966 E
D02 Birmingham Division 03/1967 M
D05 Stoke Division 08/1967 M
CE Crewe Diesel 05/1973 M
Allocation recoded CE to CD 12/1973 M
Renumbered 24034 19/03/1974 E
Store 03/08/1975 E
Stored at Crewe 03/08/75
Withdrawn 31/01/1976 E
Remained stored at Crewe, then moved to ZL Swindon Works 10/01/77 and cut up by 11/77. One of the cabs from this loco was still extant at ZE Derby Works in 11/86, but was disposed of shortly afterwards.

D5035
31B March 31/08/1959 E
30A Stratford 02/1960 M
1A Willesden 03/1961 M
30A Stratford 03/1961 M

D5035 contd.
1A Willesden 04/1961 M
1C Watford 09/1961 M
1A Willesden 01/1965 M
D01 London Division (WCML) 18/04/1966 E
D02 Birmingham Division 03/1967 M
D05 Stoke Division 08/1967 M
CE Crewe Diesel 05/1973 M
Allocation recoded CE to CD 12/1973 M
Renumbered 24035 07/04/1974 E
Store 02/11/1977 E
CD Crewe Diesel 03/11/1977 E
Returned to Service 03/11/1977 E
Withdrawn 15/10/1978 E
Moved to ZF Doncaster Works 13/12/78 and cut up in 01/79. The last date noted intact was 07/01/79.

D5036
31B March 03/09/1959 E
32B Ipswich 05/1960 M
31B March 10/1962 M
32B Ipswich 02/1963 M
D05 Stoke Division 08/1967 M
CE Crewe Diesel 05/1973 M
Allocation recoded CE to CD 12/1973 M
Renumbered 24036 05/1974 M
Store 16/10/1977 E
Stored at Crewe 16/10/77
Withdrawn 20/11/1977 E
Remained stored at Crewe, then moved to ZF Doncaster Works 11/05/78 and cut up during 06/78.

D5037
31B March 07/09/1959 E
32B Ipswich 05/1960 M
D05 Stoke Division 08/1967 M
CE Crewe Diesel 05/1973 M
Allocation recoded CE to CD 12/1973 M
Renumbered 24037 28/01/1974 E
Store 03/08/1975 E
CD Crewe Diesel 12/1975 M
Returned to Service 12/1975 M
Store 02/05/1976 E
Stored at Crewe 02/05/76
Withdrawn 17/07/1976 E
Remained stored at Crewe, then moved to ZL Swindon Works 21/03/77 and scrapped by 29/06/77.

D5038
32B Ipswich 15/09/1959 E
31B March 01/1960 M
32B Ipswich 06/1960 M

D5038 contd.
D05 Stoke Division 08/1967 M
CE Crewe Diesel 05/1973 M
Allocation recoded CE to CD 12/1973 M
Renumbered 24038 16/02/1974 E
Store 03/08/1975 E
Allocation recoded CE to CD 12/1973 M
CD Crewe Diesel 12/1975 M
Returned to Service 12/1975 M
Store 02/1976 M
Stored at Crewe Basford Hall Yard 02/76
Withdrawn 17/07/1976 E
Remained at Crewe Basford Hall Yard until 02/05/77 when it was removed en route to Swindon but stopped at Oxford, then moved to ZL Swindon Works 17/05/77 and cut up by 23/06/77.

D5039
32B Ipswich 24/09/1959 E
31B March 12/1959 M
32B Ipswich 06/1960 M
D05 Stoke Division 08/1967 M
CE Crewe Diesel 05/1973 M
Allocation recoded CE to CD 12/1973 M
Renumbered 24039 08/06/1974 E
Stored at Crewe Basford Hall Yard 02/05/76
Withdrawn 17/07/1976 E
Remained at Crewe Basford Hall Yard until 02/05/77 when it was removed en route to Swindon but stopped at Oxford, then moved to ZL Swindon Works 17/05/77 and was broken up by 20/07/78.

D5040
32B Ipswich 12/10/1959 E
31B March 11/1959 M
32B Ipswich 06/1960 M
41A Tinsley 06/1965 M
32B Ipswich 07/1965 M
D05 Stoke Division 08/1967 M
CE Crewe Diesel 05/1973 M
Allocation recoded CE to CD 12/1973 M
Renumbered 24040 04/03/1974 E
Store 12/1975 M
Stored at Crewe 12/75
Withdrawn 04/01/1976 E
Remained at Crewe, then moved to ZL Swindon Works 07/12/76 and cut up by 10/02/77.

D5041
32B Ipswich 28/09/1959 E
31B March 11/1959 M
32B Ipswich 06/1960 M

D5041 contd.
D05 Stoke Division 08/1967 M
CE Crewe Diesel 05/1973 M
Renumbered 24041 14/09/1973 E
Allocation recoded CE to CD 12/1973 M
Store 08/1975 M
CD Crewe Diesel 03/08/1975 E
Returned to Service 03/08/1975 E
Store 10/1975 M
CD Crewe Diesel 12/1975 M
Returned to Service 12/1975 M
Store 27/12/1975 E
CD Crewe Diesel 24/01/1976 E
Returned to Service 24/01/1976 E
Store 02/1976 M
Stored at Crewe Basford Hall Yard 02/76
Withdrawn 17/07/1976 E
Remained at Crewe Basford Hall Yard until 02/05/77 when it was removed en route to Swindon but stopped at Oxford, then moved to ZL Swindon Works 17/05/77 and was cut up by 15/06/78.

D5042
32B Ipswich 12/10/1959 E
31B March 10/1959 M
32B Ipswich 06/1960 M
D05 Stoke Division 08/1967 M

D5042 contd.
CE Crewe Diesel 05/1973 M
Allocation recoded CE to CD 12/1973 M
Renumbered 24042 21/01/1974 E
Store 03/08/1975 E
Withdrawn 10/08/1975 E
Stored at ZE Derby Works 03/08/75 and withdrawn while there 10/08/75. Moved to ZL Swindon Works 18/12/75 and was broken up by 26/02/76.

D5043
32B Ipswich 16/10/1959 E
31B March 10/1959 M
32B Ipswich 07/1960 M
31B March 11/1960 M
32B Ipswich 07/1961 M
D05 Stoke Division 08/1967 M
Store 07/1969 M
Stored at Chester depot following accident damage there on 09/07/69
Withdrawn 10/08/1969 E
Dismantling was begun at Chester depot on 21/02/70, it was then moved to the old yard across from the shed and the engine removed there. Moved by road to J. Cashmore, Great Bridge, West Midlands for scrap in 05/70 and finally dismantled 06/70.

The process of repainting green locomotives to the new rail blue brought a number of variations in the style and position of numbers and the double arrow symbol. However, Class 24 5021 appeared in a possibly unique version of blue as it carried the BR totem rather than the double arrows and is seen at Manchester Victoria on 1st October 1973. It had lost the 'D' prefix but the numbers were also in the original font. *(Colour-Rail.com*

D5044
32B Ipswich 23/10/1959 E
31B March 10/1959 M
32B Ipswich 07/1960 M
73C Hither Green 11/1960 M
32B Ipswich 01/1961 M
D05 Stoke Division 08/1967 M
CE Crewe Diesel 05/1973 M
Allocation recoded CE to CD 12/1973 M
Renumbered 24044 05/03/1974 E
Store 24/01/1976 E
Stored at Crewe 24/01/76
Withdrawn 31/01/1976 E
Remained stored at Crewe, then moved to ZL Swindon Works 20/10/76 and scrapped by 19/01/77.

D5045
31B March 12/11/1959 E
30A Stratford 09/1960 M
32B Ipswich 03/1961 M
D05 Stoke Division 08/1967 M
CE Crewe Diesel 05/1973 M
Allocation recoded CE to CD 12/1973 M
Renumbered 24045 13/05/1974 E
Store 08/1975 M
Withdrawn 10/08/1975 E
Stored at ZE Derby Works and withdrawn while there, then moved to ZL Swindon Works 18/12/75 and cut up by 09/12/76.

D5046
31B March 29/10/1959 E
30A Stratford 09/1960 M
32B Ipswich 03/1961 M
41A Tinsley 06/1965 M
32B Ipswich 07/1965 M
D05 Stoke Division 08/1967 M
CE Crewe Diesel 05/1973 M
Renumbered 24046 05/11/1973 E
Allocation recoded CE to CD 12/1973 M
Store 03/08/1975 E
CD Crewe Diesel 08/1975 M
Returned to Service 08/1975 M
Store 10/1975 M
CD Crewe Diesel 12/1975 M
Returned to Service 12/1975 M
Store 02/1976 M
Stored at Crewe Basford Hall Yard 02/76
Withdrawn 17/07/1976 E
Remained at Crewe Basford Hall Yard until 02/05/77 when it was removed en route to Swindon but stopped at Oxford, then moved to ZL Swindon Works 17/05/77 and was dismantled by 20/07/77.

D5047
31B March 21/11/1959 E
30A Stratford 09/1960 M
32B Ipswich 03/1961 M
41A Tinsley 06/1965 M
32B Ipswich 07/1965 M
D05 Stoke Division 08/1967 M
CE Crewe Diesel 05/1973 M
Allocation recoded CE to CD 12/1973 M
Renumbered 24047 23/02/1974 E
Store 02/11/1977 E
CD Crewe Diesel 03/11/1977 E
Returned to Service 03/11/1977 E
Withdrawn 16/11/1978 E
Moved to ZF Doncaster Works on 13/12/78 and cut up during 02/79.

D5048
31B March 05/11/1959 E
30A Stratford 09/1960 M
32B Ipswich 03/1961 M
41A Tinsley 06/1965 M
32B Ipswich 07/1965 M
D05 Stoke Division 08/1967 M
CE Crewe Diesel 05/1973 M
Allocation recoded CE to CD 12/1973 M
Renumbered 24048 09/02/1974 E
Store 08/1975 M
Withdrawn 10/08/1975 E
Stored at ZE Derby Works, moved to ZL Swindon Works on 18/12/75 and was scrapped by 18/03/76.

D5049
Completed in 11/59 but not taken into stock until 04/60.
31B March 04/04/1960 E
30A Stratford 09/1960 M
32B Ipswich 03/1961 M
41A Tinsley 06/1965 M
32B Ipswich 07/1965 M
D05 Stoke Division 08/1967 M
CE Crewe Diesel 05/1973 M
Allocation recoded CE to CD 12/1973 M
Renumbered 24049 23/02/1974 E
Store 03/08/1975 E
CD Crewe Diesel 08/1975 M
Returned to Service 08/1975 M
Store 04/01/1976 E
Stored at Crewe 04/01/76
Withdrawn 31/01/1976 E
Remained at Crewe, then moved to ZL Swindon Works 2-4/08/76 and was cut up by 24/11/76.

D5050
31B March 27/11/1959 E
30A Stratford 09/1960 M
34G Finsbury Park 03/1961 M
65A Eastfield 10/1966 M
64B Haymarket 12/1966 M
9A Longsight 01/1968 M
D09 Manchester Division 17/06/1968 E
D05 Stoke Division 09/1968 M
Store 03/1969 M
Stored at Chester 03/69.
D05 Stoke Division 04/1969 M
Returned to Service 04/1969 M
CE Crewe Diesel 05/1973 M
Allocation recoded CE to CD 12/1973 M
Renumbered 24050 22/03/1974 E
Store 08/1975 M
Stored at Crewe 08/75, then moved to ZE Derby Works 10/75 and withdrawn there.
Withdrawn 04/10/1975 E
Remained at ZE Derby Works, then moved to ZL Swindon Works 18/12/75 and broken up by 03/12/76.

D5051
31B March 05/12/1959 E
34G Finsbury Park 01/1961 M
65A Eastfield 10/1966 M
Withdrawn 02/12/1967 E
Withdrawn due to catching fire on the Waterside branch. Moved to Inverurie Works by 13/04/68 and noted still intact there on 21/09/68, but was dismantled the following month.

D5052
31B March 04/12/1959 E
34G Finsbury Park 01/1961 M
65A Eastfield 10/1966 M
12A Kingmoor Diesel 03/1968 M
Allocation to Kingmoor Diesel unconfirmed, not shown in BR official returns 03/1968 M
9A Longsight 04/1968 M
D09 Manchester Division 17/06/1968 E
D05 Stoke Division 09/1968 M
CE Crewe Diesel 05/1973 M
Allocation recoded CE to CD 12/1973 M
Renumbered 24052 29/01/1974 E
Stored at Crewe 05/76 but only officially stored 24/07/76.
Store 24/07/1976 E
Withdrawn 04/12/1976 E
Remained stored at Crewe, then moved to Oxford on 19/05/77 and on to ZL Swindon Works 30-31/05/77. Scrapped by 25/05/78.

D5053
31B March 03/12/1959 E
34G Finsbury Park 03/1961 M
65A Eastfield 10/1966 M
12A Kingmoor Diesel 03/1968 M
Allocation to Kingmoor Diesel unconfirmed, not shown in BR official returns 03/1968 M
9A Longsight 04/1968 M
D09 Manchester Division 17/06/1968 E
D05 Stoke Division 09/1968 M
CE Crewe Diesel 05/1973 M
Renumbered 24053 09/11/1973 E
Allocation recoded CE to CD 12/1973 M
Store 04/01/1976 E
Stored at Crewe 04/01/76.
Withdrawn 31/01/1976 E
Remained stored at Crewe, then moved to ZL Swindon Works 12/02/76 and cut up by 19/05/76.

D5054
31B March 18/12/1959 E
34G Finsbury Park 01/1961 M
65A Eastfield 10/1966 M
12A Kingmoor Diesel 03/1968 M
Allocation to Kingmoor Diesel unconfirmed, not shown in BR official returns 03/1968 M
9A Longsight 04/1968 M
D09 Manchester Division 17/06/1968 E
D05 Stoke Division 09/1968 M
CE Crewe Diesel 05/1973 M
Allocation recoded CE to CD 12/1973 M
Renumbered 24054 16/02/1974 E
Store 02/05/1976 E
Withdrawn 17/07/1976 E
Having been stored at Crewe from withdrawal, it was taken into Departmental Stock in 08/76, converted to an unpowered carriage heating unit and renumbered to TDB 968008.
Renumbered TDB968008 08/76 M
It first worked at Exeter and then Penzance and Newton Abbot. It was however, stored out of use by 03/79, where it remained until moved to Stratford repair shop, London on 03/08/82 and then to Norwich in 09/82, moved to Cambridge in 12/82 as a standby unit but it was moved about 15/12/82 to March, then stored.
For preservation
Sold for preservation to the East Lancs. Railway, Bury, and was hauled from March to Warrington about 09/10/83 and then onto

D5054 contd.

Bury on 13/10/83. It has carried D5054 and 24054 in preservation and was named *Phil Southern* at Bury Bolton Street Station, ELR on 28/07/07.

HQ Headquarters Pool 07/03/2002 E

Reregistered on TOPS as 89254 to allow movement by rail to galas on other heritage railways but carried D5054.

Moved to Barrow Hill for repairs 16/07/14, returned to the East Lancashire Railway 24/01/17. Repainted in BR two-tone green incorrectly as D5053, instead of the correct D5054, by 07/25. Appears at galas and possibly for longer visits at other heritage railways.

D5055

31B March 18/12/1959 E
34G Finsbury Park 01/1961 M
65A Eastfield 10/1966 M
12A Kingmoor Diesel 03/1968 M
Allocation to Kingmoor Diesel unconfirmed, not shown in BR official returns 03/1968 M
9A Longsight 04/1968 M
D09 Manchester Division 17/06/1968 E
D05 Stoke Division 09/1968 M
CE Crewe Diesel 05/1973 M
Allocation recoded CE to CD 12/1973 M
Renumbered 24055 09/02/1974 E
Withdrawn 04/10/1975 E

D5055 contd.

Stored at Crewe, then moved to ZL Swindon Works 07/09/76 and broken up by 09/12/76.

D5056

31B March 11/12/1959 E
34G Finsbury Park 02/1961 M
65A Eastfield 10/1966 M
12A Kingmoor Diesel 03/1968 M
Allocation to Kingmoor Diesel unconfirmed, not shown in BR official returns 03/1968 M
9A Longsight 04/1968 M
D09 Manchester Division 17/06/1968 E
D05 Stoke Division 09/1968 M
CE Crewe Diesel 05/1973 M
Allocation recoded CE to CD 12/1973 M
Renumbered 24056 23/02/1974 E
Withdrawn 04/10/1975 E
Stored at Crewe, then moved to ZL Swindon Works 07/09/76 and broken up by 24/11/76.

D5057

31B March 22/12/1959 E
34G Finsbury Park 02/1961 M
D01 London Division (WCML) 08/1966 M
D05 Stoke Division 04/1967 M
CE Crewe Diesel 05/1973 M
Allocation recoded CE to CD 12/1973 M
Renumbered 24057 30/03/1974 E
Withdrawn 15/01/1978 E
Stored at Crewe, then moved to ZF Doncaster Works on 11/05/78 and cut up by 31/05/78.

Not all Class 24s carried TOPS numbers but for those that did, the application of the numbers and logo were fairly consistent as here on 24052 at Stoke on 28th September 1975 having its number on one cabside with central arrow. *(K. Hughes/RCTS Photo Archive*

D5058
31B March 01/01/1960 E
34G Finsbury Park 03/1961 M
D01 London Division (WCML) 07/1966 M
D05 Stoke Division 04/1967 M
CE Crewe Diesel 05/1973 M
Allocation recoded CE to CD 12/1973 M
Renumbered 24058 16/02/1974 E
Withdrawn 04/10/1975 E
Stored at Crewe, then moved to ZL Swindon Works 04/08/76 and scrapped by 20/10/76.

D5059
31B March 29/12/1959 E
1A Willesden 10/1960 M
1B Camden 02/1961 M
34G Finsbury Park 03/1961 M
D01 London Division (WCML) 07/1966 M
D05 Stoke Division 04/1967 M
CE Crewe Diesel 05/1973 M
Allocation recoded CE to CD 12/1973 M
Renumbered 24059 25/02/1974 E
Withdrawn 04/10/1975 E
Stored at Crewe, then moved to ZL Swindon Works 07/12/76 and broken up by 02/03/77.

D5060
31B March 02/01/1960 E
9A Longsight 10/1960 M
1A Willesden 11/1960 M
9A Longsight 11/1960 M
5A Crewe North 01/1961 M
1A Willesden 02/1961 M
34G Finsbury Park 03/1961 M
D01 London Division (WCML) 07/1966 M
D05 Stoke Division 04/1967 M
Store 02/1969 M
Stored at Chester 02/69
D05 Stoke Division 04/1969 M
Returned to Service 04/1969 M
CE Crewe Diesel 05/1973 M
Allocation recoded CE to CD 12/1973 M
Renumbered 24060 30/03/1974 E
Withdrawn 04/10/1975 E
Stored at Crewe, then moved to ZL Swindon Works on 07/09/76 and cut up by 26/01/77.

D5061
31B March 15/01/1960 E
1A Willesden 10/1960 M
2A Rugby 11/1960 M
1A Willesden 03/1961 M
34G Finsbury Park 07/1961 M
64B Haymarket 08/1966 M

D5061 contd.
9A Longsight 01/1968 M
D09 Manchester Division 17/06/1968 E
D05 Stoke Division 09/1968 M
CE Crewe Diesel 05/1973 M
Allocation recoded CE to CD 12/1973 M
Renumbered 24061 05/03/1974 E
Store 08/1975 M
Withdrawn 10/08/1975 E
Following its withdrawal from revenue service on 10/08/75, it was moved to ZE Derby Works on 14/11/75, transferred to Departmental stock and became RDB968007 in 07/76.
Renumbered RDB968007 07/76 M
Formerly 24061 it was transferred to Departmental stock and became RDB968007 in 07/76. At some time in late 1978 or early 1979 the locomotive was renumbered TDB968007
Renumbered TDB968007 1979 Y
It remained powered, and was moved from Derby on 02/07/79 and arrived at ZF Doncaster Works on 04/07/79, later in July it received the engine out of 24063, after which it was renumbered to 97201 on 18/08/79, as it was self-powered.
Renumbered 97201 18/08/79 E
Formerly TDB968007 and before that RDB968007 and 24061, It was named *Experiment* at Derby RTC in 06/80.
Withdrawn 04/12/1987 E
The nameplates were removed around 07/88. Moved to Vic Berry, Leicester by 05/07/88 for asbestos removal, but remained in the scrapyard until 1991.
For preservation
Arrived at the Midland Railway Centre, Butterley on 19/07/91. Moved by road to the North Yorkshire Moors Railway and unloaded at Pickering on 01/06/94.
Sold and moved to the North Tyneside Steam Railway, Stephenson Railway Museum, West Chirton, Tyne & Wear on 21/08/92. Moved by road to the North Yorkshire Moors Railway and unloaded at Pickering on 01/06/94. The *Experiment* name was reapplied but its date of subsequent removal is unknown.
As D5061 it was named *Ian Johnson 1950 - 2014* at Grosmont Depot, NYMR on 25/08/14, a short term naming, still named 13/09/14 but nameplates removed by 06/15.

D5061 contd.
HQ Headquarters Pool 07/09/2002 E
Reregistered on TOPS as 89261 on 07/09/02 to allow movement by rail to galas at other heritage railways.

D5062
31B March 18/01/1960 E
30A Stratford 12/1960 M
34G Finsbury Park 03/1961 M
64B Haymarket 08/1966 M
9A Longsight 01/1968 M
D09 Manchester Division 17/06/1968 E
D05 Stoke Division 09/1968 M
CE Crewe Diesel 05/1973 M
Allocation recoded CE to CD 12/1973 M
Renumbered 24062 09/02/1974 E
Withdrawn 04/10/1975 E
Stored at Crewe, then moved to ZL Swindon Works on 04/08/76 and cut up by 28/10/76.

D5063
31B March 26/01/1960 E
1A Willesden 10/1960 M
1C Watford 02/1961 M
34G Finsbury Park 03/1961 M
64B Haymarket 10/1966 M
9A Longsight 01/1968 M
D09 Manchester Division 17/06/1968 E
D05 Stoke Division 11/1968 M
CE Crewe Diesel 05/1973 M
Allocation recoded CE to CD 12/1973 M
Renumbered 24063 23/03/1974 E
Store 02/11/1977 E
CD Crewe Diesel 03/11/1977 E
Returned to Service 03/11/1977 E
Withdrawn 09/04/1979 E
Withdrawn due to damage sustained in a collision at Dee Marsh Junction and stored at Crewe. Moved to Tinsley on 02/07/79 and on to ZF Doncaster Works 04/07/79 where it was finally cut up in 08/79.

D5064
31B March 27/01/1960 E
1A Willesden 10/1960 M
34G Finsbury Park 03/1961 M
64B Haymarket 08/1966 M
9A Longsight 01/1968 M
D09 Manchester Division 17/06/1968 E
D05 Stoke Division 11/1968 M
CE Crewe Diesel 05/1973 M
Allocation recoded CE to CD 12/1973 M
Renumbered 24064 16/02/1974 E
Store 04/01/1976 E

D5064 contd.
Withdrawn 31/01/1976 E
Stored at Crewe. Moved to ZL Swindon Works 05/76 and cut up by 03/12/76. The remains were moved to King's (later Mayer Newman) scrapyard, Snailwell, near Kings Lynn and noted in its yard 12/79. They were disposed of in early 1980.

D5065
31B March 02/02/1960 E
1A Willesden 10/1960 M
34G Finsbury Park 05/1961 M
64B Haymarket 08/1966 M
65A Eastfield 03/1968 M
9A Longsight 05/1968 M
D09 Manchester Division 17/06/1968 E
D05 Stoke Division 11/1968 M
64B Haymarket 11/1970 M
Allocation recoded 64B to HA 05/1973 M
Renumbered 24065 10/1973 M
ED Eastfield 05/1975 M
Store 07/07/1975 E
HA Haymarket 18/12/1975 E
Returned to Service 18/12/1975 E
Store 22/10/1976 E
Stored at Millerhill Yard 22/10/76
Withdrawn 31/12/1976 E
Remained stored at Millerhill Yard. then moved to ZL Swindon Works 04/05/77 and broken up by 02/06/77.

D5066
31B March 19/12/1959 E
1A Willesden 11/1960 M
34G Finsbury Park 03/1961 M
64B Haymarket 08/1966 M
65A Eastfield 03/1968 M
9A Longsight 05/1968 M
D09 Manchester Division 17/06/1968 E
D05 Stoke Division 11/1968 M
64B Haymarket 07/1969 M
65A Eastfield 02/1971 M
64B Haymarket 04/1971 M
Allocation recoded 64B to HA 05/1973 M
Renumbered 24066 03/1974 M
Store 08/1975 M
Stored at Haymarket 08/75, then moved to Carlisle later in the month for further storage
Withdrawn 02/02/1976 E
Remained stored at Carlisle, then moved to ZF Doncaster Works 14/02/78 and scrapped in 08/78.

D5067
31B March 24/12/1959 E
30A Stratford 01/1961 M
34G Finsbury Park 03/1961 M
64B Haymarket 09/1966 M
Withdrawn 09/10/1972 E
Withdrawn due to accident damage on an unknown date, when one cab was torn off. Moved to ZH Glasgow Works 11/72 and cut up 20/10/73.

D5068
31B March 31/12/1959 E
1A Willesden 11/1960 M
34G Finsbury Park 04/1961 M
64B Haymarket 08/1966 M
Withdrawn 09/10/1972 E
Stored at ZH Glasgow Works and broken up there 04/73.

D5069
31B March 01/01/1960 E
30A Stratford 12/1960 M
34G Finsbury Park 01/1961 M
64B Haymarket 08/1966 M
Allocation recoded 64B to HA 05/1973 M
Renumbered 24069 12/1973 M
Store 08/1975 M
Stored at Haymarket 08/75.
HA Haymarket 18/12/1975 E
Returned to Service 18/12/1975 E
Store 09/1976 M
Stored at Haymarket 09/76.
Withdrawn 01/12/1976 E
Remained stored at Haymarket, then moved to Millerhill Yard for further storage 01/77, left there on 11/06/77, noted at Tyne Yard 13/06/77 awaiting onward movement and arrived at ZF Doncaster Works about 17/06/77, where it was cut up in 09/77.

D5070
31B March 23/01/1960 E
30A Stratford 11/1960 M
73C Hither Green 11/1960 M
30A Stratford 01/1961 M
34G Finsbury Park 01/1961 M
64B Haymarket 09/1966 M
Allocation recoded 64B to HA 05/1973 M
Renumbered 24070 12/1973 M
Store 08/1975 M
Stored at Carstairs 08/75.
Withdrawn 02/02/1976 E
Remained stored at Carstairs, then moved to ZF Doncaster Works 04/04/76 and scrapped in 06/76.

D5071
31B March 06/02/1960 E
30A Stratford 11/1960 M
34G Finsbury Park 03/1961 M
64B Haymarket 10/1966 M
Allocation recoded 64B to HA 05/1973 M
Renumbered 24071 04/1974 M
Store 24/07/1975 E
Stored at Haymarket 24/07/75.
Withdrawn 16/08/1975 E
Remained stored at Haymarket, then moved to Polmadie for further storage 23/08/75. Moved to ZH Glasgow Works 10/75 and then to ZF Doncaster Works 02/05/76 and was dismantled 01/77.

D5072
31B March 17/02/1960 E
1A Willesden 03/1960 M
34G Finsbury Park 05/1961 M
64B Haymarket 08/1966 M
Allocation recoded 64B to HA 05/1973 M
Renumbered 24072 04/1974 M
Store 08/1975 M
Stored at Carlisle 08/75.
Withdrawn 05/10/1975 E
Remained stored at Carlisle 08/75 until it finally moved to ZF Doncaster Works 26/10/77 and scrapped in 12/77.

D5073
31B March 04/03/1960 E
1A Willesden 03/1960 M
D01 London Division (WCML) 18/04/1966 E
D05 Stoke Division 12/1966 M
66A Polmadie 10/1971 M
65A Eastfield 03/1972 M
Allocation recoded 65A to ED 05/1973 M
Renumbered 24073 12/1973 M
Store 08/1975 M
Stored at Carlisle 08/75
Withdrawn 02/02/1976 E
Remained stored at Carlisle. Taken into Carlisle TMD on 29/01/77 for repairs, then moved to Crewe about 17/02/77 and unofficially reinstated at Crewe Diesel 02/77, but stored from about 11/77 at Crewe, then used again during supposed storage period at the diesel depot for shunting, which finally ceased 09/78.
Moved to ZF Doncaster Works 23/10/78 and cut up 12/78.

D5074
31B March 14/03/1960 E
1A Willesden 03/1960 M
1C Watford 11/1960 M
1A Willesden 01/1965 M
D01 London Division (WCML) 18/04/1966 E
D05 Stoke Division 12/1966 M
CE Crewe Diesel 05/1973 M
Allocation recoded CE to CD 12/1973 M
Renumbered 24074 08/03/1974 E
Withdrawn 04/10/1975 E
Stored at Crewe, then moved to J. Cashmore, Great Bridge, West Midlands 05/76 and cut up 24/05/76.

D5075
31B March 26/03/1960 E
1A Willesden 04/1960 M
D01 London Division (WCML) 18/04/1966 E
D05 Stoke Division 12/1966 M
CE Crewe Diesel 05/1973 M
Allocation recoded CE to CD 12/1973 M
Renumbered 24075 23/02/1974 E
Store 04/01/1976 E
Withdrawn 31/01/1976 E
Stored at Crewe, then moved to ZL Swindon Works 12/02/76 and cut up by 01/07/76.

D5076
31B March 10/02/1960 E
1A Willesden 07/1960 M
D01 London Division (WCML) 18/04/1966 E
D05 Stoke Division 12/1966 M
CE Crewe Diesel 05/1973 M
Allocation recoded CE to CD 12/1973 M
Renumbered 24076 17/04/1974 E
Withdrawn 04/10/1975 E
Stored at Crewe, then moved to ZL Swindon Works 20/10/76 and broken up by 26/01/77.

D5077
31B March 17/02/1960 E
1A Willesden 07/1960 M
D01 London Division (WCML) 18/04/1966 E
D05 Stoke Division 12/1966 M
CE Crewe Diesel 05/1973 M
Allocation recoded CE to CD 12/1973 M
Renumbered 24077 04/1974 M
Store 02/1976 M
Withdrawn 17/07/1976 E
Stored at Crewe until moved to Oxford on 19/05/77, then on to ZL Swindon Works 31/05/77 and cut up by 22/06/78.

D5078
31B March 18/02/1960 E
1A Willesden 03/1960 M
D01 London Division (WCML) 18/04/1966 E
D05 Stoke Division 12/1966 M
CE Crewe Diesel 05/1973 M
Allocation recoded CE to CD 12/1973 M
Renumbered 24078 06/03/1974 E
Store 03/1976 M
Withdrawn 24/04/1976 E
Stored at Crewe until moved to Oxford on 19/05/77, then on to ZL Swindon Works 31/05/77 and cut up by 22/06/78.

D5079
31B March 25/02/1960 E
1A Willesden 03/1960 M
2A Rugby 08/1960 M
1A Willesden 09/1960 M
9A Longsight 10/1960 M
12B Upperby 10/1960 M
1A Willesden 05/1961 M
D01 London Division (WCML) 18/04/1966 E
D05 Stoke Division 12/1966 M
CE Crewe Diesel 05/1973 M
Allocation recoded CE to CD 12/1973 M
Renumbered 24079 08/06/1974 E
Store 02/05/1976 E
Withdrawn 17/07/1976 E
Stored at Crewe, then sent to ZL Swindon Works where it arrived 31/05/77 and was cut up by 28/09/78.

D5080
31B March 01/03/1960 E
1A Willesden 03/1960 M
2A Rugby 04/1960 M
1A Willesden 09/1960 M
D01 London Division (WCML) 18/04/1966 E
D05 Stoke Division 12/1966 M
CE Crewe Diesel 05/1973 M
Allocation recoded CE to CD 12/1973 M
Renumbered 24080 04/1974 M
Withdrawn 22/09/1976 E
Stored at Crewe, then finally moved to ZF Doncaster Works 11/05/78 and broken up by 15/06/78.

D5081
31B March 09/03/1960 E
1A Willesden 03/1960 M
2A Rugby 05/1960 M
1A Willesden 08/1960 M
1C Watford 11/1960 M

Class 24 24142 entered departmental stock in 1977 as a carriage heating unit and received the number TDB968009 and is at Worcester on 2nd September 1977 retaining its last service livery of blue with full yellow ends. *(George Staddon/RCTS Photo Archive*

D5081 contd.
1A Willesden 01/1965 M
D01 London Division (WCML) 18/04/1966 E
D05 Stoke Division 12/1966 M
CE Crewe Diesel 05/1973 M
Allocation recoded CE to CD 12/1973 M
Renumbered 24081 27/02/1974 E
Store 02/11/1977 E
CD Crewe Diesel 03/11/1977 E
Returned to Service 03/11/1977 E
Withdrawn 05/10/1980 E
For preservation
Withdrawn 05/10/80 having already been acquired for preservation by Steamport, Southport, and arrived at its premises on 17/10/80. Moved from Southport to the Llangollen Railway about 10/94.
Moved to the Gloucestershire-Warwickshire Railway about 10/98. It has visited other heritage railways for gala appearances.

D5082
31B March 29/03/1960 E
1A Willesden 04/1960 M
2A Rugby 05/1960 M
1A Willesden 07/1960 M
1C Watford 05/1962 M
5A Crewe North 01/1963 M
D05 Stoke Division 18/04/1966 E
D01 London Division (WCML) 08/1966 M
D05 Stoke Division 01/1967 M

D5082 contd.
CE Crewe Diesel 05/1973 M
Renumbered 24082 19/10/1973 E
Allocation recoded CE to CD 12/1973 M
Store 07/1976 M
Stored at Crewe 07/76
CD Crewe Diesel 10/1976 M
Returned to Service 10/1976 M
Withdrawn 01/03/1979 E
Moved to ZF Doncaster Works 20/03/79 and was scrapped 05/79.

D5083
31B March 08/04/1960 E
1A Willesden 04/1960 M
9A Longsight 05/1960 M
1A Willesden 11/1960 M
9A Longsight 11/1960 M
1A Willesden 03/1961 M
5A Crewe North 01/1963 M
1A Willesden 10/1965 M
5A Crewe Diesel 12/1965 M
D05 Stoke Division 18/04/1966 E
D01 London Division (WCML) 09/1966 M
D05 Stoke Division 01/1967 M
CE Crewe Diesel 05/1973 M
Allocation recoded CE to CD 12/1973 M
Renumbered 24083 16/03/1974 E
Store 02/1976 M
Stored at Crewe 02/76
Withdrawn 27/03/1976 E

D5083 contd.
Remained stored at Crewe, then moved to ZL Swindon Works 21/03/77 and cut up by 19/05/77.

D5084
31B March 25/04/1960 E
2A Rugby 04/1960 M
14A Cricklewood 12/1960 M
14B Cricklewood West 09/09/1963 E
Allocation recoded 14A to 14B and renamed Cricklewood West 09/09/1963 E
D14 London (Midland) Division 16/01/1965 E
1A Willesden 03/1965 M
D01 London Division (WCML) 18/04/1966 E
D05 Stoke Division 04/1967 M
CE Crewe Diesel 05/1973 M
Allocation recoded CE to CD 12/1973 M
Renumbered 24084 30/03/1974 E
Withdrawn 17/07/1976 E
Stored at Crewe until moved to Oxford on 19/05/77, then to ZL Swindon Works on 31/05/77 and was broken up by 01/12/78.

D5085
31B March 20/08/1960 E
1A Willesden 08/1960 M
14A Cricklewood 01/1961 M
14B Cricklewood West 09/09/1963 E
Allocation recoded 14A to 14B and renamed Cricklewood West 09/09/1963 E
D14 London (Midland) Division 16/01/1965 E
1A Willesden 03/1965 M
D01 London Division (WCML) 18/04/1966 E
D05 Stoke Division 03/1967 M
CE Crewe Diesel 05/1973 M
Allocation recoded CE to CD 12/1973 M
Renumbered 24085 05/1974 M
Store 02/05/1976 E
Withdrawn 17/07/1976 E
Stored at Crewe until sent to ZL Swindon Works on 31/05/77 and was scrapped by 11/10/78.

D5086
31B March 21/05/1960 E
1A Willesden 05/1960 M
14A Cricklewood 01/1961 M
14B Cricklewood West 09/09/1963 E
Allocation recoded 14A to 14B and renamed Cricklewood West 09/09/1963 E
D14 London (Midland) Division 16/01/1965 E
1A Willesden 04/1965 M
D01 London Division (WCML) 18/04/1966 E
D05 Stoke Division 03/1967 M

D5086 contd.
CE Crewe Diesel 05/1973 M
Allocation recoded CE to CD 12/1973 M
Renumbered 24086 16/02/1974 E
Store 11/1975 M
Stored at Crewe 11/75
Withdrawn 04/01/1976 E
Withdrawn due to collision damage. Remained stored at Crewe, then moved to ZE Derby Works 01/76 and stored there. Moved to ZF Doncaster Works 09/06/76 and scrapped 01/77.

D5087
31B March 09/06/1960 E
1A Willesden 06/1960 M
14A Cricklewood 12/1960 M
14B Cricklewood West 09/09/1963 E
Allocation recoded 14A to 14B and renamed Cricklewood West 09/09/1963 E
1A Willesden 12/1964 M
D01 London Division (WCML) 18/04/1966 E
D05 Stoke Division 03/1967 M
CE Crewe Diesel 05/1973 M
Allocation recoded CE to CD 12/1973 M
Renumbered 24087 09/02/1974 E
Store 07/1976 M
CD Crewe Diesel 24/07/1976 E
Returned to Service 24/07/1976 E
Withdrawn 01/02/1978 E
Stored at Crewe 02/78, then moved to ZF Doncaster Works 27/07/78 and dismantled by 09/78.

D5088
31B March 13/06/1960 E
14A Cricklewood 06/1960 M
14B Cricklewood West 09/09/1963 E
Allocation recoded 14A to 14B and renamed Cricklewood West 09/09/1963 E
D14 London (Midland) Division 16/01/1965 E
1A Willesden 02/1965 M
D01 London Division (WCML) 18/04/1966 E
D05 Stoke Division 03/1967 M
Withdrawn 27/06/1970 E
Withdrawn due to collision damage. Moved to ZE Derby Works 06/70 and stored there. Moved to G. Cohen, Kettering 15/10/71 and broken up 01/72 with some remains still in evidence on 11/02/72.

D5089
31B March 20/06/1960 E
14A Cricklewood 06/1960 M
14B Cricklewood West 09/09/1963 E

D5089 contd.
Allocation recoded 14A to 14B and renamed Cricklewood West 09/09/1963 E
1A Willesden 08/1964 M
14B Cricklewood West 09/1964 M
1A Willesden 12/1964 M
D01 London Division (WCML) 18/04/1966 E
D05 Stoke Division 03/1967 M
CE Crewe Diesel 05/1973 M
Allocation recoded CE to CD 12/1973 M
Renumbered 24089 16/03/1974 E
Store 12/1975 M
Stored at Birkenhead, Mollington Street 12/75
Withdrawn 04/01/1976 E
Withdrawn due to collision damage. Remained stored at Birkenhead Mollington Street, then to ZL Swindon Works 07/12/76 and cut up by 20/07/77.

D5090
31B March 18/06/1960 E
14A Cricklewood 06/1960 M
14B Cricklewood West 09/09/1963 E
Allocation recoded 14A to 14B and renamed Cricklewood West 09/09/1963 E
1A Willesden 12/1964 M
D01 London Division (WCML) 18/04/1966 E
D05 Stoke Division 03/1967 M
Store 09/08/1969 E
55A Leeds Holbeck 11/1969 M
Returned to Service 11/1969 M
52A Gateshead 05/1971 M
66A Polmadie 10/1971 M
65A Eastfield 03/1972 M
Allocation recoded 65A to ED 05/1973 M
Renumbered 24090 04/1974 M
Store 08/1975 M
Stored at Carlisle 8/75
Withdrawn 02/02/1976 E
Remained stored at Carlisle until finally moved to ZF Doncaster Works on 08/12/77 and scrapped by 01/78.

D5091
31B March 25/06/1960 E
14A Cricklewood 06/1960 M
14B Cricklewood West 09/09/1963 E
Allocation recoded 14A to 14B and renamed Cricklewood West 09/09/1963 E
1A Willesden 09/1964 M
D01 London Division (WCML) 18/04/1966 E
9A Longsight 12/1966 M
D01 London Division (WCML) 03/1967 M

D5091 contd.
D05 Stoke Division 03/1967 M
CE Crewe Diesel 05/1973 M
Allocation recoded CE to CD 12/1973 M
Renumbered 24091 04/1974 M
Store 10/1977 M
Stored at Crewe 10/77
Withdrawn 20/11/1977 E
Remained stored at Crewe, then moved to ZF Doncaster Works 11/05/78 and dismantled 06/78.

D5092
31B March 15/07/1960 E
14A Cricklewood 07/1960 M
14B Cricklewood West 09/09/1963 E
Allocation recoded 14A to 14B and renamed Cricklewood West 09/09/1963 E
1A Willesden 12/1964 M
D01 London Division (WCML) 18/04/1966 E
D05 Stoke Division 03/1967 M
CE Crewe Diesel 05/1973 M
Allocation recoded CE to CD 12/1973 M
Renumbered 24092 04/1974 M
Withdrawn 04/10/1975 E
Stored at Crewe until moved to ZL Swindon Works 04/08/76 and cut up by 21/12/76.

D5093
31B March 28/07/1960 E
14A Cricklewood 07/1960 M
14B Cricklewood West 09/09/1963 E
Allocation recoded 14A to 14B and renamed Cricklewood West 09/09/1963 E
1A Willesden 12/1964 M
D01 London Division (WCML) 18/04/1966 E
D05 Stoke Division 03/1967 M
Store 07/1969 M
Stored at Chester depot following accident damage there on 09/07/69.
Withdrawn 14/08/1969 E
It was then moved to the old yard across from the shed and the engine removed there. Moved to J. Cashmore, Great Bridge, West Midlands 04/70 and was still intact on 29/06/70, but was scrapped during 07/70.

D5094
31B March 18/02/1960 E
30A Stratford 03/1961 M
34G Finsbury Park 03/1961 M
64B Haymarket 08/1966 M
Allocation recoded 64B to HA 05/1973 M
Renumbered 24094 04/1974 M
Store 08/1975 M

D5094 contd.
HA Haymarket 18/12/1975 E
Stored at Haymarket 08/75, moved to Carstairs 10/75 for further storage.
Returned to Service 18/12/1975 E
Store 17/09/1976 E
Stored at Haymarket 17/09/76 after collision damage, moved to Millerhill Yard 01/77 for further storage.
Withdrawn 01/12/1976 E
Remained stored at Millerhill Yard. Moved to Tyne Yard 12/06/77 and arrived at ZF Doncaster Works 15/06/77 and was broken up in 09/77.

D5095
31B March 25/03/1960 E
34G Finsbury Park 06/1961 M
64B Haymarket 08/1966 M
Allocation recoded 64B to HA 05/1973 M
Renumbered 24095 10/1973 M
Withdrawn 16/08/1975 E
Stored at Haymarket, then moved to Cadder Yard, Glasgow 08/75 and to ZH Glasgow Works 10/75 remaining there until moved to ZF Doncaster Works on 18/02/76 and was scrapped in 06/76.

D5096
52A Gateshead 09/04/1960 E
50A York 02/1963 M
55A Leeds Holbeck 06/1967 M
52A Gateshead 05/1971 M
66A Polmadie 10/1971 M
65A Eastfield 03/1972 M
Allocation recoded 65A to ED 05/1973 M
Renumbered 24096 04/1974 M
PO Polmadie 08/1975 M
Store 08/1975 M
Withdrawn 16/08/1975 E
Stored at Polmadie 08/75, moved to Eastfield 09/75 for further storage, then to ZH Glasgow Works 10/75 and on to ZF Doncaster Works on 23/01/76 where it was cut up with just the frame left on 11/07/76. This had been removed by 29/07/76.

D5097
52A Gateshead 05/05/1960 E
55A Leeds Holbeck 10/1967 M
66A Polmadie 10/1971 M
65A Eastfield 03/1972 M
Allocation recoded 65A to ED 05/1973 M
Renumbered 24097 01/1974 M
Store 08/1975 M

D5097 contd.
Stored at Carlisle 08/75
Withdrawn 02/02/1976 E
Remained stored at Carlisle, then moved to ZH Glasgow Works 16/03/76 and held there until sent to Doncaster on 15/07/76, arriving at Doncaster shed remaining there until moved into ZF Doncaster Works by 09/76 and was scrapped in 02/77.

D5098
52A Gateshead 26/05/1960 E
50A York 03/1963 M
55A Leeds Holbeck 06/1967 M
66A Polmadie 10/1971 M
65A Eastfield 03/1972 M
Allocation recoded 65A to ED 05/1973 M
Renumbered 24098 02/1974 M
Store 08/1975 M
Withdrawn 16/08/1975 E
Stored at Cadder Yard, Glasgow 08/75, moved to ZH Glasgow Works 10/75, then moved to ZF Doncaster Works on 18/02/76 and was cut up 05/76.

D5099
52A Gateshead 03/06/1960 E
50A York 02/1963 M
55A Leeds Holbeck 06/1967 M
66A Polmadie 07/1971 M
65A Eastfield 03/1972 M
Allocation recoded 65A to ED 05/1973 M
Renumbered 24099 05/1974 M
Store 08/1975 M
Stored at Eastfield 08/75, then moved to Carstairs 10/75 for further storage.
Withdrawn 02/02/1976 E
Remained stored at Carstairs. Moved to Doncaster shed 03/04/76 and remained there until 09/76 when it entered ZF Doncaster Works and was eventually scrapped in 07/77.

D5100
52A Gateshead 25/06/1960 E
12C Carlisle Canal 05/1962 M
52A Gateshead 05/1962 M
50A York 03/1963 M
55A Leeds Holbeck 04/1967 M
66A Polmadie 07/1971 M
65A Eastfield 03/1972 M
Allocation recoded 65A to ED 05/1973 M
Renumbered 24100 10/1973 M
Store 08/1975 M
Stored at Eastfield 08/75, then moved to

D5100 contd.

Carstairs 10/75 for further storage.
Withdrawn 02/02/1976 E
Remained stored at Carstairs, then moved to ZF Doncaster Works 04/04/76 and dismantled during 05/76.

D5101

52A Gateshead 09/07/1960 E
55A Leeds Holbeck 10/1967 M
66A Polmadie 07/1971 M
65A Eastfield 03/1972 M
60A Inverness 02/1973 M
65A Eastfield 02/1973 M
Allocation recoded 65A to ED 05/1973 M
Renumbered 24101 05/1974 M
Store 08/1975 M
Stored at Eastfield 08/75, then moved to Carstairs 10/75 and to Inverness 11/75, both for further storage.
Withdrawn 02/02/1976 E
Remained stored at Inverness, then moved to ZF Doncaster Works about 01/76 and broken up by 03/76.

D5102

52A Gateshead 16/07/1960 E
Allocation recoded 52A to GD 05/1973 M
Renumbered 24102 23/11/1973 E
IS Inverness 05/1974 M
Store 10/1975 M
Stored at Carlisle 10/75, then moved to Inverness 11/75 for further storage.
Withdrawn 02/02/1976 E
Remained stored at Inverness, then moved to Carlisle about 04/03/76 and remained there until it finally left for ZF Doncaster Works on 14/02/78 and was cut up by 19/03/78 except for one cab that was scrapped later.

D5103

52A Gateshead 06/08/1960 E
Allocation recoded 52A to GD 05/1973 M
Renumbered 24103 02/1974 M
IS Inverness 05/1974 M
Store 10/1975 M
Stored at Millerhill Yard 10/75, then moved to Carlisle about 04/03/76.
HA Haymarket 13/04/1976 E

Another Class 24 to enter departmental service was 24061 which in 1976 became RDB968007 and later TDB968007 before, in August 1979, again being renumbered, this time as 97201. This number was briefly carried whilst in blue with full yellow ends but 97201 than emerged in the red and blue departmental scheme and is at Coalville in May 1981. *(Ray Reed/RCTS Photo Archive*

D5103 contd.
Returned to Service 13/04/1976 E
Store 03/08/1976 E
Stored at Motherwell 03/08/76, then moved to Polmadie 11/76 for further storage.
Withdrawn 01/12/1976 E
Remained stored at Polmadie. Moved to Tyne Yard 16/06/77 and on to ZF Doncaster Works 21/06/77 where it was scrapped during 07/77.

D5104
52A Gateshead 27/08/1960 E
Allocation recoded 52A to GD 05/1973 M
Renumbered 24104 03/1974 M
Officially renumbered 03/74 but actually renumbered 14/12/73.
IS Inverness 05/1974 M
Store 08/1975 M
Stored at Inverness 08/75, moved to Carstairs 10/75 for further storage.
HA Haymarket 13/04/1976 E
Returned to Service 13/04/1976 E
Store 22/10/1976 E
Stored at Millerhill Yard 22/10/76
Withdrawn 31/12/1976 E
Remained stored at Millerhill Yard, then moved to ZF Doncaster Works 18/06/77 and cut up 09/77.

D5105
52A Gateshead 10/09/1960 E
Allocation recoded 52A to GD 05/1973 M
Renumbered 24105 02/1974 M
ED Eastfield 05/1974 M
Store 08/1975 M
Stored at Cadder Yard, Glasgow 08/75, then moved to Carlisle 09/75 for further storage.
Withdrawn 05/10/1975 E
Remained stored at Carlisle; then moved to ZF Doncaster Works 29/12/77 and dismantled during 02/78.

D5106
52A Gateshead 24/09/1960 E
Allocation recoded 52A to GD 05/1973 M
Renumbered 24106 02/1974 M
ED Eastfield 05/1974 M
HA Haymarket 08/1975 M
Store 10/1975 M
HA Haymarket 11/1975 M
Returned to Service 11/1975 M
Store 22/10/1976 E
Stored at Millerhill Yard 22/10/76
Withdrawn 31/12/1976 E

D5106 contd.
Remained stored at Millerhill Yard, then moved to ZF Doncaster Works 18/06/77 and cut up in 10/77.

D5107
52A Gateshead 08/10/1960 E
Allocation recoded 52A to GD 05/1973 M
Renumbered 24107 01/1974 M
HA Haymarket 04/1974 M
ED Eastfield 04/1974 M
HA Haymarket 08/1975 M
Store 05/10/1976 E
Stored at Millerhill Yard 05/10/76
Withdrawn 01/12/1976 E
Remained stored at Millerhill Yard, then moved to ZF Doncaster Works 04/05/77 and cut up by 15/06/77.

D5108
52A Gateshead 22/10/1960 E
Allocation recoded 52A to GD 05/1973 M
Renumbered 24108 16/11/1973 E
HA Haymarket 04/1974 M
ED Eastfield 04/1974 M
HA Haymarket 08/1975 M
Store 10/1975 M
Stored at Millerhill Yard 10/75, then moved to Haymarket 11/75 and on to Carlisle about 04/03/76, both for further storage.
Withdrawn 18/07/1976 E
Remained stored at Carlisle, then moved to ZF Doncaster Works on 08/12/77 and scrapped during 01/78.

D5109
52A Gateshead 05/11/1960 E
Allocation recoded 52A to GD 05/1973 M
Renumbered 24109 02/1974 M
HA Haymarket 04/1974 M
ED Eastfield 04/1974 M
HA Haymarket 08/1975 M
Store 10/1975 M
Stored at Millerhill Yard 10/75.
Withdrawn 02/02/1976 E
Remained stored at Millerhill Yard, then moved to Carlisle about 04/03/76 for further storage. Moved to ZF Doncaster Works on 29/12/77 and was broken up during 03/78.

D5110
52A Gateshead 16/11/1960 E
Allocation recoded 52A to GD 05/1973 M
Renumbered 24110 10/1973 M
HA Haymarket 05/1974 M

D5110 contd.
IS Inverness 05/1975 M
HA Haymarket 10/1975 M
Store 04/10/1976 E
Stored at Millerhill 04/10/76.
Withdrawn 01/12/1976 E
Remained stored at Millerhill, then moved to ZF Doncaster Works in 02/77 and was scrapped in 04/77.

D5111
52A Gateshead 26/11/1960 E
Allocation recoded 52A to GD 05/1973 M
Renumbered 24111 02/1974 M
HA Haymarket 03/1974 M
ED Eastfield 04/1974 M
IS Inverness 12/1974 M
ED Eastfield 03/1975 M
HA Haymarket 08/1975 M
Store 10/1975 M
Stored at Millerhill Yard 10/75. then moved to Haymarket 11/75 for further storage.
Withdrawn 02/02/1976 E
Remained stored at Haymarket, moved to Carlisle about 04/03/76 for further storage, then moved to ZF Doncaster Works 29/12/77 and cut up 02/78.

D5112
52A Gateshead 30/12/1960 E
51L Thornaby 12/1961 M
52A Gateshead 06/1964 M
55A Leeds Holbeck 10/1967 M
66A Polmadie 10/1971 M
65A Eastfield 03/1972 M
Allocation recoded 65A to ED 05/1973 M
IS Inverness 02/1974 M
Renumbered 24112 07/1974 M
HA Haymarket 11/1975 M
Store 14/10/1976 E
Stored at Millerhill Yard 14/10/76.
Withdrawn 31/12/1976 E
Remained stored at Millerhill Yard, then moved to ZF Doncaster Works 17/06/77 and broken up 10/77.

D5113
52A Gateshead 29/01/1961 E
51L Thornaby 12/1961 M
52A Gateshead 06/1964 M
55A Leeds Holbeck 10/1967 M
66A Polmadie 10/1971 M
65A Eastfield 03/1972 M
60A Inverness 04/1972 M
Allocation recoded 60A to IS 05/1973 M

D5113 contd.
ED Eastfield 10/1973 M
IS Inverness 02/1974 M
Renumbered 24113 07/1974 M
HA Haymarket 10/1975 M
Store 14/10/1976 E
Stored at Millerhill Yard 14/10/76.
Withdrawn 31/12/1976 E
Remained stored at Millerhill Yard until moved to ZF Doncaster Works on 17/06/77 and dismantled during 09/77.

D5114
61A Kittybrewster 23/04/1960 E
Allocation to Kittybrewster unconfirmed, not shown in BR official returns which gave new to Inverness 23/04/1960 E
60A Inverness 04/1960 M
Withdrawn 09/10/1972 E
Withdrawn 09/10/72 due to fire or collision damage. Moved to ZH Glasgow Works 11/72 and broken up on 22/10/73.

D5115
61A Kittybrewster 30/04/1960 E
Allocation to Kittybrewster unconfirmed, not shown in BR official returns which gave as new to Inverness 30/04/1960 E
60A Inverness 05/1960 M
61A Kittybrewster 04/1961 M
60A Inverness 05/1961 M
Allocation recoded 60A to IS 05/1973 M
Renumbered 24115 07/1974 M
HA Haymarket 10/1975 M
Store 22/10/1976 E
Although officially stored on 22/10/76, 24115 worked right up to its withdrawal date.
Withdrawn 31/12/1976 E
Stored at Millerhill Yard, then moved to ZL Swindon Works 04/05/77 and cut up by 09/06/77.

D5116
61A Kittybrewster 07/05/1960 E
Allocation to Kittybrewster unconfirmed, not shown in BR official returns which gave new to Inverness 07/05/1960 E
60A Inverness 05/1960 M
66A Polmadie 12/1960 M
60A Inverness 05/1961 M
Allocation recoded 60A to IS 05/1973 M
Renumbered 24116 04/1974 M
HA Haymarket 10/1975 M
Store 05/09/1976 E
Withdrawn 15/09/1976 E

D5116 contd.
Stored at Polmadie 09/76, then moved to ZF Doncaster Works 05/77 and scrapped during 07/77.

D5117
60A Inverness 14/05/1960 E
65A Eastfield 11/1960 M
64H Leith Central 04/1961 M
Allocation to Leith Central unconfirmed, not shown in BR official returns which gave transferred to Inverness 04/61 04/1961 M
60A Inverness 06/1961 M
Allocation recoded 60A to IS 05/1973 M
Renumbered 24117 07/1974 M
HA Haymarket 11/1975 M
Store 09/01/1976 E
Withdrawn 02/02/1976 E
Moved to ZH Glasgow Works 02/76 and remained there until moved to ZF Doncaster Works 02/05/76 and broken up during 01/77.

D5118
60A Inverness 21/05/1960 E
Allocation recoded 60A to IS 05/1973 M
Renumbered 24118 07/1974 M
HA Haymarket 10/1975 M
Store 31/10/1976 E
Stored at Millerhill Yard 31/10/76.
Withdrawn 31/12/1976 E
Remained stored at Millerhill Yard, then moved to ZF Doncaster Works 03/77 and dismantled 05/77.

D5119
60A Inverness 28/05/1960 E
Allocation recoded 60A to IS 05/1973 M
Renumbered 24119 03/1974 M
HA Haymarket 11/1975 M
Store 13/04/1976 E
Stored at Haymarket 13/04/76.
Withdrawn 18/07/1976 E
Remained stored at Haymarket, then moved to ZF Doncaster Works in 03/77 and cut up 05/77.

D5120
60A Inverness 04/06/1960 E
Allocation recoded 60A to IS 05/1973 M
Renumbered 24120 07/1974 M
HA Haymarket 10/1975 M
Store 31/10/1976 E
Stored at Haymarket 31/10/76.
Withdrawn 31/12/1976 E
Remained stored at Haymarket, then moved to Millerhill Yard 01/77 for further storage,

D5120 contd.
moved to ZF Doncaster Works 15/06/77 and broken up 07/77.

D5121
60A Inverness 11/06/1960 E
Allocation recoded 60A to IS 05/1973 M
Renumbered 24121 02/05/1974 E
HA Haymarket 10/1975 M
Store 22/10/1976 E
Stored 22/10/76 but reinstated the same day due to locomotive shortage, stored again 31/10/76.
Withdrawn 31/12/1976 E
Stored at Polmadie 01/77, then moved to Carlisle 11/77 for further storage. Moved to ZF Doncaster Works 14/02/78 and cut up in 05/78.

D5122
60A Inverness 18/06/1960 E
Withdrawn 02/10/1968 E
Withdrawn 02/10/68 due to damage and fire sustained in an accident at Castlecary, Scotland with a railcar on 09/09/68. Moved to ZH Glasgow Works; noted 30/03/69 minus both cabs and finally broken up 03/71.

D5123
60A Inverness 25/06/1960 E
Allocation recoded 60A to IS 05/1973 M
Renumbered 24123 18/04/1974 E
HA Haymarket 10/1975 M
Store 06/1976 M
Stored at Polmadie 06/76.
Withdrawn 18/07/1976 E
Remained stored at Polmadie, then moved to ZF Doncaster Works during 04/77 and scrapped in 08/77.

D5124
60A Inverness 02/07/1960 E
Allocation recoded 60A to IS 05/1973 M
Renumbered 24124 17/04/1974 E
HA Haymarket 11/1975 M
Store 07/1976 M
Stored at Haymarket 07/76.
Withdrawn 01/12/1976 E
Remained stored at Haymarket, then moved to Millerhill Yard 01/77 for further storage. Moved to ZL Swindon Works 04/05/77 and was cut up immediately, with completion by 25/05/77.

D5125
60A Inverness 14/07/1960 E

A relatively small number of Class 24s and Class 25s survived into preservation given the size of the classes. D5032 had been sent for scrap at T. J. Thompson's yard on Teesside but was loaned to the North Yorkshire Moors Railway and later became resident there. It was painted in two-tone green and is seen on the top of the moors hauling a two-car DMU set on 23rd April 1978.
(Colour-Rail.com

D5125 contd.
Allocation recoded 60A to IS 05/1973 M
Renumbered 24125 17/04/1974 E
HA Haymarket 10/1975 M
Store 11/1975 M
Stored at Haymarket 11/75, then believed to have been moved to Millerhill Yard 01/76 for further storage.
Withdrawn 27/03/1976 E
Remained stored at Millerhill Yard. Moved to Doncaster depot about 05/76 and stored there until moved into ZF Doncaster Works 12/76 and scrapped in 08/77.

D5126
60A Inverness 23/07/1960 E
Allocation recoded 60A to IS 05/1973 M
Renumbered 24126 07/1974 M
HA Haymarket 10/1975 M
Store 18/12/1975 E
Stored 18/12/75, believed to have been at Millerhill Yard.
Withdrawn 02/02/1976 E
Remained stored at Millerhill Yard. Moved

D5126 contd.
to Doncaster depot about 05/76 and stored there until moved into ZF Doncaster Works about 12/76 and broken up 08/77.

D5127
60A Inverness 30/07/1960 E
Allocation recoded 60A to IS 05/1973 M
Renumbered 24127 10/1974 M
HA Haymarket 11/1975 M
Store 18/12/1975 E
Withdrawn 02/02/1976 E
Moved to Doncaster depot about 05/76 and stored there until moved to ZF Doncaster Works about 12/76 and dismantled 04/77.

D5128
60A Inverness 13/08/1960 E
Allocation recoded 60A to IS 05/1973 M
Renumbered 24128 01/05/1974 E
HA Haymarket 10/1975 M
Store 05/1976 M
Withdrawn 18/07/1976 E
Stored at Carstairs 07/76, then moved to York 08/77 and remained there until moved

D51286 contd.
to ZF Doncaster Works 09/77 and cut up during 10/77.

D5129
60A Inverness 27/08/1960 E
Allocation recoded 60A to IS 05/1973 M
Renumbered 24129 04/1974 M
HA Haymarket 11/1975 M
Store 11/10/1976 E
Stored at Millerhill Yard 11/10/76.
Withdrawn 31/12/1976 E
Remained stored at Millerhill Yard, then moved to ZF Doncaster Works in 03/77 and cut up 04/77.

D5130
60A Inverness 03/09/1960 E
Allocation recoded 60A to IS 05/1973 M
Renumbered 24130 04/1974 M
HA Haymarket 11/1975 M
Store 07/10/1976 E
Stored at Haymarket 07/10/76.
Withdrawn 01/12/1976 E
Remained stored at Haymarket, then moved to Millerhill Yard 01/77 for further storage. Moved to ZF Doncaster Works 15/06/77 and scrapped during 09/77.

D5131
60A Inverness 17/09/1960 E
Moved to ZH Glasgow Works about 06/71, believed to be due to accident damage at Inverness Depot about 06/71.
Withdrawn 11/09/1971 E
D5131 was dismantled in 02/72 at ZH Glasgow Works.

D5132
60A Inverness 23/09/1960 E
Allocation recoded 60A to IS 05/1973 M
Renumbered 24132 10/1974 M
Store 10/1975 M
Stored at Inverness 10/75.
Withdrawn 02/02/1976 E
Remained stored at Inverness, then to ZH Glasgow Works 02/76 but moved straight to ZF Doncaster Works on 06/02/76 and was broken up in 03/76.

D5133
9A Longsight 24/09/1960 E
5A Crewe North 11/1960 M
1A Willesden 12/1960 M
12C Carlisle Canal 05/1962 M
1A Willesden 07/1962 M

D5133 contd.
9A Longsight 07/1962 M
5A Crewe North 09/1962 M
1E Bletchley 03/1966 M
D01 London Division (WCML) 18/04/1966 E
D05 Stoke Division 09/1966 M
CE Crewe Diesel 05/1973 M
Allocation recoded CE to CD 12/1973 M
Renumbered 24133 02/1974 M
Store 02/1978 M
Stored at Crewe 02/78.
Withdrawn 21/03/1978 E
Remained stored at Crewe, then moved to ZF Doncaster Works 27/07/78 and scrapped by 10/78.

D5134
9A Longsight 08/10/1960 E
1B Camden 01/1962 M
9A Longsight 10/1962 M
1F Rugby 12/1964 M
9A Longsight 04/1965 M
1F Rugby 11/1965 M
D01 London Division (WCML) 04/1966 M
9A Longsight 04/1966 M
D01 London Division (WCML) 12/1966 M
9A Longsight 03/1967 M
D09 Manchester Division 17/06/1968 E
D05 Stoke Division 11/1968 M
CE Crewe Diesel 05/1973 M
Allocation recoded CE to CD 12/1973 M
Renumbered 24134 02/1974 M
Store 02/10/1976 E
Stored at Crewe 02/10/76.
Withdrawn 04/12/1976 E
Remained stored, then moved to ZL Swindon Works 31/05/77 and cut up by 13/09/78.

D5135
9A Longsight 08/10/1960 E
1B Camden 04/1962 M
9A Longsight 10/1962 M
D09 Manchester Division 17/06/1968 E
D05 Stoke Division 11/1968 M
CE Crewe Diesel 05/1973 M
Allocation recoded CE to CD 12/1973 M
Renumbered 24135 22/04/1974 E
Store 12/1975 M
Withdrawn 04/01/1976 E
Withdrawn 04/01/76 due to collision damage. Stored at Birkenhead Mollington Street, then moved to ZL Swindon Works 07/12/76 and cut up by 02/07/77.

D5136
9A Longsight 22/10/1960 E
D09 Manchester Division 17/06/1968 E
D05 Stoke Division 11/1968 M
CE Crewe Diesel 05/1973 M
Allocation recoded CE to CD 12/1973 M
Renumbered 24136 04/1974 M
Withdrawn 04/10/1975 E
Stored at Crewe 10/75, then moved to ZL Swindon Works 07/09/76 and broken up by 13/01/77.

D5137
9A Longsight 15/10/1960 E
D09 Manchester Division 17/06/1968 E
D05 Stoke Division 11/1968 M
Store 03/1969 M
D05 Stoke Division 04/1969 M
Returned to Service 04/1969 M
CE Crewe Diesel 05/1973 M
Allocation recoded CE to CD 12/1973 M
Renumbered 24137 04/1974 M
Store 02/1976 M
CD Crewe Diesel 03/1976 M
Returned to Service 03/1976 M
Store 02/05/1976 E
Withdrawn 17/07/1976 E
Stored at Bescot 05/76, then towed to Toton 01/78 for derailing/rerailing exercises, then stored there. Moved to ZF Doncaster Works 27/07/78 and cut up during 10/78.

D5138
9A Longsight 29/10/1960 E
D09 Manchester Division 17/06/1968 E
D05 Stoke Division 11/1968 M
Store 07/1969 M
Stored at Chester depot following accident damage there on 09/07/69.
Withdrawn 10/08/1969 E
It was then moved to the old yard across from the shed and the engine removed there. Moved to J. Cashmore, Great Bridge, West Midlands 04/70 and cut up 06/70.

D5139
9A Longsight 29/10/1960 E
D09 Manchester Division 17/06/1968 E
D05 Stoke Division 11/1968 M
Store 07/1969 M
Stored at Chester depot following accident damage there on 09/07/69.
Withdrawn 10/08/1969 E
It was then moved to the old yard across from the shed and the engine removed

D5139 contd.
there. Moved to J. Cashmore, Great Bridge, West Midlands 04/70 and scrapped 06/70.

D5140
9A Longsight 05/11/1960 E
1B Camden 10/1962 M
1E Bletchley 12/1965 M
D01 London Division (WCML) 18/04/1966 E
D05 Stoke Division 09/1966 M
CE Crewe Diesel 05/1973 M
Allocation recoded CE to CD 12/1973 M
Renumbered 24140 02/1974 M
Store 04/01/1976 E
Stored at Crewe 04/01/76.
Withdrawn 31/01/1976 E
Remained stored at Crewe, then moved to ZL Swindon Works 11/05/76 and cut up by 22/09/76.

D5141
9A Longsight 12/11/1960 E
1B Camden 10/1962 M
2F Bescot 12/1965 M
D02 Birmingham Division 18/04/1966 E
D05 Stoke Division 09/1966 M
CE Crewe Diesel 05/1973 M
Allocation recoded CE to CD 12/1973 M
Renumbered 24141 02/1974 M
Store 02/1976 M
Stored at Crewe 02/76.
Withdrawn 17/07/1976 E
Remained stored at Crewe, then moved to ZL Swindon Works 31/05/77 and broken up by 09/06/78.

D5142
9A Longsight 19/11/1960 E
1B Camden 01/1962 M
17A Derby 03/1962 M
1B Camden 03/1962 M
9A Longsight 04/1962 M
16C Derby 03/1964 M
9A Longsight 03/1964 M
D09 Manchester Division 17/06/1968 E
D05 Stoke Division 11/1968 M
CE Crewe Diesel 05/1973 M
Allocation recoded CE to CD 12/1973 M
Renumbered 24142 04/1974 M
Store 02/1976 M
Withdrawn 17/07/1976 E
Stored at Crewe after withdrawal and was taken into Departmental Stock and converted to an unpowered carriage heating unit.

D5142 contd.
To stock as a Departmental unit at Exeter on 31/08/76 but still numbered as 24142.
Renumbered TDB968009 01/77 M
Moved to Worcester on 09/05/77 and during 1978 it was towed to Oxford for use but was stored by 02/79, then moved to Reading and stored from 09/79, but then it was hauled to Cardiff for further use on 25/07/81. It then moved to Ebbw Junction in 10/81 and on to Swansea Maliphant carriage sidings on 05/11/81 with its final move being to Stratford in 09/82 for storage.
Withdrawn 10/1982 M
Hauled from Stratford to Healey Mills Yard on 21/02/83 for further storage, before being sold for scrap to Cooper's Metals, Attercliffe, Sheffield in 05/84. It was towed to its yard in 09/84 and was broken up almost immediately.

D5143

1A Willesden 26/11/1960 E
5A Crewe Diesel 07/1965 M
1A Willesden 10/1965 M
5A Crewe Diesel 12/1965 M
D05 Stoke Division 18/04/1966 E
D01 London Division (WCML) 08/1966 M
D05 Stoke Division 09/1966 M
CE Crewe Diesel 05/1973 M
Allocation recoded CE to CD 12/1973 M
Renumbered 24143 03/1974 M
Store 04/01/1976 E
Withdrawn 31/01/1976 E
Stored at Crewe 01/76, then moved to ZL Swindon Works 12/02/76 and cut up there by 06/05/76.

D5144

1A Willesden 03/12/1960 E
5A Crewe North 11/1964 M
1F Rugby 01/1965 M
D01 London Division (WCML) 18/04/1966 E
D05 Stoke Division 09/1966 M
9A Longsight 04/1968 M
D09 Manchester Division 17/06/1968 E
D05 Stoke Division 11/1968 M
CE Crewe Diesel 05/1973 M
Allocation recoded CE to CD 12/1973 M
Renumbered 24144 15/05/1974 E
Store 04/01/1976 E
Stored at Crewe 04/01/76.
Withdrawn 31/01/1976 E
Remained stored at Crewe, then moved to

D5144 contd.
ZL Swindon Works 11/05/76 and cut up by 30/09/76.

D5145

1A Willesden 10/12/1960 E
5A Crewe North 11/1964 M
1F Rugby 01/1965 M
D01 London Division (WCML) 18/04/1966 E
D05 Stoke Division 09/1966 M
9A Longsight 04/1968 M
D09 Manchester Division 17/06/1968 E
D05 Stoke Division 11/1968 M
CE Crewe Diesel 05/1973 M
Allocation recoded CE to CD 12/1973 M
Renumbered 24145 05/1974 M
Store 04/01/1976 E
Stored at Crewe 04/01/76.
Withdrawn 31/01/1976 E
Remained stored at Crewe, then moved to ZL Swindon Works 12/02/76 with 24143 and was broken up by 15/05/76.

D5146

1A Willesden 10/12/1960 E
21E Monument Lane 05/1961 M
1A Willesden 07/1961 M
9A Longsight 04/1964 M
D09 Manchester Division 17/06/1968 E
D05 Stoke Division 11/1968 M
CE Crewe Diesel 05/1973 M
Allocation recoded CE to CD 12/1973 M
Renumbered 24146 19/03/1974 E
Store 04/01/1976 E
Stored at Crewe 04/01/76.
Withdrawn 31/01/1976 E
Remained stored at Crewe, then moved to ZL Swindon Works 11/05/76 and broken up by 14/10/76.

D5147

52A Gateshead 17/12/1960 E
55A Leeds Holbeck 11/1967 M
66A Polmadie 10/1971 M
65A Eastfield 03/1972 M
Allocation recoded 65A to ED 05/1973 M
Renumbered 24147 04/1974 M
HA Haymarket 08/1975 M
Store 13/04/1976 E
Stored at Haymarket with collision damage 02/04/76; officially stored 13/04/76.
Withdrawn 18/07/1976 E
Remained stored at Haymarket, moved to

D5147 contd.

Carstairs 07/76, then to York 09/77, both for further storage. Moved to ZF Doncaster Works 11/77 and scrapped by 25/11/77.

D5148

52A Gateshead 23/12/1960 E
55A Leeds Holbeck 09/1968 M
66A Polmadie 10/1971 M
65A Eastfield 03/1972 M
Allocation recoded 65A to ED 05/1973 M
Renumbered 24148 04/1974 M
Store 08/1975 M
Stored at Carlisle 08/75.
Withdrawn 05/10/1975 E
Remained stored at Carlisle, then moved to Carstairs 07/76 for further storage. Moved to ZF Doncaster Works 26/10/77 and dismantled during 12/77.

D5149

52A Gateshead 07/02/1961 E
55A Leeds Holbeck 09/1968 M
65A Eastfield 10/1971 M

D5149 contd.

Withdrawn 09/10/1972 E
Withdrawn 09/10/72 due to collision or fire damage. Moved to ZH Glasgow Works and noted 10/02/73; although cutting started in 04/73, it stopped almost immediately. Still intact but cabless on 15/09/73 and remains still extant on 15/10/73, but had been removed by 11/73.

D5150

52A Gateshead 27/02/1961 E
55A Leeds Holbeck 09/1968 M
65A Eastfield 10/1971 M
Allocation recoded 65A to ED 05/1973 M
Renumbered 24150 16/04/1974 E
HA Haymarket 08/1975 M
Store 04/10/1976 E
Stored at Millerhill Yard 04/10/76.
Withdrawn 01/12/1976 E
Remained stored at Millerhill Yard, then moved to ZF Doncaster Works 17/06/77 and cut up during 07/77.

A goodly number of Cl. 24s met there end at Swindon Works and down at the old C shop little remained of 24041 on 11th June 1978 and it was reported as completely cut up four days later. It had been withdrawn almost two years previously. *(Colour-Rail.com*

CLASS 25

The Class 25 Bo-Bo Type 2 diesel-electrics were a 'logical development' of the Class 24s D5000-D5150, again having a Sulzer engine although this was the more powerful 1,250hp 6LDA28B version. However, the traction motors fitted evolved over time with D5151-75 having BTH equipment with subsequent builds receiving AEI motors paired with various versions of GEC-designed other equipment, the various sub-batches thus being D5176-D5232, D5233-99, D7500-97 and D7598-D7677. These also did not coincide with works building batches. Whilst Derby Works built the majority, Darlington Works contributed D5151-85, D5223-32 and D7578-97 whilst D7624-66 were to be constructed by Beyer Peacock although eventually D7660-66 came from Derby Works.

During the build period, which was from 1961 to 1967 the fitting of end doors was discontinued giving the front ends of the locomotives a radically different appearance but as deliveries were not in numerical order the two varieties were mixed numerically with D7597 being the highest numbered with doors whilst many D52xx locomotives had the new front end design. The various equipment differences saw internal class classifications of 25/0 (D5151-75), 25/1 (D5176-D5232), 25/2 D5233-99, D7500-97 and 25/3 for the remainder. The class were permitted to run at 90mph unlike the Class 24s which had a nominal top speed of 75mph.

The North Eastern Region was the first recipient of the class but the vast majority were employed on the Midland with large numbers being allocated to the Nottingham area but they could be found anywhere from London to the Scottish border on that region. Many of the final build, from D7598 upwards, were allocated new to Tinsley whilst 23 were new to Eastfield although these soon migrated to the LMR. The contraction of the work for which the class were primarily designed, being transfer freights and light passenger duties, saw some become surplus and, with the Western Region being required to withdraw its D63xx diesel-hydraulics, a small number of Class 25s moved west to cover some of their duties whilst the demise of Class 24 saw the 25s return north of the border although primarily to southern Scotland rather than Highland line duties.

In later years, with the decision to replace some DMUs with loco-hauled trains, the Class 25s found themselves regularly employed on 'express duties' such as on the Marches line from Crewe to Cardiff but generally it was freight traffic that kept them busy.

D7605 was the first of the class to be condemned, that being in March 1972, being due to accident damage. It was only when the last Class 24s had been condemned that serious inroads were made to the Class 25s and the last was withdrawn in 1987 only for the class to return in the shape of D7672 from 1989 to 1991. A number were cut up at BR works but the majority met their end at the hands of Vic Berry of Leicester. Some twenty class members survived into the preservation arena.

The TOPS renumbering of the class was simple but needing some thought to translate between old and new numbers with D5151-D5299 becoming 25001-149 and D7500-D7677 becoming 25150-25327. Class 25/9 numbers were applied to twelve class members all of these being from the Class 25/3 sub type, originally intended for workings on an ICI contract and based at Kingmoor, but it seems that work did not materialise and they could soon be found anywhere on the LMR.

It seems that the class went through the full palette of green and blue livery variations including it is reported blue with small yellow panels. However, many also sported two-tone green in combination with the new front end design with both yellow panels and full yellow ends. A few of the class carried names towards the end of their careers, almost all deemed to be unofficial appendages. Three locomotives enjoyed a new life as carriage heating units as 97250-2 and in the process acquired both a blue and grey livery and Intercity colours to blend in with the coaching stock with which they were paired.

D5151
51L Thornaby 15/04/1961 E
52A Gateshead 09/1967 M
12A Kingmoor 11/1967 M
8F Springs Branch 01/1968 M
9A Longsight 05/1968 M
D09 Manchester Division 17/06/1968 E
64B Haymarket 10/1972 M
Allocation recoded 64B to HA 05/1973 M
ED Eastfield 12/1973 M
HA Haymarket 02/1974 M
Renumbered 25001 04/1974 M
TI Tinsley 05/1974 M
ED Eastfield 07/1975 M
Store 10/1977 M
Withdrawn 25/09/1980 E
Moved to ZL Swindon Works 16/10/80 and cut up by 03/12/80.

D5152
51L Thornaby 01/05/1961 E
12A Kingmoor 11/1967 M
8F Springs Branch 01/1968 M
9A Longsight 05/1968 M
D09 Manchester Division 17/06/1968 E
64B Haymarket 10/1972 M
Allocation recoded 64B to HA 05/1973 M
Renumbered 25002 03/1974 M
TI Tinsley 05/1974 M
ED Eastfield 07/1975 M
Store 10/06/1977 E
ED Eastfield 21/06/1977 E
Returned to Service 21/06/1977 E
Withdrawn 01/12/1980 E
Moved to ZL Swindon Works 07/03/81 and broken up by 14/04/81.

D5153
51L Thornaby 10/05/1961 E
12A Kingmoor 11/1967 M
8F Springs Branch 01/1968 M
9A Longsight 05/1968 M
D09 Manchester Division 17/06/1968 E
64B Haymarket 10/1972 M
Allocation recoded 64B to HA 05/1973 M
Renumbered 25003 03/1974 M
TI Tinsley 05/1974 M
ED Eastfield 07/1975 M
Withdrawn 18/08/1976 E
Withdrawn due to collision damage. Moved to ZH Glasgow Works by 02/10/76 and scrapped 01/79.

D5154
51L Thornaby 20/05/1961 E
50A York 12/1966 M
55A Leeds Holbeck 06/1967 M
51L Thornaby 09/1967 M
12A Kingmoor 12/1967 M
8F Springs Branch 01/1968 M
9A Longsight 05/1968 M
D09 Manchester Division 17/06/1968 E
64B Haymarket 10/1972 M
Allocation recoded 64B to HA 05/1973 M
Renumbered 25004 04/1974 M
TI Tinsley 05/1974 M
ED Eastfield 07/1975 M
Withdrawn 15/09/1976 E
Stored at Polmadie 11/76, then moved to ZH Glasgow Works 05/77 and dismantled 09/77 with only the frame visible on 01/10/77.

D5155
51L Thornaby 03/06/1961 E
50A York 12/1966 M
55A Leeds Holbeck 06/1967 M
51L Thornaby 09/1967 M
12A Kingmoor 11/1967 M
8F Springs Branch 01/1968 M
9A Longsight 05/1968 M
D09 Manchester Division 17/06/1968 E
65A Eastfield 03/1972 M
Allocation recoded 65A to ED 05/1973 M
HA Haymarket 05/1973 M
Renumbered 25005 01/1974 M
TI Tinsley 10/1974 M
ED Eastfield 08/1975 M
Withdrawn 01/12/1980 E
Moved to ZL Swindon Works 07/03/81 and cut up by 08/08/81.

D5156
51L Thornaby 17/06/1961 E
52A Gateshead 12/1961 M
51L Thornaby 09/1964 M
12A Kingmoor 11/1967 M
8F Springs Branch 01/1968 M
9A Longsight 05/1968 M
D09 Manchester Division 17/06/1968 E
65A Eastfield 03/1972 M
Allocation recoded 65A to ED 05/1973 M
Renumbered 25006 03/1974 M
HA Haymarket 04/1974 M
TI Tinsley 02/1975 M
ED Eastfield 08/1975 M
HA Haymarket 05/1980 M

D5156 contd.
Store 28/09/1980 E
Withdrawn 01/12/1980 E
Moved with 25007 to ZL Swindon Works 06/11/80. Dismantled during 07/83.

D5157
51L Thornaby 07/07/1961 E
52A Gateshead 12/1961 M
51L Thornaby 09/1964 M
55A Leeds Holbeck 07/1971 M
65A Eastfield 10/1971 M
Allocation recoded 65A to ED 05/1973 M
HA Haymarket 04/1974 M
Renumbered 25007 05/1974 M
TI Tinsley 02/1975 M
ED Eastfield 08/1975 M
HA Haymarket 05/1980 M
Store 28/09/1980 E
Withdrawn 12/1980 M
Moved with 25006 to ZL Swindon Works 06/11/80. Broken up by 21/09/82.

D5158
51L Thornaby 10/07/1961 E
55A Leeds Holbeck 07/1971 M
65A Eastfield 01/1972 M
Allocation recoded 65A to ED 05/1973 M
HA Haymarket 04/1974 M
Renumbered 25008 09/1974 M
TI Tinsley 02/1975 M
ED Eastfield 08/1975 M
HA Haymarket 01/1980 M
Withdrawn 09/06/1980 E
Withdrawn due to collision damage. Stored at ZH Glasgow Works by 28/05/80 and dismantled by 08/80.

D5159
51L Thornaby 27/07/1961 E
55A Leeds Holbeck 08/1971 M
65A Eastfield 01/1972 M
Allocation recoded 65A to ED 05/1973 M
Renumbered 25009 04/1974 M
HA Haymarket 04/1974 M
TI Tinsley 10/1974 M
ED Eastfield 08/1975 M
Store 01/02/1976 E
ED Eastfield 06/1976 M
Returned to Service 06/1976 M
HA Haymarket 01/1980 M
Withdrawn 07/07/1980 E
Moved to ZH Glasgow Works and scrapped by 10/80.

D5160
51L Thornaby 19/08/1961 E
55A Leeds Holbeck 08/1971 M
65A Eastfield 01/1972 M
Allocation recoded 65A to ED 05/1973 M
Renumbered 25010 04/1974 M
HA Haymarket 05/1974 M
TI Tinsley 10/1974 M
ED Eastfield 08/1975 M
HA Haymarket 05/1978 M
Store 30/12/1980 E
Stored at Millerhill Yard 30/12/80.
Withdrawn 11/02/1981 E
Withdrawn 11/02/81 and it was moved immediately to ZL Swindon Works arriving there about 14/02/81; cut up by 01/06/81.

D5161
51L Thornaby 02/09/1961 E
65A Eastfield 10/1971 M
Allocation recoded 65A to ED 05/1973 M
Renumbered 25011 10/1973 M
HA Haymarket 05/1974 M
TI Tinsley 03/1975 M
ED Eastfield 08/1975 M
HA Haymarket 10/1976 M
Withdrawn 01/12/1980 E
Moved to ZL Swindon Works 11/02/81 and broken up by 04/03/81.

D5162
51L Thornaby 09/09/1961 E
55A Leeds Holbeck 10/1971 M
41A Tinsley 10/1972 M
Allocation recoded 41A to TI 05/1973 M
Renumbered 25012 02/1974 M
ED Eastfield 08/1975 M
Store 01/02/1976 E
HA Haymarket 05/1976 M
Returned to Service 05/1976 M
Withdrawn 04/02/1977 E
Moved to ZH Glasgow Works by 31/05/77; scrapped 09/77, with just the frame extant on 01/10/77, which was disposed of by 10/10/77.

D5163
51L Thornaby 23/09/1961 E
55A Leeds Holbeck 10/1971 M
41A Tinsley 10/1972 M
Allocation recoded 41A to TI 05/1973 M
Renumbered 25013 03/1974 M
ED Eastfield 08/1975 M
Store 02/1976 M

D5163 contd.
ED Eastfield 06/1976 M
Returned to Service 06/1976 M
HA Haymarket 10/1976 M
Withdrawn 10/09/1980 E
Moved to ZL Swindon Works 16/10/80 and broken up by 08/01/81.

D5164
51L Thornaby 07/10/1961 E
55A Leeds Holbeck 10/1971 M
41A Tinsley 10/1972 M
55A Leeds Holbeck 11/1972 M
Allocation recoded 55A to HO 05/1973 M
TI Tinsley 05/1973 M
Renumbered 25014 02/05/1974 E
ED Eastfield 08/1975 M
Store 01/02/1976 E
Stored at Haymarket 01/02/76 marked as CM&EE Training Locomotive.
HA Haymarket 06/1976 M
Returned to Service 06/1976 M
Withdrawn 20/07/1977 E
Moved to ZH Glasgow Works by 06/08/77 and cut up completely by 09/10/77.

D5165
51L Thornaby 19/10/1961 E
55A Leeds Holbeck 05/1969 M
51L Thornaby 03/1970 M
55A Leeds Holbeck 01/1972 M
41A Tinsley 10/1972 M
Allocation recoded 41A to TI 05/1973 M
Renumbered 25015 03/05/1974 E
Withdrawn 18/12/1975 E
Withdrawn due to collision damage. Moved to ZE Derby Works 12/75 and stored there, then moved to ZF Doncaster Works 10/06/76 and dismantled during 02/77.

D5166
51L Thornaby 02/11/1961 E
52A Gateshead 06/1967 M
51L Thornaby 11/1967 M
55A Leeds Holbeck 10/1968 M
51L Thornaby 05/1970 M
55A Leeds Holbeck 01/1972 M
41A Tinsley 10/1972 M
55A Leeds Holbeck 11/1972 M
Allocation recoded 55A to HO 05/1973 M
TI Tinsley 05/1973 M
HO Leeds Holbeck 10/1973 M
Renumbered 25016 02/1974 M
TI Tinsley 03/1974 M
Withdrawn 25/01/1976 E

D5166 contd.
Stored at Barrow Hill, then moved with 25017 to ZL Swindon Works 10/03/76 and cut up by 16/12/76.

D5167
51L Thornaby 25/11/1961 E
52A Gateshead 06/1967 M
51L Thornaby 11/1967 M
55A Leeds Holbeck 10/1968 M
51L Thornaby 05/1970 M
55A Leeds Holbeck 11/1970 M
51L Thornaby 11/1971 M
55A Leeds Holbeck 01/1972 M
41A Tinsley 10/1972 M
Allocation recoded 41A to TI 05/1973 M
Renumbered 25017 02/1974 M
Withdrawn 25/01/1976 E
Stored at Barrow Hill, then moved with 25016 to ZL Swindon Works on 10/03/76 and broken up by 29/07/76.

D5168
51L Thornaby 01/12/1961 E
52A Gateshead 07/1967 M
51L Thornaby 11/1967 M
55A Leeds Holbeck 11/1967 M
51L Thornaby 05/1970 M
55A Leeds Holbeck 11/1970 M
52A Gateshead 10/1971 M
55A Leeds Holbeck 04/1972 M
41A Tinsley 10/1972 M
Allocation recoded 41A to TI 05/1973 M
HO Leeds Holbeck 10/1973 M
Renumbered 25018 02/1974 M
TI Tinsley 03/1974 M
ED Eastfield 02/1976 M
Overran a signal at danger on 09/11/76 and was derailed on catch points alongside Ayr TMD with the locomotive rolling over onto its side and hitting 20125 causing it slight damage.
Store 18/11/1976 E
Withdrawn 22/11/1976 E
Stored at Ayr, then moved to ZH Glasgow Works 05/08/77 and scrapped during 06/78.

D5169
51L Thornaby 15/12/1961 E
52A Gateshead 07/1967 M
51L Thornaby 11/1967 M
55A Leeds Holbeck 12/1967 M
52A Gateshead 04/1972 M
41A Tinsley 07/1972 M
Allocation recoded 41A to TI 05/1973 M

D5169 contd.
Renumbered 25019 16/11/1973 E
ED Eastfield 02/1976 M
HA Haymarket 01/1980 M
Withdrawn 03/09/1980 E
Moved to ZL Swindon Works 16/10/80 and cut up by 08/01/81.

D5170
51L Thornaby 29/12/1961 E
55A Leeds Holbeck 12/1967 M
51L Thornaby 01/1971 M
55A Leeds Holbeck 03/1971 M
51L Thornaby 11/1971 M
55A Leeds Holbeck 01/1972 M
52A Gateshead 04/1972 M
41A Tinsley 10/1972 M
Allocation recoded 41A to TI 05/1973 M
Renumbered 25020 03/1974 M
Withdrawn 25/01/1976 E
Stored at Barrow Hill, then moved to ZL Swindon Works on 10/03/76 and was broken up by 19/08/76.

D5171
51L Thornaby 03/02/1962 E
55A Leeds Holbeck 12/1967 M
51L Thornaby 01/1971 M
55A Leeds Holbeck 03/1971 M
52A Gateshead 10/1971 M
41A Tinsley 08/1972 M
Allocation recoded 41A to TI 05/1973 M
Renumbered 25021 02/1974 M
ED Eastfield 02/1976 M
HA Haymarket 05/1978 M
Withdrawn 03/09/1980 E
Moved to ZL Swindon Works 16/10/80 and cut up by 16/12/80.

D5172
51L Thornaby 17/02/1962 E
55A Leeds Holbeck 10/1966 M
52A Gateshead 10/1967 M
55A Leeds Holbeck 12/1967 M
51L Thornaby 11/1971 M
55A Leeds Holbeck 01/1972 M
52A Gateshead 08/1972 M
41A Tinsley 10/1972 M
Allocation recoded 41A to TI 05/1973 M
Renumbered 25022 03/1974 M
Store 11/01/1976 E
Withdrawn 25/01/1976 E
Stored at Barrow Hill, then moved to ZH Glasgow Works 18/03/76 and cut up by 29/01/78.

D5173
51L Thornaby 17/03/1962 E
55A Leeds Holbeck 10/1966 M
52A Gateshead 08/1972 M
41A Tinsley 10/1972 M
Allocation recoded 41A to TI 05/1973 M
Renumbered 25023 02/1974 M
ED Eastfield 02/1976 M
HA Haymarket 01/1980 M
Withdrawn 28/09/1980 E
Stored at Millerhill Yard, then moved to ZL Swindon Works 11/02/81 and cut up by 29/03/83.

D5174
51L Thornaby 30/03/1962 E
55A Leeds Holbeck 10/1966 M
52A Gateshead 08/1972 M
41A Tinsley 08/1972 M
Allocation recoded 41A to TI 05/1973 M
Renumbered 25024 03/1974 M
Store 11/01/1976 E
Withdrawn 25/01/1976 E
Stored at Barrow Hill, then moved to ZH Glasgow Works and dismantled during 12/76.

D5175
51L Thornaby 21/04/1962 E
55A Leeds Holbeck 10/1966 M
41A Tinsley 10/1972 M
Allocation recoded 41A to TI 05/1973 M
Renumbered 25025 02/1974 M
ED Eastfield 02/1976 M
Store 09/1976 M
Withdrawn 15/04/1977 E
Stored at Polmadie 09/76. Withdrawn 15/04/77 due to fire damage. Moved to ZH Glasgow Works 02/78 and was scrapped in 06/78.

D5176
55A Leeds Holbeck 08/01/1963 E
50A York 06/1963 M
LMML LM Midland Lines 08/1965 M
50A York 09/1965 M
51L Thornaby 12/1966 M
55A Leeds Holbeck 09/1967 M
65A Eastfield 07/1971 M
D09 Manchester Division 09/1972 M
LO Longsight 05/1973 M
Renumbered 25026 02/1974 M
TI Tinsley 08/1974 M
HA Haymarket 02/1975 M
TO Toton 10/1980 M

D5176 contd.
Withdrawn 24/10/1980 E
Moved to ZL Swindon Works 12/01/81 and cut up by 25/03/81.

D5177
55A Leeds Holbeck 04/02/1963 E
52A Gateshead 06/1963 M
50A York 10/1965 M
55A Leeds Holbeck 04/1967 M
65A Eastfield 07/1971 M
D09 Manchester Division 09/1972 M
LO Longsight 05/1973 M
Renumbered 25027 12/10/1973 E
CD Crewe Diesel 08/1980 M
Withdrawn 09/05/1983 E
Stored at Saltley, then moved to ZL Swindon Works on 25/03/85 where it remained until the closure of the works, departing 26/05/87 to Swindon Cocklebury Yard, on to Oxford Hinksey Yard 02/06/87 and arrived at Vic Berry, Leicester 11/06/87 where it was broken up by 04/10/87.

D5178
55A Leeds Holbeck 08/02/1963 E
52A Gateshead 06/1963 M
50A York 10/1965 M
51L Thornaby 12/1966 M
55A Leeds Holbeck 09/1967 M
65A Eastfield 07/1971 M
Allocation recoded 65A to ED 05/1973 M
Renumbered 25028 04/1974 M
HA Haymarket 05/1974 M
ED Eastfield 05/1978 M
HA Haymarket 01/1980 M
Store 28/10/1980 E
Withdrawn 01/12/1980 E
Stored at Millerhill, then at Polmadie 09/81 for further storage before moving to ZH Glasgow Works in 02/83. Remained there until sold to Vic Berry, Leicester in 01/87. Moved by rail to Thornton Junction on 29/01/87, to Mossend Yard 03/06/87, to Carlisle 04/06/87, to Basford Hall Yard 05/06/87 and on to Leicester Humberstone Road on 08/06/87. Moved into Berry's Yard on 09/06/87 and quickly cut up by 14/06/87, with only the cabs left, which were soon disposed of.

D5179
52A Gateshead 11/02/1963 E
55A Leeds Holbeck 01/1967 M
86B Ebbw Junction 11/1970 M

D5179 contd.
Allocation recoded 86B to EJ 05/1973 M
Renumbered 25029 04/1974 M
CF Cardiff (Canton) 05/1974 M
HA Haymarket 10/1975 M
IS Inverness 11/1975 M
TO Toton 05/1976 M
Withdrawn 07/08/1977 E
Stored at ZE Derby Works, then moved to ZH Glasgow Works by 01/10/77 and broken up by 03/78. The cabs were still there on 25/06/84, but were disposed of by 12/84.

D5180
52A Gateshead 19/02/1963 E
55A Leeds Holbeck 01/1967 M
86B Ebbw Junction 11/1970 M
84A Laira 10/1971 M
86B Ebbw Junction 01/1972 M
Allocation recoded 86B to EJ 05/1973 M
Renumbered 25030 08/02/1974 E
CF Cardiff (Canton) 05/1974 M
HA Haymarket 10/1975 M
IS Inverness 11/1975 M
ED Eastfield 05/1976 M
CW Cricklewood East 05/1976 M
25030 was in collision with 25174 at Aylesbury on 05/08/76 and moved to ZE Derby Works on 09/08/76 for assessment.
Withdrawn 21/08/1976 E
It remained at Derby Works until 05/80 before being scrapped. The official Derby Works scrap list recorded it as being cut up on 04/08/76, the day before its accident that led to its withdrawal!

D5181
52A Gateshead 04/03/1963 E
55A Leeds Holbeck 01/1967 M
86B Ebbw Junction 11/1970 M
Allocation recoded 86B to EJ 05/1973 M
Renumbered 25031 11/1973 M
CF Cardiff (Canton) 05/1974 M
HA Haymarket 10/1975 M
IS Inverness 11/1975 M
ED Eastfield 05/1976 M
SP Springs Branch 05/1976 M
ED Eastfield 10/1977 M
Store 17/10/1977 E
Withdrawn 31/12/1977 E
Moved to ZH Glasgow Works about 03/78 and was cut up 06/78, with just the cabs left 07/78.

Coinciding with the decision to stop fitting end doors the Class 25s were outshopped new in two-tone green livery with yellow warning panels. D5282 is ex-works in this livery at Derby Works in June 1964. *(Trevor Owen/Colour-Rail.com*

D5182
52A Gateshead 19/03/1963 E
55A Leeds Holbeck 12/1967 M
86B Ebbw Junction 11/1970 M
Allocation recoded 86B to EJ 05/1973 M
Renumbered 25032 03/1974 M
CF Cardiff (Canton) 05/1974 M
BS Bescot 10/1976 M
LO Longsight 03/1983 M
CD Crewe Diesel 07/1983 M
Withdrawn 10/03/1986 E
Stored at Toton until moved to Humberstone Road, Leicester on 14/07/88. Taken into Vic Berry, Leicester on 15/07/88 and was still intact on 17/12/88, but had been cut up completely by 02/01/89.

D5183
18A Toton 13/04/1963 E
Allocation recoded 18A to 16A 09/1963 M
41D Canklow 29/12/1963 E
16A Toton 02/1964 M
2E Saltley 04/1964 M
D02 Birmingham Division 04/1966 M
LMML LM Midland Lines 04/1966 M
D16 Nottingham Division 17/06/1968 E

D5183 contd.
D01 London Division 07/1969 M
55A Leeds Holbeck 08/1972 M
41A Tinsley 10/1972 M
Allocation recoded 41A to TI 05/1973 M
Renumbered 25033 02/1974 M
HA Haymarket 02/1975 M
BS Bescot 02/1981 M
Withdrawn 25/04/1983 E
Stored at Birkenhead Mollington Street, then moved to ZE Derby Works 27/08/83, but on 23/09/83 it was moved to Etches Park depot and stored there in a damaged and derelict condition until it was broken up on site there by staff from Vic Berry, Leicester on 22/02/86.

D5184
18A Toton 04/05/1963 E
Allocation recoded 18A to 16A 09/1963 M
41C Wath 02/1964 M
16A Toton 05/1964 M
14B Cricklewood West 09/1964 M
LMML LM Midland Lines 16/01/1965 E
D15 Leicester Division 06/1965 M
LMML LM Midland Lines 07/1965 M

D5184 contd.
D16 Nottingham Division 17/06/1968 E
D01 London Division 07/1969 M
55A Leeds Holbeck 08/1972 M
41A Tinsley 10/1972 M
Allocation recoded 41A to TI 05/1973 M
Renumbered 25034 01/1974 M
HA Haymarket 02/1975 M
ED Eastfield 08/1975 M
HA Haymarket 05/1977 M
BS Bescot 02/1981 M
Store 23/08/1983 E
BS Bescot 21/06/1984 E
Returned to Service 21/06/1984 E
CD Crewe Diesel 07/1985 M
Unofficially named *Castell Aberystwyth/ Aberystwyth Castle* sometime between mid-1985 and the end of 1986.
Withdrawn 22/12/1986 E
Stored at Basford Hall Yard. Sold to Vic Berry, Leicester and moved to Berry's Yard on 29/05/87 and where it was part dismantled and put in the 'pyramid' by 10/10/87. The body was cut up by 04/03/88.

D5185
18A Toton 25/05/1963 E
Allocation recoded 18A to 16A 09/1963 M
15A Leicester (Midland) 01/1964 M
16A Toton 05/1964 M
14B Cricklewood West 09/1964 M
LMML LM Midland Lines 16/01/1965 E
D16 Nottingham Division 17/06/1968 E
D01 London Division 07/1969 M
55A Leeds Holbeck 07/1972 M
41A Tinsley 10/1972 M
Allocation recoded 41A to TI 05/1973 M
Renumbered 25035 02/1974 M
HA Haymarket 02/1975 M
Store 19/06/1979 E
HA Haymarket 06/1980 M
Returned to Service 06/1980 M
CD Crewe Diesel 11/1980 M
Unofficially named *Castell Dinas Bran* - date unknown but post 01/81, painted name later replaced by cast nameplates.
Withdrawn 15/03/1987 E
Stored at Basford Hall Yard until sold to Vic Berry, Leicester. Moved to Humberstone Road, Leicester on 14/07/87 and remained there until moved into Berry's Yard on 11/09/87 where it remained intact.

D5185 contd.
For preservation
Sold for preservation in 1988 and moved 14/07/88 to the Northampton & Lamport Railway, also known as the Northampton Steam Railway, at Pitsford. Repainted as 25735 in 03/95 and painted back to 25035 in 04/97. Moved to the Great Central Railway, Loughborough about 03/03 for bodywork repairs, it was due to return to Northampton & Lamport Railway. However, it appears to have remained at the GCR since 03/03 apart from appearing at galas on other heritage railways. It was repainted as D5185 in 04/06.

D5186
18A Toton 23/03/1963 E
Allocation recoded 18A to 16A 09/1963 M
15A Leicester (Midland) 02/1964 M
LMML LM Midland Lines 16/01/1965 E
D16 Nottingham Division 02/1965 M
D15 Leicester Division 06/1965 M
LMML LM Midland Lines 09/1965 M
D16 Nottingham Division 17/06/1968 E
D10 Preston Division 11/1968 M
D01 London Division 11/1969 M
CD Cricklewood East 05/1973 M
Allocation recoded CD to CW 12/1973 M
Renumbered 25036 03/1974 M
WN Willesden 05/1974 M
CW Cricklewood East 08/1974 M
SP Springs Branch 12/1974 M
LA Laira 05/1978 M
SP Springs Branch 05/1978 M
KD Kingmoor Diesel 08/1980 M
BS Bescot 02/1982 M
Withdrawn 20/12/1982 E
Moved to ZE Derby Works 01/83 and remained until sent to ZL Swindon Works on 05/02/85 and was cut up by 07/06/85.

D5187
18A Toton 23/03/1963 E
Allocation recoded 18A to 16A 09/1963 M
2E Saltley 01/1964 M
16A Toton 09/1964 M
16D Nottingham 10/1964 M
D16 Nottingham Division 16/01/1965 E
D15 Leicester Division 06/1965 M
LMML LM Midland Lines 09/1965 M
D16 Nottingham Division 17/06/1968 E
D10 Preston Division 11/1968 M
D01 London Division 09/1972 M
CD Cricklewood East 05/1973 M

D5187 contd.
TO Toton 09/1973 M
Renumbered 25037 03/1974 M
ED Eastfield 10/1976 M
HA Haymarket 05/1977 M
ED Eastfield 05/1982 M
CD Crewe Diesel 10/1982 M
Withdrawn 19/01/1987 E
Stored at Basford Hall Yard. Sold to Vic Berry, Leicester and moved to Berry's Yard on 29/05/87. It was cut up completely by 14/06/87.

D5188
18A Toton 23/03/1963 E
Allocation recoded 18A to 16A 09/1963 M
2E Saltley 04/1964 M
16C Derby 06/1964 M
D16 Nottingham Division 16/01/1965 E
D15 Leicester Division 06/1965 M
LMML LM Midland Lines 09/1965 M
D16 Nottingham Division 17/06/1968 E
D10 Preston Division 11/1968 M
KM Kingmoor Diesel 05/1973 M
BS Bescot 05/1973 M
Renumbered 25038 25/02/1974 E
KD Kingmoor Diesel 11/1980 M
Withdrawn 05/06/1981 E
Stored at Crewe Diesel, then moved to Gateshead 01/82 for further storage. Moved to ZE Derby Works 19/02/82 and scrapped during 09/82.

D5189
18A Toton 30/03/1963 E
Allocation recoded 18A to 16A 09/1963 M
16C Derby 03/1964 M
D16 Nottingham Division 16/01/1965 E
D15 Leicester Division 06/1965 M
LMML LM Midland Lines 12/1965 M
D16 Nottingham Division 17/06/1968 E
D10 Preston Division 11/1968 M
KM Kingmoor Diesel 05/1973 M
BS Bescot 05/1973 M
Renumbered 25039 02/1974 M
LO Longsight 01/1980 M
Withdrawn 15/06/1981 E
Stored at Bescot. Moved to ZL Swindon Works on 03/08/81 and broken up by 10/12/81.

D5190
18A Toton 06/04/1963 E
Allocation recoded 18A to 16A 09/1963 M
16C Derby 03/1964 M

D5190 contd.
D16 Nottingham Division 16/01/1965 E
LMML LM Midland Lines 06/1965 M
D16 Nottingham Division 17/06/1968 E
D10 Preston Division 11/1968 M
KM Kingmoor Diesel 05/1973 M
BS Bescot 05/1973 M
Renumbered 25040 10/04/1974 E
LO Longsight 11/1980 M
Withdrawn 10/11/1980 E
Moved to ZL Swindon Works 19/12/80 and dismantled by 10/02/82, the cabs were still in evidence on 01/11/87 but disposed of soon afterwards.

D5191
18A Toton 04/05/1963 E
Allocation recoded 18A to 16A 09/1963 M
15A Leicester (Midland) 02/1964 M
LMML LM Midland Lines 16/01/1965 E
D16 Nottingham Division 17/06/1968 E
D10 Preston Division 11/1968 M
KM Kingmoor Diesel 05/1973 M
Renumbered 25041 02/1974 M
Allocation recoded KM-KD 01/1975 M
CD Crewe Diesel 02/1976 M
TO Toton 05/1977 M
KD Kingmoor Diesel 08/1977 M
Withdrawn 31/05/1981 E
Moved to ZL Swindon Works 08/12/81 and broken up by 22/06/83.

D5192
18A Toton 04/05/1963 E
Allocation recoded 18A to 16A 09/1963 M
15A Leicester (Midland) 02/1964 M
LMML LM Midland Lines 16/01/1965 E
D16 Nottingham Division 17/06/1968 E
D10 Preston Division 11/1968 M
KM Kingmoor Diesel 05/1973 M
Renumbered 25042 27/02/1974 E
Allocation recoded KM to KD 01/1975 M
LO Longsight 03/1975 M
CD Crewe Diesel 05/1976 M
Withdrawn 08/05/1986 E
Stored at Crewe Diesel, moved to Gresty Lane 03/87, then to Basford Hall Yard 06/87. Sold to Vic Berry, Leicester and moved to Humberstone Road Yard, Leicester on 16/07/87 and into Berry's Yard on 24/07/87. Noted being cut up on 10/10/87 and completed by 24/10/87.

D5193
18A Toton 04/05/1963 E

D5193 contd.
Allocation recoded 18A to 16A 09/1963 M
16D Nottingham 03/1964 M
16C Derby 10/1964 M
D16 Nottingham Division 16/01/1965 E
2E Saltley 06/1965 M
D02 Birmingham Division 04/1966 M
LMML LM Midland Lines 04/1966 M
D16 Nottingham Division 17/06/1968 E
D08 Liverpool Division 07/1968 M
D10 Preston Division 05/1970 M
KM Kingmoor Diesel 05/1973 M
Renumbered 25043 18/04/1974 E
LO Longsight 09/1974 M
CD Crewe Diesel 05/1976 M
Withdrawn 01/02/1981 E
Taken out of use and moved to Derby 01/81, where it was withdrawn on 01/02/81. Subsequently moved to ZE Derby Works. Mostly dismantled and the shell only left on 01/08/81, which was scrapped on 25/09/81.

D5194
18A Toton 04/05/1963 E
Allocation recoded 18A to 16A 09/1963 M
15A Leicester (Midland) 02/1964 M
LMML LM Midland Lines 16/01/1965 E
D14 London (Midland) Division 01/1967 M
D01 London Division 17/06/1968 E
D08 Liverpool Division 11/1968 M
D10 Preston Division 05/1970 M
KM Kingmoor Diesel 05/1973 M
SP Springs Branch 05/1973 M
Renumbered 25044 03/1974 M
ED Eastfield 10/1976 M
HA Haymarket 01/1980 M
CW Cricklewood East 02/1981 M
KD Kingmoor Diesel 11/1981 M
Withdrawn 09/07/1985 E
Stored at Kingmoor Diesel, then moved to Springs Branch 10/85 for further storage. Moved to ZF Doncaster Works on 16/04/86 and broken up by 12/07/86.

D5195
18A Toton 04/05/1963 E
Allocation recoded 18A to 16A 09/1963 M
16D Nottingham 02/1964 M
D16 Nottingham Division 16/01/1965 E
40E Colwick 05/1965 M
Allocation recoded 40E to 16B 01/1966 M
D16 Nottingham Division 01/1966 M
LMML LM Midland Lines 10/1966 M
D16 Nottingham Division 17/06/1968 E

D5195 contd.
D08 Liverpool Division 07/1968 M
D10 Preston Division 05/1970 M
KM Kingmoor Diesel 05/1973 M
SP Springs Branch 05/1973 M
Renumbered 25045 28/02/1974 E
Store 08/1975 M
Withdrawn 04/10/1975 E
The official scrap list for ZE Derby Works reported that it was cut up there on 17/03/79. but remains were still there on 01/09/79 and were later disposed of.

D5196
18A Toton 11/05/1963 E
Allocation recoded 18A to 16A 09/1963 M
16C Derby 03/1964 M
LMML LM Midland Lines 16/01/1965 E
D14 London (Midland) Division 01/1966 M
D16 Nottingham Division 01/1967 M
LMML LM Midland Lines 06/1968 M
D16 Nottingham Division 17/06/1968 E
D08 Liverpool Division 07/1968 M
D10 Preston Division 05/1970 M
D08 Liverpool Division 07/1972 M
SP Springs Branch 05/1973 M
TO Toton 09/1973 M
Renumbered 25046 25/02/1974 E
SP Springs Branch 08/1976 M
HA Haymarket 05/1977 M
Withdrawn 03/02/1981 E
Stored at Haymarket 02/81, then to Millerhill Yard for further storage. Moved to Mossend Yard by 22/10/81, to Polmadie 26/10/81 and was due to go to ZL Swindon Works, but the locomotive stayed in Scotland being unfit to travel to Swindon. Moved from Polmadie to Shawfield Sidings and remained until sold to Vic Berry, Leicester 04/87 for scrap. Moved to Mossend Yard 10/06/87, to Carlisle 11/06/87, on to Basford Hall on 22/06/87 and to Humberstone Road, Leicester 23/06/87 and into Berry's yard 30/06/87. Cutting up started on 04/07/87 and was completed by 10/07/87.

D5197
18A Toton 11/05/1963 E
Allocation recoded 18A to 16A 09/1963 M
16D Nottingham 01/1964 M
2E Saltley 04/1964 M
D02 Birmingham Division 04/1966 M
LMML LM Midland Lines 04/1966 M
9A Longsight 03/1968 M

D5197 contd.
D09 Manchester Division 17/06/1968 E
LO Longsight 05/1973 M
Renumbered 25047 08/03/1974 E
TO Toton 10/1975 M
SP Springs Branch 08/1976 M
Withdrawn 26/08/1980 E
Stored at Springs Branch. Moved to ZL Swindon Works on 21/11/80 and scrapped by 13/01/81.

D5198
18A Toton 18/05/1963 E
Allocation recoded 18A to 16A 09/1963 M
15A Leicester (Midland) 02/1964 M
LMML LM Midland Lines 16/01/1965 E
8F Springs Branch 10/1967 M
9A Longsight 05/1968 M
D09 Manchester Division 17/06/1968 E
LO Longsight 05/1973 M
Renumbered 25048 02/1974 M
SP Springs Branch 10/1975 M
LA Laira 05/1978 M
BS Bescot 11/1980 M
CW Cricklewood East 01/1983 M
BS Bescot 11/1984 M
CD Crewe Diesel 07/1985 M
Store 21/02/1986 E
Withdrawn 24/02/1986 E
Stored at Crewe Diesel until sold to Vic Berry, Leicester 12/86 for scrap. Moved to Knighton Sidings, Leicester on 23/01/87 and into Berry's Yard on 26/01/87. It was dismantled by 11/04/87.

D5199
18A Toton 18/05/1963 E
Allocation recoded 18A to 16A 09/1963 M
16D Nottingham 02/1964 M
LMML LM Midland Lines 16/01/1965 E
8F Springs Branch 10/1967 M
9A Longsight 05/1968 M
D09 Manchester Division 17/06/1968 E
LO Longsight 05/1973 M
Renumbered 25049 04/1974 M
TO Toton 10/1975 M
CD Crewe Diesel 07/1976 M
ED Eastfield 10/1976 M
HA Haymarket 02/1978 M
CD Crewe Diesel 10/1982 M
Withdrawn 08/01/1984 E
Moved to ZE Derby Works with collision damage 11/83 and withdrawn 08/01/84. Sent to ZL Swindon Works on 05/02/85 and scrapped by 05/06/85.

D5200
18A Toton 01/06/1963 E
Allocation recoded 18A to 16A 09/1963 M
16C Derby 03/1964 M
LMML LM Midland Lines 16/01/1965 E
52A Gateshead 08/1965 M
50A York 08/1965 M
LMML LM Midland Lines 09/1965 M
8F Springs Branch 10/1967 M
9A Longsight 05/1968 M
D09 Manchester Division 17/06/1968 E
LO Longsight 05/1973 M
Renumbered 25050 21/03/1974 E
KD Kingmoor Diesel 03/1975 M
HA Haymarket 05/1977 M
ED Eastfield 12/1978 M
HA Haymarket 01/1980 M
TO Toton 02/1981 M
KD Kingmoor Diesel 05/1981 M
CW Cricklewood East 11/1981 M
Withdrawn 25/04/1983 E
Moved to ZE Derby Works about 30/04/83 and stored there until moved to ZL Swindon Works 04/02/85 and was cut up by 02/04/85.

D5201
18A Toton 25/05/1963 E
Allocation recoded 18A to 16A 09/1963 M
16D Nottingham 02/1964 M
LMML LM Midland Lines 16/01/1965 E
8F Springs Branch 10/1967 M
D08 Liverpool Division 17/06/1968 E
SP Springs Branch 05/1973 M
LO Longsight 09/1973 M
Renumbered 25051 27/02/1974 E
CW Cricklewood East 10/1976 M
BS Bescot 08/1980 M
CD Crewe Diesel 07/1985 M
Withdrawn 18/09/1985 E
Stored at Kingmoor Diesel until at least 04/86, then moved to Kingmoor New Yard for further storage. Sold for scrap to Vic Berry, Leicester about 02/87. Towed to Warrington Arpley on 09/03/87, then to Basford Hall Yard on 10/03/87, on to Humberstone Road, Leicester 11/03/87 and into Berry's Yard 12/03/87. It was cut up by 03/04/87 but cabs still in existence on 16/06/87, which were later disposed of.

D5202
18A Toton 01/06/1963 E
Allocation recoded 18A to 16A 09/1963 M
9A Longsight 01/1964 M

D5202 contd.
10G Skipton 05/1964 M
9A Longsight 07/1964 M
16A Toton 09/1964 M
16D Nottingham 12/1964 M
D16 Nottingham Division 16/01/1965 E
2E Saltley 06/1965 M
D02 Birmingham Division 04/1966 M
LMML LM Midland Lines 04/1966 M
8F Springs Branch 11/1967 M
D08 Liverpool Division 17/06/1968 E
82A Bristol Bath Road 01/1972 M
Allocation recoded 82A to BR 05/1973 M
Renumbered 25052 02/1974 M
LA Laira 05/1976 M
Withdrawn 05/10/1980 E
Moved to ZL Swindon Works 08/10/80 and scrapped on 12/11/80.

D5203
18A Toton 01/06/1963 E
14A Cricklewood 07/1963 M
18A Toton 08/1963 M
Allocation recoded 18A to 16A 09/1963 M
16D Nottingham 03/1964 M
LMML LM Midland Lines 16/01/1965 E
8F Springs Branch 11/1967 M

D5203 contd.
D08 Liverpool Division 17/06/1968 E
D09 Manchester Division 11/1970 M
LO Longsight 05/1973 M
Renumbered 25053 02/1974 M
CW Cricklewood East 05/1977 M
BS Bescot 08/1980 M
Store 03/11/1980 E
Stored at ZL Swindon Works 03/11/80
Withdrawn 01/12/1980 E
Remained in store at Swindon Works until broken up by 18/11/81.

D5204
18A Toton 08/06/1963 E
14A Cricklewood 07/1963 M
14B Cricklewood West 09/09/1963 E
Allocation recoded 14A to 14B and renamed Cricklewood West 09/09/1963 E
LMML LM Midland Lines 16/01/1965 E
8F Springs Branch 11/1967 M
12A Kingmoor Diesel 01/1968 M
D05 Stoke Division 05/1968 M
D08 Liverpool Division 11/1968 M
D09 Manchester Division 02/1972 M
LO Longsight 05/1973 M
Renumbered 25054 03/1974 M

A general livery development was the adoption of full yellow ends across the locomotive fleet and all of classes 24 and 25 were so treated. Class 25 D7579 shows this variant at Polmadie in 1967.
(Colour-Rail.com

D5204 contd.
CW Cricklewood East 05/1977 M
BS Bescot 08/1980 M
CD Crewe Diesel 03/1983 M
Withdrawn 12/05/1985 E
Stored at Gresty Lane, Crewe 06/10/85. Moved to ZF Doncaster Works 24/01/86 and cut up by 13/09/86.

D5205
18A Toton 15/06/1963 E
14A Cricklewood 07/1963 M
18A Toton 08/1963 M
Allocation recoded 18A to 16A 09/1963 M
16C Derby 03/1964 M
LMML LM Midland Lines 16/01/1965 E
8F Springs Branch 11/1967 M
12A Kingmoor Diesel 01/1968 M
D05 Stoke Division 05/1968 M
D08 Liverpool Division 11/1968 M
D09 Manchester Division 11/1970 M
LO Longsight 05/1973 M
Renumbered 25055 19/03/1974 E
CD Crewe Diesel 05/1976 M
CF Cardiff (Canton) 12/1976 M
CD Crewe Diesel 11/1977 M
KD Kingmoor Diesel 08/1980 M
Withdrawn 12/11/1980 E
Moved to ZL Swindon Works 27/02/81 and cut up by 24/12/81.

D5206
18A Toton 22/06/1963 E
14A Cricklewood 07/1963 M
14B Cricklewood West 09/09/1963 E
Allocation recoded 14A to 14B and renamed Cricklewood West 09/09/1963 E
LMML LM Midland Lines 16/01/1965 E
8F Springs Branch 12/1967 M
D08 Liverpool Division 17/06/1968 E
D10 Preston Division 09/1968 M
D08 Liverpool Division 11/1968 M
SP Springs Branch 05/1973 M
Renumbered 25056 06/03/1974 E
LO Longsight 01/1975 M
CD Crewe Diesel 05/1976 M
KD Kingmoor Diesel 05/1977 M
Withdrawn 01/08/1982 E
Stored at Tinsley 02/83 and moved to Toton on 09/03/83 for further storage. Moved to Swindon Cocklebury Yard 12/07/84 and into ZL Swindon Works on 25/07/84 with scrapping taking place by 06/03/85.

D5207
18A Toton 22/06/1963 E
14A Cricklewood 07/1963 M
18A Toton 08/1963 M
Allocation recoded 18A to 16A 09/1963 M
16C Derby 03/1964 M
LMML LM Midland Lines 16/01/1965 E
8F Springs Branch 12/1967 M
D08 Liverpool Division 17/06/1968 E
D10 Preston Division 09/1968 M
D08 Liverpool Division 11/1968 M
D09 Manchester Division 01/1972 M
D08 Liverpool Division 02/1972 M
SP Springs Branch 05/1973 M
Renumbered 25057 04/1974 M
LA Laira 05/1978 M
LO Longsight 11/1980 M
CD Crewe Diesel 05/1985 M
Withdrawn 15/03/1987 E
Stored at Basford Hall Yard until sold to Vic Berry, Leicester and moved to Humberstone Road, Leicester on 14/07/87. Shunted into Berry's Yard on 11/09/87 and remained intact.
For preservation
Sold for preservation. Moved to Buckinghamshire Railway Centre, Quainton Road arriving there 05/08/88. Later sold to a private individual and moved to the North Norfolk Railway by road on 03/04/91.
Acquired by HNRC, moved from the North Norfolk Railway to Worksop 27/11/19.

D5208
18A Toton 22/06/1963 E
14A Cricklewood 07/1963 M
14B Cricklewood West 09/09/1963 E
Allocation recoded 14A to 14B and renamed Cricklewood West 09/09/1963 E
LMML LM Midland Lines 16/01/1965 E
On loan to the Scottish Region 07/65 - shed not notified.
LMML LM Midland Lines 08/1965 M
D16 Nottingham Division 08/1965 M
LMML LM Midland Lines 10/1966 M
9A Longsight 01/1968 M
12A Kingmoor Diesel 03/1968 M
D10 Preston Division 17/06/1968 E
D08 Liverpool Division 11/1968 M
D09 Manchester Division 11/1970 M
D08 Liverpool Division 05/1971 M
D09 Manchester Division 01/1972 M
LO Longsight 05/1973 M
Renumbered 25058 27/02/1974 E

D5208 contd.
SP Springs Branch 01/1975 M
LA Laira 05/1978 M
BS Bescot 10/1980 M
CD Crewe Diesel 07/1985 M
Unofficially named *Castell Criccieth/ Cricceth Castle*, date unknown but probably in late 1985 or early 1986.
Withdrawn 03/02/1987 E
Stored at Basford Hall Yard, Crewe by 27/03/87 and remained until moved to Humberstone Road, Leicester on 16/07/87 and into Vic Berry, Leicester on 24/07/87. Scrapping was completed by 28/01/89.

D5209
18A Toton 22/06/1963 E
14A Cricklewood 07/1963 M
14B Cricklewood West 09/09/1963 E
Allocation recoded 14A to 14B and renamed Cricklewood West 09/09/1963 E
LMML LM Midland Lines 16/01/1965 E
9A Longsight 01/1968 M
12A Kingmoor Diesel 03/1968 M
D10 Preston Division 17/06/1968 E
D08 Liverpool Division 11/1968 M
D09 Manchester Division 11/1970 M
86B Ebbw Junction 01/1972 M
82A Bristol Bath Road 07/1972 M
Allocation recoded 82A to BR 05/1973 M
Renumbered 25059 07/02/1974 E
CF Cardiff (Canton) 05/1974 M
BR Bristol Bath Road 10/1974 M
HA Haymarket 05/1976 M
ED Eastfield 05/1978 M
HA Haymarket 01/1980 M
SP Springs Branch 09/1982 M
CD Crewe Diesel 10/1982 M
Withdrawn 20/03/1987 E
Stored at Crewe Basford Hall Yard. Moved to Humberstone Road, Leicester on 03/07/87, then into Vic Berry, Leicester on 06/07/87.

For preservation

Sold for preservation to the Keighley & Worth Valley Railway 09/87 and moved there on 09/10/87. Suffered water damage from floods on the K&WVR line in 09/04. Having last been used there in 2019 it was moved to Barrow Hill on 16/03/24 for a major overhaul.

D5210
18A Toton 22/06/1963 E
14A Cricklewood 07/1963 M
18A Toton 08/1963 M

D5210 contd.
Allocation recoded 18A to 16A 09/1963 M
14B Cricklewood West 10/1963 M
LMML LM Midland Lines 16/01/1965 E
9A Longsight 02/1968 M
12A Kingmoor Diesel 03/1968 M
D10 Preston Division 17/06/1968 E
D09 Manchester Division 11/1968 M
LO Longsight 05/1973 M
Renumbered 25060 02/1974 M
SP Springs Branch 10/1975 M
CD Crewe Diesel 08/1980 M
Withdrawn 09/12/1985 E
Moved to ZF Doncaster Works about 29/01/86 and then to Goole Docks on 14/08/86 for storage. Sold to Vic Berry, Leicester 10/86 for scrap. Moved to Humberstone Road, Leicester on 29/10/86 and into Berry's Yard on 30/10/86. Although still intact on 13/03/87, it was cut up by 03/04/87.

D5211
18A Toton 29/06/1963 E
14A Cricklewood 07/1963 M
14B Cricklewood West 09/09/1963 E
Allocation recoded 14A to 14B and renamed Cricklewood West 09/09/1963 E
LMML LM Midland Lines 16/01/1965 E
9A Longsight 02/1968 M
D09 Manchester Division 17/06/1968 E
LO Longsight 05/1973 M
Renumbered 25061 30/05/1974 E
CD Crewe Diesel 05/1976 M
The locomotive was nominally loaned to the Scottish Region in 05/77 but was in works at the time and returned to Crewe Diesel on release.
LO Longsight 08/1980 M
Withdrawn 02/11/1980 E
Moved to ZL Swindon Works 14/01/81 and scrapped by 11/03/83.

D5212
18A Toton 29/06/1963 E
14A Cricklewood 07/1963 M
14B Cricklewood West 09/09/1963 E
Allocation recoded 14A to 14B and renamed Cricklewood West 09/09/1963 E
LMML LM Midland Lines 16/01/1965 E
9A Longsight 03/1968 M
D09 Manchester Division 17/06/1968 E
D01 London Division 08/1972 M
CD Cricklewood East 05/1973 M

D5212 contd.
LO Longsight 05/1973 M
Renumbered 25062 26/02/1974 E
ED Eastfield 08/1975 M
HA Haymarket 05/1976 M
IS Inverness 06/1976 M
ED Eastfield 06/1979 M
LO Longsight 11/1980 M
KD Kingmoor Diesel 07/1981 M
Withdrawn 20/12/1982 E
Moved to ZE Derby Works 01/83 and then to ZL Swindon Works on 04/02/85, broken up by 30/04/85.

D5213
18A Toton 06/07/1963 E
14A Cricklewood 08/1963 M
14B Cricklewood West 09/09/1963 E
Allocation recoded 14A to 14B and renamed Cricklewood West 09/09/1963 E
D14 London (Midland) Division 16/01/1965 E
D01 London Division 17/06/1968 E
86B Ebbw Junction 01/1972 M
82A Bristol Bath Road 07/1972 M
Allocation recoded 82A to BR 05/1973 M
Renumbered 25063 02/1974 M
CF Cardiff (Canton) 05/1974 M
BR Bristol Bath Road 10/1974 M
LA Laira 10/1975 M
CF Cardiff (Canton) 01/1976 M
LA Laira 10/1976 M
CF Cardiff (Canton) 12/1976 M
CD Crewe Diesel 11/1977 M
Withdrawn 17/11/1980 E
Moved to ZL Swindon Works 19/12/80 and cut up by 03/03/83.

D5214
18A Toton 06/07/1963 E
14A Cricklewood 08/1963 M
14B Cricklewood West 09/09/1963 E
Allocation recoded 14A to 14B and renamed Cricklewood West 09/09/1963 E
D14 London (Midland) Division 16/01/1965 E
D01 London Division 17/06/1968 E
55A Leeds Holbeck 08/1972 M
41A Tinsley 10/1972 M
Allocation recoded 41A to TI 05/1973 M
Renumbered 25064 03/1974 M
SP Springs Branch 03/1975 M
IS Inverness 06/1976 M
ED Eastfield 12/1978 M
HA Haymarket 01/1980 M
ED Eastfield 05/1982 M

D5214 contd.
CD Crewe Diesel 10/1982 M
Withdrawn 09/12/1985 E
Stored at Crewe Diesel, until sold to Vic Berry, Leicester in 12/86. Moved to Berry's Yard 12/01/87 and cut up by 06/03/87, with the cabs still in evidence on 16/06/87.

D5215
18A Toton 20/07/1963 E
14A Cricklewood 08/1963 M
14B Cricklewood West 09/09/1963 E
Allocation recoded 14A to 14B and renamed Cricklewood West 09/09/1963 E
D14 London (Midland) Division 16/01/1965 E
D01 London Division 17/06/1968 E
CD Cricklewood East 05/1973 M
Allocation recoded CD to CW 12/1973 M
Renumbered 25065 22/03/1974 E
TO Toton 01/1975 M
SP Springs Branch 10/1976 M
HA Haymarket 05/1977 M
Withdrawn 01/02/1981 E
Stored at Kingmoor Diesel 06/81, then moved to ZL Swindon Works 25/06/81 and cut up by 03/02/82.

D5216
18A Toton 13/07/1963 E
14A Cricklewood 08/1963 M
14B Cricklewood West 09/09/1963 E
Allocation recoded 14A to 14B and renamed Cricklewood West 09/09/1963 E
D14 London (Midland) Division 16/01/1965 E
D01 London Division 17/06/1968 E
CD Cricklewood East 05/1973 M
Allocation recoded CD to CW 12/1973 M
Renumbered 25066 03/1974 M
TO Toton 10/1975 M
SP Springs Branch 10/1976 M
HA Haymarket 05/1977 M
IS Inverness 12/1978 M
ED Eastfield 06/1979 M
Involved in a major accident, also involving 47208 , near Invergowrie on 22/10/79.
TO Toton 12/1980 M
CW Cricklewood East 03/1981 M
Withdrawn 21/06/1981 E
Stored at Toton 01/82, then moved to ZE Derby Works 02/82 and scrapped by 02/83 with the remains noted loaded in wagons at the works on 08/03/83 for final disposal.

D5217
18A Toton 03/08/1963 E

D5217 contd.

14A Cricklewood 08/1963 M
14B Cricklewood West 09/09/1963 E
Allocation recoded 14A to 14B and renamed Cricklewood West 09/09/1963 E
D14 London (Midland) Division 16/01/1965 E
D01 London Division 17/06/1968 E
CD Cricklewood East 05/1973 M
Allocation recoded CD to CW 12/1973 M
Renumbered 25067 03/1974 M
TO Toton 01/1981 M
CW Cricklewood East 02/1982 M
Withdrawn 13/12/1982 E
Stored at Bescot until 10/83. Moved to Wellington 11/10/83 for 'Rail Week' and later back to Bescot, then to Wolverhampton in early 1984. Moved to Swindon Cocklebury Yard 16/07/84 and to ZL Swindon Works 23/07/84 and stored intact.

For preservation
Sold for preservation 22/03/85 to the Mid-Hants Railway, but remained at Swindon Works until moved on 26/11/85. Repainted as D5217 while there. It was moved to the Battlefield Line, Shackerstone in 04/95 for further use.
Resold and moved by road to Barrow Hill Roundhouse Museum on 06/05/99. Following various repairs and other work there including reinstatement of the steam heat boiler, moved in 12/07 to the Weardale Railway. Moved back to the Battlefield Line in 12/08 for use and to stay on the line apart from visiting galas on other heritage railways. To Nemesis Rail, Burton-upon-Trent, date unknown.

D5218

14A Cricklewood 03/08/1963 E
14B Cricklewood West 09/09/1963 E
Allocation recoded 14A to 14B and renamed Cricklewood West 09/09/1963 E
D14 London (Midland) Division 16/01/1965 E
D01 London Division 17/06/1968 E
WN Willesden 05/1973 M
Renumbered 25068 08/03/1974 E
CW Cricklewood East 06/1975 M
ED Eastfield 06/1976 M
IS Inverness 05/1977 M
ED Eastfield 06/1979 M
Withdrawn 14/07/1980 E
Moved to ZH Glasgow Works 04/10/80 and broken up by 07/10/81.

D5219

18A Toton 10/08/1963 E
Allocation recoded 18A to 16A 09/1963 M
14B Cricklewood West 10/1963 M
D14 London (Midland) Division 16/01/1965 E
D01 London Division 17/06/1968 E
WN Willesden 05/1973 M
Renumbered 25069 02/1974 M
CW Cricklewood East 06/1975 M
Withdrawn 18/12/1983 E
Stored at Springs Branch. Moved to ZL Swindon Works 21/02/85 and cut up by 20/06/86.

D5220

14B Cricklewood West 21/09/1963 E
D14 London (Midland) Division 16/01/1965 E
D01 London Division 17/06/1968 E
CD Cricklewood East 05/1973 M
Allocation recoded CD to CW 12/1973 M
Renumbered 25070 07/03/1974 E
WN Willesden 01/1975 M
CW Cricklewood East 06/1975 M
BS Bescot 01/1976 M
SP Springs Branch 10/1976 M
Withdrawn 02/11/1980 E
Moved to ZL Swindon Works 03/03/81 and broken up by 25/05/83.

D5221

14A Cricklewood 31/08/1963 E
14B Cricklewood West 09/09/1963 E
Allocation recoded 14A to 14B and renamed Cricklewood West 09/09/1963 E
D14 London (Midland) Division 16/01/1965 E
D01 London Division 17/06/1968 E
WN Willesden 05/1973 M
Renumbered 25071 09/04/1974 E
CW Cricklewood East 06/1975 M
Withdrawn 21/06/1981 E
Stored at Crewe until moved to Gloucester 12/81, then to ZL Swindon Works 06/01/82 and cut up by 31/01/83.

D5222

14B Cricklewood West 21/09/1963 E
D14 London (Midland) Division 16/01/1965 E
LMML LM Midland Lines 09/1965 M
D15 Leicester Division 12/1965 M
D14 London (Midland) Division 01/1967 M
D01 London Division 17/06/1968 E
CD Cricklewood East 05/1973 M
Allocation recoded CD to CW 12/1973 M
Renumbered 25072 21/03/1974 E

D5222 contd.
WN Willesden 08/1974 M
CW Cricklewood East 06/1975 M
ED Eastfield 10/1976 M
HA Haymarket 01/1980 M
ED Eastfield 03/1982 M
CD Crewe Diesel 10/1982 M
Withdrawn 05/12/1985 E
Stored at Toton until moved to Humberstone Road, Leicester on 02/12/87 and then into Vic Berry, Leicester the same day where it was stored.

For preservation

Sold for preservation to Hazet Tools of Gloucestershire and moved by road 17/03/88 to the Swindon & Cricklade Railway, Blunsdon. Moved by road to Whatley Quarry on 01/03/92 and used on shunting work following failure of the regular ARC shunter, and to stay about four weeks. Sold to Pete Waterman 10/93 and arrived at The Railway Age, Crewe on 03/12/93, then sold to the Yeovil Country Railway 11/96, but then moved to the West Somerset Railway on 09/12/96. Moved again to the Swindon & Cricklade Railway 12/05/97.
Sold in 08/98 and to move to the Dartmoor Railway, but sold again in 05/99 and moved by road to RMS Locotec, Dewsbury 10/05/99 for repairs. After completion of these, the locomotive remained at Dewsbury until moved to Meldon Quarry in 05/02 for storage. Sold again and arrived by road at the Caledonian Railway, Brechin on 24/02/04.

D5223
18A Toton 06/07/1963 E
Allocation recoded 18A to 16A 09/1963 M
14B Cricklewood West 10/1963 M
LMML LM Midland Lines 16/01/1965 E
D16 Nottingham Division 02/1965 M
2E Saltley 06/1965 M
D02 Birmingham Division 04/1966 M
LMML LM Midland Lines 04/1966 M
D14 London (Midland) Division 02/1968 M
D01 London Division 17/06/1968 E
D16 Nottingham Division 07/1972 M
TO Toton 05/1973 M
Renumbered 25073 07/03/1974 E
Withdrawn 08/09/1981 E
Stored at Bescot 12/81, then moved to ZL Swindon Works 24/12/81 and cut up by 21/08/82.

D5224
18A Toton 20/07/1963 E
Allocation recoded 18A to 16A 09/1963 M
16D Nottingham 02/1964 M
LMML LM Midland Lines 16/01/1965 E
D14 London (Midland) Division 02/1968 M
D01 London Division 17/06/1968 E
D16 Nottingham Division 11/1969 M
TO Toton 05/1973 M
Renumbered 25074 03/1974 M
Store 27/08/1980 E
Stored at Springs Branch 27/08/80
Withdrawn 14/10/1980 E
Moved to ZL Swindon Works 21/11/80 and broken up by 25/05/82.

D5225
18A Toton 27/07/1963 E
Allocation recoded 18A to 16A 09/1963 M
16D Nottingham 01/1964 M
15A Leicester (Midland) 05/1964 M
LMML LM Midland Lines 16/01/1965 E
D16 Nottingham Division 02/1966 M
LMML LM Midland Lines 03/1967 M
D14 London (Midland) Division 02/1968 M
D01 London Division 17/06/1968 E
D16 Nottingham Division 12/1968 M
TO Toton 05/1973 M
Renumbered 25075 12/12/1974 E
HA Haymarket 05/1977 M
BS Bescot 11/1980 M
CW Cricklewood East 07/1981 M
Withdrawn 27/03/1983 E
Stored at Cricklewood, then moved to Acton 03/05/85, on to Swindon on 14/05/85 and into ZL Swindon Works the next day. Due to Swindon Works imminent closure, the locomotive was sold to Vic Berry, Leicester and departed for Cocklebury Yard, Swindon on 26/05/87, then to Hinksey Yard, Oxford on 02/06/87 and into Vic Berry, Leicester on 11/06/87. Cutting started about 29/06/87 and completed 03/07/87 except for the cabs, which were cut later.

D5226
18A Toton 24/08/1963 E
Allocation recoded 18A to 16A 09/1963 M
16C Derby 03/1964 M
2E Saltley 06/1964 M
D02 Birmingham Division 04/1966 M
LMML LM Midland Lines 04/1966 M
D16 Nottingham Division 02/1968 M
D01 London Division 10/1968 M

D5226 contd.
D16 Nottingham Division 12/1968 M
TO Toton 05/1973 M
Renumbered 25076 20/03/1974 E
HA Haymarket 05/1977 M
ED Eastfield 12/1978 M
HA Haymarket 02/1981 M
ED Eastfield 03/1982 M
KD Kingmoor Diesel 10/1982 M
Withdrawn 12/11/1984 E
Stored at Bescot, then moved to ZL Swindon Works 27/03/85 and scrapped by 18/08/86. The cabs were taken to Vic Berry, Leicester and noted there on 06/11/86, being disposed of later.

D5227
16A Toton 07/09/1963 E
Allocation recoded 18A to 16A 09/1963 M
14B Cricklewood West 10/1963 M
LMML LM Midland Lines 16/01/1965 E
D16 Nottingham Division 02/1966 M
D01 London Division 10/1968 M
D16 Nottingham Division 12/1968 M
86B Ebbw Junction 01/1972 M
82A Bristol Bath Road 07/1972 M
64B Haymarket 10/1972 M
Allocation recoded 64B to HA 05/1973 M
Renumbered 25077 04/1974 M
BR Bristol Bath Road 05/1974 M
LA Laira 08/1975 M
CF Cardiff (Canton) 11/1975 M
ED Eastfield 10/1976 M
Withdrawn 06/05/1978 E
Withdrawn due to extensive fire damage. Stored at Polmadie, then moved to ZH Glasgow Works 03/07/78 and cut up by 14/08/78.

D5228
16A Toton 14/09/1963 E
14B Cricklewood West 10/1963 M
LMML LM Midland Lines 16/01/1965 E
D16 Nottingham Division 09/1967 M
55A Leeds Holbeck 04/1972 M
41A Tinsley 10/1972 M
Allocation recoded 41A to TI 05/1973 M
Renumbered 25078 02/1974 M
SP Springs Branch 03/1975 M
HA Haymarket 05/1976 M
TO Toton 05/1976 M
ED Eastfield 10/1976 M
HA Haymarket 02/1981 M
ED Eastfield 03/1982 M

D5228 contd.
CD Crewe Diesel 10/1982 M
Withdrawn 22/09/1985 E
Stored at Bescot, then to Toton 10/85 for further storage. Moved to ZF Doncaster Works 03/03/86 and then to Goole Docks 15/08/86 for further storage. Sold for scrap 10/86 and moved to Humberstone Road, Leicester on 29/10/86 and on to Vic Berry, Leicester on 30/10/86. Still intact 20/03/87, but was dismantled completely by 04/04/87.

D5229
14B Cricklewood West 05/10/1963 E
LMML LM Midland Lines 16/01/1965 E
D16 Nottingham Division 02/1968 M
55A Leeds Holbeck 04/1972 M
41A Tinsley 10/1972 M
Allocation recoded 41A to TI 05/1973 M
Renumbered 25079 02/1974 M
SP Springs Branch 03/1975 M
HA Haymarket 05/1976 M
ED Eastfield 05/1978 M
HA Haymarket 02/1981 M
ED Eastfield 03/1982 M
LO Longsight 09/1982 M
Withdrawn 28/08/1983 E
To ZL Swindon Works 29/09/83 and cut up by 23/12/83.

D5230
14B Cricklewood West 19/10/1963 E
LMML LM Midland Lines 16/01/1965 E
D16 Nottingham Division 02/1968 M
LMML LM Midland Lines 05/1968 M
D16 Nottingham Division 17/06/1968 E
82A Bristol Bath Road 01/1972 M
Allocation recoded 82A to BR 05/1973 M
Renumbered 25080 29/01/1974 E
LA Laira 05/1976 M
CD Crewe Diesel 05/1978 M
LA Laira 05/1978 M
LO Longsight 10/1980 M
CD Crewe Diesel 05/1984 M
Withdrawn 02/09/1985 E
Stored at Toton. Moved via Leicester shed on 17/08/88 to Vic Berry, Leicester by 09/88 and stored intact, but derelict. Moved to Basford Hall, Crewe on 12/05/89 and stored until moved again, this time into Crewe Heritage Centre on 07/11/91 and remained until moved back to Basford Hall Yard on 17/02/92. Held there and then moved by road to MC Metal Processing, Glasgow

The final twenty or so Class 25s were delivered in the then new BR blue livery with full yellow ends as here on D7663 accompanied by D7662 at Willesden on 4th December 1966. The D prefix was retained at this time. *(R. Mabey/Colour-Rail.com*

D5230 contd.
arriving there 28/05/93 and cut up immediately, being completed by 01/06/93.

D5231
16A Toton 14/12/1963 E
16D Nottingham 03/1964 M
LMML LM Midland Lines 16/01/1965 E
D16 Nottingham Division 02/1968 M
LMML LM Midland Lines 05/1968 M
D16 Nottingham Division 17/06/1968 E
TO Toton 05/1973 M
Renumbered 25081 23/02/1974 E
CD Crewe Diesel 05/1976 M
CW Cricklewood East 12/1976 M
Withdrawn 07/02/1982 E
Stored at Kingmoor Diesel 19/02/82, then moved to ZL Swindon Works 25/02/82 and broken up by 03/07/82.

D5232
16A Toton 09/11/1963 E
2E Saltley 04/1964 M
D02 Birmingham Division 04/1966 M
LMML LM Midland Lines 04/1966 M
D16 Nottingham Division 02/1968 M
LMML LM Midland Lines 05/1968 M

D5232 contd.
D16 Nottingham Division 17/06/1968 E
D09 Manchester Division 10/1972 M
LO Longsight 05/1973 M
Renumbered 25082 04/1974 M
ED Eastfield 10/1976 M
HA Haymarket 11/1980 M
Withdrawn 10/05/1981 E
Stored at Haymarket, moved to Millerhill Yard 07/81 and on to Mossend Yard 10/81, then to Carlisle New Yard 04/11/81, all for further storage. Moved to ZL Swindon Works on 08/06/82 and scrapped by 11/01/83.

D5233
16A Toton 21/12/1963 E
16C Derby 01/1964 M
2E Saltley 04/1964 M
D02 Birmingham Division 04/1966 M
LMML LM Midland Lines 04/1966 M
D16 Nottingham Division 03/1968 M
LMML LM Midland Lines 05/1968 M
D16 Nottingham Division 17/06/1968 E
TO Toton 05/1973 M
HA Haymarket 09/1973 M

D5233 contd.
ED Eastfield 09/1973 M
TI Tinsley 10/1973 M
Renumbered 25083 02/1974 M
BS Bescot 03/1975 M
ED Eastfield 07/1975 M
IS Inverness 06/1976 M
ED Eastfield 05/1978 M
HA Haymarket 12/1978 M
SP Springs Branch 12/1980 M
CD Crewe Diesel 10/1982 M
Store 09/07/1984 E
Withdrawn 09/07/1984 E
Stored at Crewe Diesel 07/84 and used for apprentice training, then moved to Crewe Electric Depot sidings 26/08/84. Moved to the Heritage Centre 18/05/88, to Basford Hall Yard 03/94 then to Crewe Carriage Shed in 1996.

For preservation

Sold for preservation and moved by rail to the Caledonian Railway, Brechin arriving there 12/10/00.
HQ Headquarters Pool 15/11/2000 E.

D5234

16A Toton 14/12/1963 E
16D Nottingham 12/1963 M
2E Saltley 04/1964 M
D02 Birmingham Division 04/1966 M
LMML LM Midland Lines 04/1966 M
D16 Nottingham Division 03/1968 M
LMML LM Midland Lines 05/1968 M
D16 Nottingham Division 17/06/1968 E
TO Toton 05/1973 M
HA Haymarket 09/1973 M
ED Eastfield 09/1973 M
TI Tinsley 10/1973 M
Renumbered 25084 02/1974 M
CF Cardiff (Canton) 03/1975 M
HA Haymarket 08/1975 M
KD Kingmoor Diesel 10/1980 M
Withdrawn 18/12/1983 E
Stored at Kingmoor Diesel 12/83, then moved to Newton Heath by 02/06/84 for further storage. Moved to ZL Swindon Works 19/02/85 and broken up by 04/07/86.

D5235

16A Toton 21/12/1963 E
16D Nottingham 02/1964 M
LMML LM Midland Lines 16/01/1965 E
D16 Nottingham Division 03/1968 M
LMML LM Midland Lines 05/1968 M

D5235 contd.
D16 Nottingham Division 17/06/1968 E
TO Toton 05/1973 M
ED Eastfield 08/1973 M
TI Tinsley 10/1973 M
Renumbered 25085 20/04/1974 E
CF Cardiff (Canton) 03/1975 M
HA Haymarket 08/1975 M
SP Springs Branch 10/1980 M
TO Toton 01/1981 M
KD Kingmoor Diesel 05/1981 M
Withdrawn 21/03/1982 E
Moved to ZE Derby Works by 04/82 and remained there until cutting started on 05/05/83 and was completed by 28/05/83.

D5236

16A Toton 21/12/1963 E
16C Derby 01/1964 M
2E Saltley 04/1964 M
D02 Birmingham Division 04/1966 M
LMML LM Midland Lines 04/1966 M
D16 Nottingham Division 17/06/1968 E
TO Toton 05/1973 M
ED Eastfield 08/1973 M
KM Kingmoor Diesel 11/1973 M
Renumbered 25086 27/02/1974 E
LO Longsight 03/1974 M
ED Eastfield 07/1975 M
HA Haymarket 02/1978 M
Store 28/11/1980 E
Stored at Millerhill Yard 28/11/80, then moved to Springs Branch 12/80.
SP Springs Branch 12/1980 M
Returned to Service 12/1980 M
KD Kingmoor Diesel 05/1982 M
BS Bescot 11/1982 M
CD Crewe Diesel 03/1983 M
Withdrawn 09/10/1983 E
Stored at Crewe Diesel, then moved to Newton Heath by 02/06/84 for further storage. Moved to ZL Swindon Works 19/02/85 and was cut up by 28/03/86, the cabs being sent to Vic Berry, Leicester on 04/06/86 and disposed of.

D5237

16A Toton 21/12/1963 E
16D Nottingham 12/1964 M
D16 Nottingham Division 16/01/1965 E
LMML LM Midland Lines 03/1965 M
D16 Nottingham Division 17/06/1968 E
TO Toton 05/1973 M
Renumbered 25087 02/1974 M

D5237 contd.
ED Eastfield 07/1975 M
HA Haymarket 02/1978 M
Withdrawn 28/09/1980 E
Stored at Millerhill Yard 12/80. Moved to ZL Swindon Works 11/02/81 and broken up by 01/04/81.

D5238
16A Toton 21/12/1963 E
D16 Nottingham Division 16/01/1965 E
LMML LM Midland Lines 03/1967 M
D05 Stoke Division 08/1967 M
10D Lostock Hall 08/1967 M
D10 Preston Division 17/06/1968 E
D16 Nottingham Division 05/1969 M
D09 Manchester Division 06/1972 M
LO Longsight 05/1973 M
TO Toton 08/1973 M
LO Longsight 09/1973 M
Renumbered 25088 18/04/1974 E
Withdrawn 16/09/1981 E
Withdrawn due to collision damage. Stored at Willesden, then moved to Acton 10/12/81 for further storage. Moved to ZE Derby Works 10/06/82 and then stored at Etches Park, Derby in heavily damaged condition until broken up on site by staff from Vic Berry, Leicester on 15/02/86 with parts taken back to Berry's Yard by road.

D5239
16A Toton 21/12/1963 E
16D Nottingham 05/1964 M
16A Toton 12/1964 M
D16 Nottingham Division 16/01/1965 E
2E Saltley 01/1965 M
D02 Birmingham Division 04/1966 M
LMML LM Midland Lines 04/1966 M
D14 London (Midland) Division 08/1966 M
D16 Nottingham Division 11/1966 M
LMWL LM Western Lines 03/1967 M
LMML LM Midland Lines 03/1967 M
D16 Nottingham Division 17/06/1968 E
TO Toton 05/1973 M
TI Tinsley 09/1973 M
Renumbered 25089 20/04/1974 E
ED Eastfield 07/1975 M
LO Longsight 07/1975 M
BS Bescot 01/1980 M
CW Cricklewood East 08/1980 M
SP Springs Branch 11/1980 M
CD Crewe Diesel 10/1982 M
KD Kingmoor Diesel 01/1983 M

D5239 contd.
CD Crewe Diesel 07/1983 M
Withdrawn 24/02/1986 E
Stored at Crewe Diesel then at Gresty Lane until moved to Basford Hall in early 1987. Moved to Humberstone Road, Leicester 15/07/87 and into Vic Berry, Leicester on 20/07/87 where it was dismantled by 17/10/87.

D5240
16A Toton 04/01/1964 E
14B Cricklewood West 04/1964 M
15A Leicester (Midland) 06/1964 M
15B Wellingborough 07/1964 M
16A Toton 09/1964 M
Loaned to the Southern Region 09/64, exact shed not known, returning to 16A 12/64.
16A Toton 12/1964 M
D16 Nottingham Division 16/01/1965 E
LMML LM Midland Lines 02/1965 M
D14 London (Midland) Division 11/1965 M
LMML LM Midland Lines 02/1968 M
D16 Nottingham Division 17/06/1968 E
D10 Preston Division 10/1968 M
D16 Nottingham Division 05/1969 M
TO Toton 05/1973 M
TI Tinsley 09/1973 M
Renumbered 25090 02/1974 M
ED Eastfield 07/1975 M
LO Longsight 07/1975 M
BS Bescot 07/1977 M
ED Eastfield 10/1977 M
SP Springs Branch 10/1980 M
CD Crewe Diesel 10/1982 M
BS Bescot 11/1982 M
Withdrawn 22/05/1983 E
Stored at Toton by 22/10/83, then moved to Gloucester 10/07/84, to Swindon Cocklebury Yard 13/07/84 and into ZL Swindon Works 25/07/84 and was broken up by 26/02/85.

D5241
16A Toton 04/01/1964 E
14B Cricklewood West 04/1964 M
15A Leicester (Midland) 06/1964 M
15B Wellingborough 07/1964 M
16A Toton 09/1964 M
Loaned to the Southern Region in 09/64 (specific shed not known) returning to 16A in 12/64.
16A Toton 12/1964 M
D16 Nottingham Division 16/01/1965 E
D14 London (Midland) Division 07/1965 M

D5241 contd.
LMML LM Midland Lines 09/1965 M
D14 London (Midland) Division 11/1965 M
D01 London Division 17/06/1968 E
D16 Nottingham Division 05/1969 M
TO Toton 05/1973 M
TI Tinsley 09/1973 M
Renumbered 25091 20/04/1974 E
ED Eastfield 07/1975 M
BS Bescot 07/1975 M
LA Laira 08/1975 M
HA Haymarket 10/1975 M
Withdrawn 15/10/1978 E
Stored at Eastfield. Moved to ZH Glasgow Works 30/05/79 and scrapped by 10/79. The cabs were still in evidence on 26/05/84 and disposed of later.

D5242
16A Toton 04/01/1964 E
14B Cricklewood West 04/1964 M
15A Leicester (Midland) 06/1964 M
15B Wellingborough 07/1964 M
16C Derby 09/1964 M
14B Cricklewood West 12/1964 M
D14 London (Midland) Division 16/01/1965 E
2E Saltley 04/1965 M
LMML LM Midland Lines 08/1965 M
D16 Nottingham Division 02/1966 M
LMML LM Midland Lines 04/1967 M
D05 Stoke Division 08/1967 M
9A Longsight 08/1967 M
8F Springs Branch 05/1968 M
D08 Liverpool Division 17/06/1968 E
D16 Nottingham Division 05/1969 M
TO Toton 05/1973 M
TI Tinsley 09/1973 M
Renumbered 25092 02/1974 M
ED Eastfield 07/1975 M
TO Toton 07/1975 M
LA Laira 08/1975 M
HA Haymarket 10/1975 M
ED Eastfield 05/1976 M
IS Inverness 07/1976 M
ED Eastfield 07/1976 M
LO Longsight 10/1976 M
TO Toton 12/1976 M
CW Cricklewood East 04/1977 M
ED Eastfield 10/1977 M
CD Crewe Diesel 11/1978 M
CW Cricklewood East 01/1980 M
Withdrawn 11/05/1980 E
Stored at Toton 06/80. Moved to ZE Derby

D5242 contd.
Works by 03/81 and dismantled by 07/82. The official Derby Works cutting up list recorded that as being on 23/07/82.

D5243
16A Toton 08/01/1964 E
Loaned to the Southern Region in 09/64 (depot unknown) and returned to 16A 12/64.
16A Toton 12/1964 M
LMML LM Midland Lines 16/01/1965 E
2E Saltley 04/1965 M
D02 Birmingham Division 04/1966 M
LMML LM Midland Lines 04/1966 M
D14 London (Midland) Division 08/1966 M
D16 Nottingham Division 11/1966 M
LMWL LM Western Lines 03/1967 M
LMML LM Midland Lines 03/1967 M
D16 Nottingham Division 17/06/1968 E
TO Toton 05/1973 M
ED Eastfield 02/1974 M
HA Haymarket 02/1974 M
Renumbered 25093 04/1974 M
SP Springs Branch 10/1974 M
TO Toton 02/1975 M
LO Longsight 02/1975 M
BR Bristol Bath Road 05/1975 M
LA Laira 08/1975 M
HA Haymarket 10/1975 M
IS Inverness 11/1975 M
ED Eastfield 05/1976 M
IS Inverness 07/1976 M
ED Eastfield 07/1976 M
CD Crewe Diesel 11/1978 M
TO Toton 03/1980 M
CW Cricklewood East 07/1980 M
TO Toton 11/1980 M
CW Cricklewood East 04/1981 M
BS Bescot 11/1981 M
Withdrawn 07/11/1982 E
Stored at Bescot. Moved to ZL Swindon Works by 22/10/83 and stored intact. Due to imminent closure of the works, 25093 was sold to Vic Berry, Leicester, moved to Swindon Cocklebury Yard 03/06/87, and on to Humberstone Road, Leicester the same day, arrived at Berry's Yard on 04/06/87 and put into the 'pyramid', partly dismantled, by 10/87. It was noted being cut up on 13/02/88 and was completed by 04/03/88.

D5244
16A Toton 20/01/1964 E
Loaned to the Southern Region in 09/64

D5244 contd.
(depot unknown) and returned to 16A 12/64.
16A Toton 12/1964 M
LMML LM Midland Lines 16/01/1965 E
D16 Nottingham Division 02/1966 M
LMML LM Midland Lines 04/1967 M
D05 Stoke Division 08/1967 M
D02 Birmingham Division 08/1967 M
9A Longsight 01/1968 M
8F Springs Branch 05/1968 M
D08 Liverpool Division 17/06/1968 E
D16 Nottingham Division 05/1969 M
TO Toton 05/1973 M
Renumbered 25094 04/1974 M
ED Eastfield 03/1974 M
HA Haymarket 05/1974 M
SP Springs Branch 10/1974 M
TO Toton 02/1975 M
LO Longsight 02/1975 M
SP Springs Branch 03/1975 M
BR Bristol Bath Road 05/1975 M
LA Laira 08/1975 M
HA Haymarket 10/1975 M
ED Eastfield 08/1976 M
TO Toton 10/1976 M
KD Kingmoor Diesel 08/1977 M
CD Crewe Diesel 10/1977 M
TO Toton 03/1980 M
CW Cricklewood East 08/1980 M
TO Toton 11/1980 M
Withdrawn 01/02/1981 E
Stored at Derby until at least 10/02/81, then moved to ZE Derby Works. Derby Works official list reported that it was cut up on 05/05/82.

D5245
16A Toton 21/01/1964 E
Loaned to the Southern Region in 09/64 (depot unknown) and returned to 16A 12/64.
16A Toton 12/1964 M
LMML LM Midland Lines 16/01/1965 E
2E Saltley 01/1965 M
D02 Birmingham Division 04/1966 M
LMML LM Midland Lines 04/1966 M
D14 London (Midland) Division 08/1966 M
D16 Nottingham Division 11/1966 M
LMWL LM Western Lines 03/1967 M
LMML LM Midland Lines 03/1967 M
D16 Nottingham Division 17/06/1968 E
D08 Liverpool Division 07/1968 M
D16 Nottingham Division 05/1969 M

D5245 contd.
TO Toton 05/1973 M
Renumbered 25095 04/1974 M
CW Cricklewood East 11/1977 M
TO Toton 02/1982 M
CW Cricklewood East 01/1983 M
BS Bescot 01/1984 M
CD Crewe Diesel 07/1985 M
Withdrawn 28/07/1986 E
Stored at Crewe Diesel, then moved to Basford Hall Yard 03/87 for further storage. Sold to Vic Berry, Leicester and moved there on 29/05/87 and was put in the 'pyramid' in 10/87. Cutting up started about 20/01/89 and was completed by 18/02/89.

D5246
16A Toton 24/01/1964 E
16C Derby 08/1964 M
14B Cricklewood West 12/1964 M
D14 London (Midland) Division 16/01/1965 E
2E Saltley 04/1965 M
D02 Birmingham Division 04/1966 M
LMML LM Midland Lines 04/1966 M
D14 London (Midland) Division 08/1966 M
D16 Nottingham Division 11/1966 M
LMWL LM Western Lines 03/1967 M
LMML LM Midland Lines 03/1967 M
D16 Nottingham Division 17/06/1968 E
D08 Liverpool Division 07/1968 M
D16 Nottingham Division 05/1969 M
TO Toton 05/1973 M
ED Eastfield 03/1974 M
Renumbered 25096 04/1974 M
HA Haymarket 05/1974 M
BS Bescot 10/1974 M
BR Bristol Bath Road 05/1975 M
LA Laira 08/1975 M
HA Haymarket 10/1975 M
IS Inverness 11/1975 M
ED Eastfield 05/1976 M
TO Toton 10/1976 M
ED Eastfield 10/1977 M
Store 25/10/1977 E
Withdrawn 31/12/1977 E
Moved to ZH Glasgow Works and stored there until 06/78, when it was scrapped except the cabs which were still there in 07/78.

D5247
16A Toton 31/01/1964 E
Loaned to the Southern Region in 09/64 (Depot unknown) and returned to 16A 12/64.
16A Toton 12/1964 M

D5247 contd.
LMML LM Midland Lines 16/01/1965 E
2E Saltley 04/1965 M
D02 Birmingham Division 04/1966 M
LMML LM Midland Lines 04/1966 M
D16 Nottingham Division 17/06/1968 E
D08 Liverpool Division 07/1968 M
D16 Nottingham Division 06/1969 M
D09 Manchester Division 06/1972 M
LO Longsight 05/1973 M
Renumbered 25097 05/1974 M
SP Springs Branch 11/1980 M
KD Kingmoor Diesel 11/1981 M
TO Toton 02/1982 M
Withdrawn 13/11/1983 E
Moved to ZL Swindon Works 10/02/84 and cut up by 10/01/85.

D5248
16A Toton 06/02/1964 E
LMML LM Midland Lines 16/01/1965 E
D15 Leicester Division 04/1965 M
51L Thornaby 12/1965 M
D15 Leicester Division 12/1965 M
51L Thornaby 01/1966 M
55A Leeds Holbeck 05/1966 M
12A Kingmoor 11/1967 M
8F Springs Branch 01/1968 M
8J Allerton 05/1968 M
D08 Liverpool Division 17/06/1968 E
D16 Nottingham Division 10/1969 M
D08 Liverpool Division 10/1970 M
D16 Nottingham Division 11/1970 M
TO Toton 05/1973 M
Renumbered 25098 02/1974 M
BR Bristol Bath Road 05/1975 M
LA Laira 08/1975 M
HA Haymarket 10/1975 M
ED Eastfield 08/1976 M
Withdrawn 15/10/1978 E
Stored at Polmadie. Moved to ZH Glasgow Works by 04/79 and dismantled by 06/79.

D5249
16A Toton 07/02/1964 E
15E Coalville 11/1964 M
D15 Leicester Division 16/01/1965 E
51L Thornaby 12/1965 M
D15 Leicester Division 12/1965 M
51L Thornaby 01/1966 M
55A Leeds Holbeck 05/1966 M
12A Kingmoor 12/1967 M
8F Springs Branch 01/1968 M
8J Allerton 05/1968 M

D5249 contd.
D08 Liverpool Division 17/06/1968 E
D16 Nottingham Division 10/1969 M
D08 Liverpool Division 06/1970 M
D16 Nottingham Division 11/1970 M
TO Toton 05/1973 M
Renumbered 25099 07/03/1974 E
CW Cricklewood East 11/1977 M
Store 03/11/1980 E
Stored at Springs Branch 03/11/80
Withdrawn 01/12/1980 E
Moved to ZL Swindon Works 21/11/80 and cut up by 25/02/81.

D5250
16A Toton 14/02/1964 E
LMML LM Midland Lines 16/01/1965 E
D15 Leicester Division 04/1965 M
51L Thornaby 12/1965 M
D15 Leicester Division 12/1965 M
51L Thornaby 01/1966 M
55A Leeds Holbeck 05/1966 M
12A Kingmoor 12/1967 M
8F Springs Branch 01/1968 M
8J Allerton 05/1968 M
D08 Liverpool Division 17/06/1968 E
D16 Nottingham Division 11/1970 M
TO Toton 05/1973 M
Renumbered 25100 04/1974 M
LO Longsight 01/1976 M
Withdrawn 01/02/1981 E
Stored at Reddish. Moved to ZL Swindon Works 27/02/81 and broken up by 09/02/83.

D5251
16A Toton 19/02/1964 E
LMML LM Midland Lines 16/01/1965 E
D15 Leicester Division 08/1965 M
51L Thornaby 12/1965 M
D15 Leicester Division 12/1965 M
51L Thornaby 01/1966 M
55A Leeds Holbeck 05/1966 M
12A Kingmoor 12/1967 M
8J Allerton 05/1968 M
D08 Liverpool Division 17/06/1968 E
D16 Nottingham Division 11/1970 M
D08 Liverpool Division 10/1971 M
D16 Nottingham Division 01/1972 M
D08 Liverpool Division 06/1972 M
D16 Nottingham Division 12/1972 M
TO Toton 05/1973 M
TI Tinsley 12/1973 M
Renumbered 25101 05/12/1973 E
ED Eastfield 07/1975 M

Whilst a number of Class 24s received blue livery prior to the two-tone green, Class 25s were less common in blue with full yellow ends relative to the class size in the pre-TOPS era, but one to gain the livery was 5254 having the numbers on the cabside along with a central arrow, this differing from those delivered new in blue. Taken at Carnforth. *(K. Nuttal/Colour-Rail.com*

D5251 contd.
BS Bescot 10/1976 M
TO Toton 10/1977 M
CW Cricklewood East 08/1980 M
TO Toton 11/1980 M
CW Cricklewood East 04/1981 M
BS Bescot 11/1981 M
Withdrawn 16/01/1983 E
Moved to Swindon Cocklebury Yard 11/07/84 and into ZL Swindon Works on 25/07/84 where it was cut up by 18/11/85.

D5252
16A Toton 21/02/1964 E
16D Nottingham 05/1964 M
D16 Nottingham Division 16/01/1965 E
LMML LM Midland Lines 02/1965 M
D15 Leicester Division 04/1965 M
51L Thornaby 12/1965 M
D15 Leicester Division 12/1965 M
51L Thornaby 01/1966 M
55A Leeds Holbeck 05/1966 M
12A Kingmoor 12/1967 M
8J Allerton 05/1968 M
D08 Liverpool Division 17/06/1968 E
D16 Nottingham Division 11/1970 M
D08 Liverpool Division 03/1971 M

D5252 contd.
D16 Nottingham Division 04/1972 M
D08 Liverpool Division 06/1972 M
D16 Nottingham Division 12/1972 M
TO Toton 05/1973 M
Renumbered 25102 04/1974 M
LO Longsight 01/1976 M
Withdrawn 11/05/1980 E
Moved to ZL Swindon Works 14/08/80 and broken up by 29/10/80.

D5253
16A Toton 26/02/1964 E
16D Nottingham 05/1964 M
D16 Nottingham Division 16/01/1965 E
51L Thornaby 12/1965 M
D16 Nottingham Division 12/1965 M
51L Thornaby 01/1966 M
55A Leeds Holbeck 05/1966 M
12A Kingmoor 12/1967 M
8J Allerton 05/1968 M
D08 Liverpool Division 17/06/1968 E
D16 Nottingham Division 12/1972 M
TO Toton 05/1973 M
SP Springs Branch 05/1973 M
Renumbered 25103 02/03/1974 E
Withdrawn 03/09/1980 E

D5253 contd.
Stored at Toton. Moved to ZL Swindon Works 12/01/81 and cut up by 24/03/83.

D5254
16A Toton 28/02/1964 E
LMML LM Midland Lines 16/01/1965 E
D16 Nottingham Division 11/1965 M
51L Thornaby 12/1965 M
D16 Nottingham Division 12/1965 M
51L Thornaby 01/1966 M
55A Leeds Holbeck 06/1966 M
12A Kingmoor 12/1967 M
8J Allerton 05/1968 M
D08 Liverpool Division 17/06/1968 E
SP Springs Branch 05/1973 M
Renumbered 25104 10/04/1974 E
TI Tinsley 11/1974 M
BS Bescot 01/1975 M
LO Longsight 07/1975 M
Withdrawn 26/09/1982 E
Stored at Crewe Diesel. Moved to Gloucester 28/03/84 and into ZL Swindon Works 30/03/84 and scrapped by 05/12/86.

D5255
16A Toton 06/03/1964 E
9E Trafford Park 03/1964 M
16A Toton 04/1964 M
D16 Nottingham Division 16/01/1965 E
D15 Leicester Division 08/1965 M
51L Thornaby 12/1965 M
D15 Leicester Division 12/1965 M
51L Thornaby 01/1966 M
55A Leeds Holbeck 06/1966 M
12A Kingmoor 12/1967 M
8F Springs Branch 05/1968 M
D08 Liverpool Division 17/06/1968 E
SP Springs Branch 05/1973 M
Renumbered 25105 01/02/1974 E
TI Tinsley 10/1974 M
BS Bescot 01/1975 M
LO Longsight 07/1975 M
Withdrawn 04/04/1982 E
Stored at Tyseley. Moved to ZE Derby Works 05/82 and stored intact, then moved to ZL Swindon Works 24/07/85 and broken up by 25/11/85.

D5256
16A Toton 13/03/1964 E
16C Derby 08/1964 M
D16 Nottingham Division 16/01/1965 E
51L Thornaby 12/1965 M
D16 Nottingham Division 12/1965 M

D5256 contd.
51L Thornaby 01/1966 M
55A Leeds Holbeck 10/1966 M
12A Kingmoor 12/1967 M
8F Springs Branch 05/1968 M
D08 Liverpool Division 17/06/1968 E
SP Springs Branch 05/1973 M
Renumbered 25106 17/05/1974 E
TI Tinsley 10/1974 M
BS Bescot 01/1975 M
LO Longsight 07/1975 M
TO Toton 10/1980 M
BS Bescot 05/1981 M
CD Crewe Diesel 09/1981 M
KD Kingmoor Diesel 01/1983 M
Withdrawn 09/10/1983 E
Stored at Springs Branch, then moved to Bescot 28/10/83 for further storage. Moved to ZL Swindon Works 16/11/83 and was cut up by 06/02/84.

D5257
16A Toton 17/03/1964 E
D16 Nottingham Division 16/01/1965 E
31B March 09/1965 M
D16 Nottingham Division 01/1966 M
LMML LM Midland Lines 04/1967 M
D05 Stoke Division 08/1967 M
9A Longsight 03/1968 M
8F Springs Branch 05/1968 M
D08 Liverpool Division 17/06/1968 E
SP Springs Branch 05/1973 M
Renumbered 25107 04/03/1974 E
TI Tinsley 10/1974 M
BS Bescot 01/1975 M
TO Toton 08/1976 M
Store 04/1981 M
Withdrawn 30/04/1981 E
Moved to ZL Swindon Works 03/08/81 and scrapped by 09/09/81.

D5258
16A Toton 20/03/1964 E
16D Nottingham 09/1964 M
D16 Nottingham Division 16/01/1965 E
D15 Leicester Division 10/1965 M
D16 Nottingham Division 08/1967 M
D05 Stoke Division 08/1967 M
8J Allerton 05/1968 M
D08 Liverpool Division 17/06/1968 E
SP Springs Branch 05/1973 M
Renumbered 25108 05/03/1974 E
TI Tinsley 06/1974 M
ED Eastfield 07/1975 M

D5258 contd.
Withdrawn 14/07/1980 E
Stored at ZH Glasgow Works 11/80 and was cut up by 12/80. However, about a third of the locomotive remained, was noted there on 26/05/84 and was not cut up until 11/88.

D5259
16A Toton 25/03/1964 E
16C Derby 08/1964 M
D16 Nottingham Division 16/01/1965 E
8F Springs Branch 10/1967 M
8J Allerton 05/1968 M
D08 Liverpool Division 17/06/1968 E
SP Springs Branch 05/1973 M
Renumbered 25109 02/1974 M
ED Eastfield 02/1978 M
HA Haymarket 03/1981 M
CD Crewe Diesel 10/1982 M
Unofficially named *Castell Trefaldwyn/ Montgomery Castle* - date not recorded but post 1982.
Withdrawn 11/03/1987 E
Stored at Basford Hall Yard. Moved to Humberstone Road, Leicester on 14/07/87 and held there before entering Vic Berry, Leicester on 11/09/87 and was broken up by 23/12/87.

D5260
16A Toton 26/03/1964 E
16C Derby 05/1964 M
D16 Nottingham Division 16/01/1965 E
8F Springs Branch 10/1967 M
8J Allerton 05/1968 M
D08 Liverpool Division 17/06/1968 E
D16 Nottingham Division 03/1972 M
TO Toton 05/1973 M
SP Springs Branch 05/1973 M
Renumbered 25110 02/1974 M
Withdrawn 27/10/1980 E
Moved to ZL Swindon Works on 30/10/80 and was cut up by 25/03/82.

D5261
16A Toton 02/04/1964 E
D16 Nottingham Division 16/01/1965 E
8F Springs Branch 10/1967 M
8J Allerton 05/1968 M
D08 Liverpool Division 17/06/1968 E
SP Springs Branch 05/1973 M
Renumbered 25111 07/03/1974 E
TI Tinsley 10/1974 M
ED Eastfield 07/1975 M
CD Crewe Diesel 10/1976 M

D5261 contd.
CW Cricklewood East 05/1977 M
TO Toton 10/1977 M
CW Cricklewood East 03/1978 M
Withdrawn 30/03/1980 E
Moved to ZL Swindon Works on 06/05/80 and scrapped by 29/10/80.

D5262
16A Toton 10/04/1964 E
D16 Nottingham Division 16/01/1965 E
8F Springs Branch 10/1967 M
8J Allerton 05/1968 M
D08 Liverpool Division 17/06/1968 E
SP Springs Branch 05/1973 M
Renumbered 25112 04/1974 M
KD Kingmoor Diesel 10/1975 M
SP Springs Branch 05/1976 M
CD Crewe Diesel 10/1977 M
CW Cricklewood East 05/1978 M
Withdrawn 13/11/1980 E
Moved to ZL Swindon Works 20/03/81 and cut up by 10/30/82.

D5263
16A Toton 14/04/1964 E
D16 Nottingham Division 16/01/1965 E
8F Springs Branch 10/1967 M
9A Longsight 03/1968 M
8F Springs Branch 05/1968 M
D08 Liverpool Division 17/06/1968 E
SP Springs Branch 05/1973 M
Renumbered 25113 07/04/1974 E
KD Kingmoor Diesel 10/1975 M
SP Springs Branch 02/1981 M
CD Crewe Diesel 10/1982 M
Withdrawn 26/06/1983 E
Stored at Kingmoor Diesel. Moved to ZL Swindon Works on 27/08/83 and broken up by 18/10/83.

D5264
16A Toton 17/04/1964 E
16D Nottingham 05/1964 M
16A Toton 12/1964 M
D16 Nottingham Division 16/01/1965 E
8F Springs Branch 10/1967 M
9A Longsight 03/1968 M
8F Springs Branch 05/1968 M
D08 Liverpool Division 17/06/1968 E
SP Springs Branch 05/1973 M
Renumbered 25114 02/1974 M
KD Kingmoor Diesel 10/1975 M
SP Springs Branch 05/1976 M
CD Crewe Diesel 10/1977 M

D5264 contd.
CW Cricklewood East 05/1978 M
Withdrawn 01/02/1981 E
Stored at Cricklewood. Moved to ZL Swindon Works 20/03/81 and broken up by 22/07/81.

D5265
16A Toton 22/04/1964 E
16C Derby 05/1964 M
D16 Nottingham Division 16/01/1965 E
8F Springs Branch 10/1967 M
9A Longsight 03/1968 M
8F Springs Branch 05/1968 M
D08 Liverpool Division 17/06/1968 E
SP Springs Branch 05/1973 M
Renumbered 25115 04/1974 M
KD Kingmoor Diesel 10/1975 M
SP Springs Branch 05/1976 M
TO Toton 10/1977 M
CW Cricklewood East 04/1981 M
CD Crewe Diesel 11/1981 M
CW Cricklewood East 11/1982 M
Store 08/1983 M
Withdrawn 02/10/1983 E
Stored at Bletchley 08/83, then moved to Toton by 12/83 for further storage. Moved to Gloucester 10/07/84, to Swindon Cocklebury Yard 24/07/84 and into ZL Swindon Works next day. Stored intact and reported sold to the North Yorkshire Moors Railway for preservation on 22/03/85 but, despite this, the locomotive was cut up at Swindon Works by 16/12/85.

D5266
16A Toton 29/04/1964 E
16C Derby 05/1964 M
D16 Nottingham Division 16/01/1965 E
2E Saltley 01/1965 M
D02 Birmingham Division 04/1966 M
LMML LM Midland Lines 04/1966 M
D16 Nottingham Division 12/1967 M
LMML LM Midland Lines 04/1968 M
D16 Nottingham Division 17/06/1968 E
D08 Liverpool Division 07/1968 M
D09 Manchester Division 12/1969 M
D16 Nottingham Division 11/1970 M
TO Toton 05/1973 M
Renumbered 25116 27/02/1974 E
KD Kingmoor Diesel 02/1976 M
CW Cricklewood East 05/1976 M
TO Toton 10/1976 M
CW Cricklewood East 05/1978 M

D5266 contd.
Withdrawn 13/11/1980 E
Moved to ZL Swindon Works 21/11/80 where it and 25197 were put to use starting stored locomotives. It was eventually scrapped by 31/07/82.

D5267
16A Toton 29/04/1964 E
16C Derby 05/1964 M
16A Toton 08/1964 M
D16 Nottingham Division 16/01/1965 E
TO Toton 05/1973 M
Renumbered 25117 02/1974 M
CW Cricklewood East 11/1977 M
TO Toton 02/1982 M
CW Cricklewood East 03/1983 M
Withdrawn 22/01/1984 E
Stored at Cricklewood. Moved to Acton on 09/02/84 and on to ZL Swindon Works 14/02/84 and cut up by 21/05/84.

D5268
16A Toton 08/05/1964 E
16C Derby 09/1964 M
D16 Nottingham Division 16/01/1965 E
TO Toton 05/1973 M
Renumbered 25118 18/03/1974 E
Withdrawn 04/01/1981 E
Stored at Toton. Moved to ZL Swindon Works 24/10/81 and dismantled by 06/08/83.

D5269
16A Toton 06/05/1964 E
15B Wellingborough 05/1964 M
16A Toton 09/1964 M
D16 Nottingham Division 16/01/1965 E
D15 Leicester Division 10/1965 M
D16 Nottingham Division 08/1967 M
D09 Manchester Division 03/1972 M
LO Longsight 05/1973 M
Renumbered 25119 02/1974 M
KD Kingmoor Diesel 10/1975 M
TO Toton 11/1980 M
CD Crewe Diesel 11/1983 M
Withdrawn 14/06/1985 E
Stored at Basford Hall Yard. Moved to ZF Doncaster Works on 16/04/86 and was cut up by 12/07/86.

D5270
16A Toton 14/05/1964 E
15B Wellingborough 05/1964 M
16A Toton 09/1964 M
D16 Nottingham Division 16/01/1965 E

D5270 contd.
LMML LM Midland Lines 09/1967 M
D16 Nottingham Division 02/1968 M
D14 London (Midland) Division 04/1968 M
D01 London Division 17/06/1968 E
D02 Birmingham Division 01/1969 M
D01 London Division 02/1970 M
D16 Nottingham Division 07/1970 M
TO Toton 05/1973 M
Renumbered 25120 08/03/1974 E
CW Cricklewood East 11/1977 M
SP Springs Branch 06/1982 M
CD Crewe Diesel 10/1982 M
Withdrawn 27/11/1983 E
Withdrawn due to accident damage. Stored at Springs Branch, then moved to Crewe Diesel 08/02/84 and on to ZL Swindon Works 16/02/84 and broken up by 31/05/84.

D5271
16A Toton 15/05/1964 E
15B Wellingborough 07/1964 M
16A Toton 09/1964 M
D16 Nottingham Division 16/01/1965 E
D14 London (Midland) Division 01/1966 M
D01 London Division 17/06/1968 E
D02 Birmingham Division 01/1969 M
D01 London Division 02/1970 M
D08 Liverpool Division 03/1971 M
D16 Nottingham Division 10/1972 M
TO Toton 05/1973 M
Renumbered 25121 28/02/1974 E
Withdrawn 02/11/1980 E
Stored at Toton, then moved to Bletchley in 01/82 for further storage. Moved to ZL Swindon Works on 21/06/82 and cut up by 14/08/82.

D5272
16A Toton 22/05/1964 E
15B Wellingborough 06/1964 M
16A Toton 09/1964 M
D16 Nottingham Division 16/01/1965 E
LMML LM Midland Lines 09/1967 M
D16 Nottingham Division 17/06/1968 E
D08 Liverpool Division 07/1968 M
D01 London Division 11/1968 M
D02 Birmingham Division 10/1969 M
D09 Manchester Division 02/1970 M
D08 Liverpool Division 01/1971 M
D16 Nottingham Division 10/1972 M
TO Toton 05/1973 M
Renumbered 25122 29/01/1974 E
Withdrawn 02/11/1980 E

D5272 contd.
Stored at Newton Heath. Moved to ZL Swindon Works 27/02/81 and broken up by 20/06/83.

D5273
16A Toton 22/05/1964 E
15B Wellingborough 06/1964 M
16D Nottingham 09/1964 M
D16 Nottingham Division 16/01/1965 E
D15 Leicester Division 09/1965 M
8B Warrington 07/1967 M
8F Springs Branch 10/1967 M
9A Longsight 12/1967 M
D09 Manchester Division 17/06/1968 E
D08 Liverpool Division 03/1972 M
D16 Nottingham Division 10/1972 M
TO Toton 05/1973 M
Renumbered 25123 05/1974 M
CD Crewe Diesel 10/1981 M
Withdrawn 01/05/1983 E
Moved to Bristol Bath Road and stored there until moved into ZL Swindon Works on 14/11/84 and stored awaiting scrap. Due to closure of Swindon Works, was resold to Vic Berry, Leicester 05/87 and left for Swindon Cocklebury Yard on 26/05/87, then to Oxford Hinksey Yard 02/06/87 and to Berry's Yard on 11/06/87. It was partly cut up 27/06/87, with completion by 11/07/87, except for the cabs still there on 02/11/87, but disposed of later.

D5274
16A Toton 29/05/1964 E
9E Trafford Park 06/1964 M
9A Longsight 03/1968 M
D09 Manchester Division 17/06/1968 E
D16 Nottingham Division 04/1972 M
TO Toton 05/1973 M
Renumbered 25124 03/10/1973 E
BS Bescot 02/1982 M
CW Cricklewood East 01/1983 M
Withdrawn 20/10/1983 E
Stored until moved to Gloucester on 28/03/84 and then to ZL Swindon Works 30/03/84 and remained there until cut up by 12/12/86.

D5275
16A Toton 03/06/1964 E
9E Trafford Park 06/1964 M
9A Longsight 03/1968 M
D09 Manchester Division 17/06/1968 E
D16 Nottingham Division 04/1972 M

D5275 contd.
TO Toton 05/1973 M
Renumbered 25125 17/04/1974 E
Withdrawn 06/12/1981 E
Reported seen at Crewe 13/12/81, may have then been moved to Toton and stored there. Moved to ZL Swindon Works on 26/04/82, and scrapped by 12/04/83.

D5276
16A Toton 05/06/1964 E
9E Trafford Park 06/1964 M
9A Longsight 03/1968 M
D09 Manchester Division 17/06/1968 E
D16 Nottingham Division 04/1972 M
TO Toton 05/1973 M
Renumbered 25126 04/1974 M
BS Bescot 02/1982 M
CD Crewe Diesel 09/1982 M
Withdrawn 28/11/1982 E
Stored at Newton Heath. Moved to ZL Swindon Works 25/06/84 and held intact until sold to Vic Berry, Leicester 05/87 due to Swindon Works closure. Moved to Swindon Cocklebury Yard on 03/06/87, to Humberstone Road, Leicester 05/06/87 and to Berry's Yard the next day. It was put in the 'pyramid' by 10/87 where it remained, last

D5276 contd.
noted on 17/11/87, but definitely cut up by 12/12/87.

D5277
16A Toton 11/06/1964 E
16C Derby 07/1964 M
9E Trafford Park 07/1964 M
9A Longsight 03/1968 M
D09 Manchester Division 17/06/1968 E
D16 Nottingham Division 04/1972 M
TO Toton 05/1973 M
Renumbered 25127 01/03/1974 E
Withdrawn 02/11/1980 E
Moved to ZL Swindon Works 14/01/81 and cut up by 29/06/83, with parts of this locomotive being noted at Vic Berry, Leicester on 16/08/83.

D5278
16A Toton 12/06/1964 E
16C Derby 07/1964 M
9E Trafford Park 07/1964 M
9A Longsight 03/1968 M
D09 Manchester Division 17/06/1968 E
Withdrawn 02/05/1971 E
Withdrawn due to severe damage sustained in a head-on crash at Great Rocks in 02/71.

With the advent of TOPS numbering, further livery variants could be noted such as 25252 carrying its new TOPS number but still in two-tone green with full yellow ends at Sutton Park on 30th May 1974. *(Michael Mensing/RCTS Photo Archive*

D5278 contd.

Cut up at Peak Forest in 10/71 by staff from G. Cohen, Tinsley.

D5279

16A Toton 18/06/1964 E
9E Trafford Park 07/1964 M
9A Longsight 03/1968 M
D09 Manchester Division 17/06/1968 E
D16 Nottingham Division 03/1972 M
TO Toton 05/1973 M
Renumbered 25129 04/1974 M
Withdrawn 07/02/1982 E
Withdrawn due to collision damage at Roade on 10/01/82 with 25215, which was undamaged. Moved to ZE Derby Works about 04/82 and held in deteriorating condition, then moved to ZL Swindon Works on 04/02/85 and broken up by 24/03/85.

D5280

16A Toton 20/06/1964 E
16C Derby 07/1964 M
D16 Nottingham Division 16/01/1965 E
LMML LM Midland Lines 09/1967 M
D16 Nottingham Division 17/06/1968 E
D08 Liverpool Division 07/1968 M
D10 Preston Division 11/1968 M
D16 Nottingham Division 04/1972 M
TO Toton 05/1973 M
Renumbered 25130 01/03/1974 E
Derailed near Chapel-en-le-Frith and rolled over onto its side on 10/12/74; rerailed 13/12/74 and repaired.
CW Cricklewood East 02/1982 M
Withdrawn 06/12/1982 E
Stored at Springs Branch. Moved to ZL Swindon Works 27/06/84 and finally dismantled by 09/01/87.

D5281

16A Toton 26/06/1964 E
16C Derby 07/1964 M
14B Cricklewood West 10/1964 M
D14 London (Midland) Division 16/01/1965 E
2E Saltley 04/1965 M
D02 Birmingham Division 04/1966 M
LMML LM Midland Lines 04/1966 M
D16 Nottingham Division 17/06/1968 E
D08 Liverpool Division 07/1968 M
D10 Preston Division 11/1968 M
D16 Nottingham Division 04/1972 M
TO Toton 05/1973 M
SP Springs Branch 07/1973 M
TO Toton 08/1973 M

D5281 contd.

Renumbered 25131 10/04/1974 E
CW Cricklewood East 02/1982 M
Withdrawn 19/12/1982 E
Stored at Toton 02/83
Reinstated 10/1983 M
Taken into Departmental service 01/10/83 still carrying the external number 25131.
Renumbered 97202 01/84 M
Although it had been officially renumbered in 10/83, the external number was not apparently changed to 97202 until the loco returned to store. Departmental service was brief as it was stored at Toton being noted 26/12/83-14/1/84 (by then renumbered 97202).
Renumbered 25131 01/1984 M
TO Toton 01/1984 M
When Departmental use as 97202 was finished in 01/84 (officially), the locomotive was reinstated to capital stock as 25131 (but only on paper) so as to effect its disposal and was then promptly withdrawn again.
Withdrawn 01/1984 M
Moved to Swindon Transfer Yard on 12/07/84 and stored at ZL Swindon Works North Yard from 23/07/84 (still externally as 97202). Sold to Vic Berry, Leicester, due to Swindon Works impending closure. Moved to Swindon Cocklebury Yard on 26/05/87, to Oxford Hinksey Yard 02/06/87 and to Berry's Yard 11/06/87. Noted being cut up on 20/06/87 and completed by 25/06/87.

D5282

16A Toton 10/07/1964 E
16D Nottingham 08/1964 M
D16 Nottingham Division 16/01/1965 E
LMML LM Midland Lines 09/1967 M
D16 Nottingham Division 17/06/1968 E
D08 Liverpool Division 07/1968 M
D10 Preston Division 11/1968 M
D16 Nottingham Division 04/1972 M
TO Toton 05/1973 M
SP Springs Branch 07/1973 M
TO Toton 08/1973 M
Renumbered 25132 02/1974 M
LO Longsight 04/1982 M
Withdrawn 20/12/1982 E
Stored at Crewe Diesel 01/83. Moved to Gloucester 29/03/84 and to ZL Swindon Works on 02/04/84 and was scrapped by 15/11/84.

D5283
16A Toton 02/07/1964 E
14B Cricklewood West 07/1964 M
16A Toton 09/1964 M
16D Nottingham 09/1964 M
D16 Nottingham Division 16/01/1965 E
LMML LM Midland Lines 07/1965 M
D16 Nottingham Division 11/1965 M
D14 London (Midland) Division 01/1966 M
LMML LM Midland Lines 11/1966 M
D05 Stoke Division 08/1967 M
8J Allerton 05/1968 M
D08 Liverpool Division 17/06/1968 E
D10 Preston Division 11/1968 M
D16 Nottingham Division 04/1972 M
TO Toton 05/1973 M
SP Springs Branch 07/1973 M
TO Toton 09/1973 M
Renumbered 25133 10/10/1973 E
KD Kingmoor Diesel 04/1982 M
TO Toton 11/1982 M
KD Kingmoor Diesel 01/1983 M
Withdrawn 28/08/1983 E
Moved to ZE Derby Works and stored until moved to ZL Swindon Works on 04/02/85 where it remained intact. Due to the impending Swindon Works closure, it was sold to Vic Berry, Leicester 05/87. Moved to Swindon Cocklebury Yard on 26/05/87, then to Hinksey Yard, Oxford on 02/06/87 and to Berry's Yard on 11/06/87; was noted partly cut up 27/06/87 and, other than the cabs, was completed by 01/07/87.

D5284
16A Toton 09/07/1964 E
14B Cricklewood West 07/1964 M
16A Toton 09/1964 M
16C Derby 09/1964 M
14B Cricklewood West 10/1964 M
D14 London (Midland) Division 16/01/1965 E
2E Saltley 04/1965 M
D02 Birmingham Division 04/1966 M
LMML LM Midland Lines 04/1966 M
D16 Nottingham Division 17/06/1968 E
D08 Liverpool Division 07/1968 M
D10 Preston Division 10/1968 M
D16 Nottingham Division 04/1972 M
TO Toton 05/1973 M
SP Springs Branch 07/1973 M
TO Toton 09/1973 M
Renumbered 25134 28/05/1974 E
BS Bescot 10/1982 M

D5284 contd.
Withdrawn 20/12/1982 E
Stored at Newton Heath. Moved to ZL Swindon Works awaiting scrap, but with Swindon Works impending closure, the loco was sold to Vic Berry, Leicester and moved to Swindon Cocklebury Yard on 03/06/87, to Humberstone Road, Leicester on 05/06/87 and to Berry's Yard on 08/06/87 and was cut up by 04/03/88.

D5285
16A Toton 09/07/1964 E
14B Cricklewood West 07/1964 M
16A Toton 09/1964 M
16C Derby 09/1964 M
14B Cricklewood West 10/1964 M
D14 London (Midland) Division 16/01/1965 E
LMML LM Midland Lines 06/1965 M
D16 Nottingham Division 04/1966 M
LMML LM Midland Lines 03/1967 M
D05 Stoke Division 08/1967 M
12A Kingmoor Diesel 05/1968 M
D10 Preston Division 17/06/1968 E
D08 Liverpool Division 05/1970 M
D10 Preston Division 01/1972 M
D16 Nottingham Division 10/1972 M
TO Toton 05/1973 M
SP Springs Branch 07/1973 M
TO Toton 10/1973 M
Renumbered 25135 03/1974 M
BS Bescot 10/1982 M
Withdrawn 16/01/1983 E
Stored at Bescot. Moved to Gloucester 24/03/84 and to ZL Swindon Works 02/04/84 and was broken up by 31/07/86, with the cabs removed to Vic Berry, Leicester and still on site 02/11/87.

D5286
16A Toton 29/07/1964 E
16C Derby 09/1964 M
14B Cricklewood West 10/1964 M
D14 London (Midland) Division 16/01/1965 E
LMML LM Midland Lines 06/1965 M
D16 Nottingham Division 04/1966 M
LMML LM Midland Lines 03/1967 M
D05 Stoke Division 08/1967 M
12A Kingmoor Diesel 05/1968 M
D10 Preston Division 17/06/1968 E
D08 Liverpool Division 01/1970 M
D16 Nottingham Division 03/1973 M
TO Toton 05/1973 M
SP Springs Branch 07/1973 M

D5286 contd.
TO Toton 03/1974 M
Renumbered 25136 03/1974 M
CW Cricklewood East 01/1983 M
Withdrawn 28/03/1983 E
Stored at Crewe Diesel. Moved to Gloucester and to ZL Swindon Works 02/04/84, and was scrapped by 10/09/86. The cabs were taken to Vic Berry, Leicester and were still extant on 02/11/87.

D5287
16A Toton 29/07/1964 E
16C Derby 09/1964 M
14B Cricklewood West 10/1964 M
D14 London (Midland) Division 16/01/1965 E
LMML LM Midland Lines 06/1965 M
D16 Nottingham Division 11/1965 M
LMML LM Midland Lines 03/1967 M
D02 Birmingham Division 08/1967 M
D05 Stoke Division 11/1967 M
D10 Preston Division 09/1968 M
D08 Liverpool Division 01/1970 M
SP Springs Branch 05/1973 M
TO Toton 09/1973 M
Renumbered 25137 04/1974 M
WN Willesden 05/1975 M
TO Toton 06/1975 M
SP Springs Branch 02/1976 M
TO Toton 11/1977 M
Withdrawn 02/11/1980 E
Moved to ZE Derby Works by 04/11/80 and stored there. Moved to ZL Swindon Works on 12/01/81 and was dismantled by 18/05/83.

D5288
16A Toton 30/07/1964 E
16C Derby 08/1964 M
14B Cricklewood West 10/1964 M
D14 London (Midland) Division 16/01/1965 E
LMML LM Midland Lines 06/1965 M
D16 Nottingham Division 04/1966 M
LMML LM Midland Lines 03/1967 M
D02 Birmingham Division 08/1967 M
D05 Stoke Division 11/1967 M
D08 Liverpool Division 11/1968 M
SP Springs Branch 05/1973 M
Renumbered 25138 26/02/1974 E
CD Crewe Diesel 10/1982 M
Withdrawn 11/12/1983 E
Stored at Crewe Diesel. Moved to ZL Swindon Works 21/02/85 and cut up by 28/11/86. The cabs were sent to Vic Berry, Leicester and still there on 02/11/87.

D5289
16A Toton 13/08/1964 E
15A Leicester (Midland) 08/1964 M
D15 Leicester Division 16/01/1965 E
LMML LM Midland Lines 03/1967 M
D02 Birmingham Division 08/1967 M
D05 Stoke Division 11/1967 M
D08 Liverpool Division 11/1968 M
SP Springs Branch 05/1973 M
Renumbered 25139 02/1974 M
CD Crewe Diesel 01/1979 M
TO Toton 03/1980 M
Withdrawn 07/11/1982 E
Stored at Toton. Moved to Gloucester 10/07/84, then to ZL Swindon Works 25/07/84 and was cut up by 10/10/86.

D5290
16A Toton 17/08/1964 E
16C Derby 09/1964 M
14B Cricklewood West 10/1964 M
D14 London (Midland) Division 16/01/1965 E
LMML LM Midland Lines 06/1965 M
D16 Nottingham Division 02/1966 M
LMML LM Midland Lines 03/1967 M
D02 Birmingham Division 08/1967 M
D05 Stoke Division 11/1967 M
D08 Liverpool Division 11/1968 M
SP Springs Branch 05/1973 M
Renumbered 25140 03/1974 M
CD Crewe Diesel 01/1979 M
CW Cricklewood East 03/1980 M
KD Kingmoor Diesel 11/1981 M
Withdrawn 18/12/1983 E
Stored at Carlisle. Moved to ZL Swindon Works 03/04/85 and broken up 10/09/86. The cabs were removed to Vic Berry, Leicester and still on site 06/87, but disposed of by 09/87.

D5291
16A Toton 24/08/1964 E
16C Derby 09/1964 M
14B Cricklewood West 10/1964 M
D14 London (Midland) Division 16/01/1965 E
LMML LM Midland Lines 09/1965 M
D16 Nottingham Division 04/1966 M
LMML LM Midland Lines 03/1967 M
D02 Birmingham Division 08/1967 M
D05 Stoke Division 11/1967 M
D08 Liverpool Division 11/1968 M
D02 Birmingham Division 02/1973 M
BS Bescot 05/1973 M

D5291 contd.
TO Toton 01/1974 M
Renumbered 25141 19/03/1974 E
LO Longsight 09/1974 M
SP Springs Branch 10/1976 M
BS Bescot 11/1977 M
CW Cricklewood East 01/1980 M
LO Longsight 11/1981 M
Withdrawn 19/09/1982 E
Stored at Longsight, then moved to Springs Branch 01/83 for further storage. Moved to ZL Swindon Works 27/06/84 and was finally scrapped by 23/01/87.

D5292
16A Toton 26/08/1964 E
16C Derby 09/1964 M
14B Cricklewood West 10/1964 M
D14 London (Midland) Division 16/01/1965 E
LMML LM Midland Lines 09/1965 M
D16 Nottingham Division 04/1966 M
LMML LM Midland Lines 03/1967 M
D02 Birmingham Division 08/1967 M
D05 Stoke Division 11/1967 M
D08 Liverpool Division 11/1968 M
D09 Manchester Division 10/1969 M
D08 Liverpool Division 12/1969 M
D02 Birmingham Division 02/1973 M
BS Bescot 05/1973 M
Renumbered 25142 03/1974 M
KD Kingmoor Diesel 01/1976 M
Withdrawn 16/10/1981 E
Stored at Carlisle Kingmoor. Moved to ZL Swindon Works 08/12/81 and scrapped by 24/11/82.

D5293
16A Toton 02/09/1964 E
16C Derby 09/1964 M
14B Cricklewood West 10/1964 M
D14 London (Midland) Division 16/01/1965 E
LMML LM Midland Lines 09/1965 M
D16 Nottingham Division 11/1965 M
LMML LM Midland Lines 03/1967 M
D02 Birmingham Division 08/1967 M
8F Springs Branch 11/1967 M
9A Longsight 12/1967 M
D09 Manchester Division 17/06/1968 E
D02 Birmingham Division 01/1971 M
D09 Manchester Division 02/1971 M
D16 Nottingham Division 04/1972 M
D01 London Division 08/1972 M
D09 Manchester Division 09/1972 M
LO Longsight 05/1973 M

D5293 contd.
BS Bescot 08/1973 M
Renumbered 25143 02/1974 M
TO Toton 05/1980 M
Withdrawn 14/11/1982 E
Stored at Crewe Diesel. Moved to Gloucester 29/03/84 and on to ZL Swindon Works 02/04/84 and was cut up by 30/10/84.

D5294
16A Toton 07/09/1964 E
16C Derby 09/1964 M
16D Nottingham 10/1964 M
D16 Nottingham Division 16/01/1965 E
LMML LM Midland Lines 03/1967 M
D02 Birmingham Division 08/1967 M
D09 Manchester Division 03/1972 M
LO Longsight 05/1973 M
Renumbered 25144 15/05/74 E
KD Kingmoor Diesel 10/1975 M
BS Bescot 06/1981 M
Store 06/04/1983 E
Withdrawn 18/04/1983 E
Withdrawn, probably due to collision damage sustained in Watford Yard about 04/04/83. Moved to Swindon Transfer Yard 12/07/84 and into ZL Swindon Works 23/07/84, where it remained stored. Sold to Vic Berry, Leicester in 05/87, due to Swindon Works imminent closure. Moved to Berry's Yard on 11/06/87 and was cut up by 01/07/87, except the cabs, still there on 02/11/87.

D5295
16A Toton 10/09/1964 E
16C Derby 09/1964 M
16D Nottingham 10/1964 M
D16 Nottingham Division 16/01/1965 E
LMML LM Midland Lines 03/1967 M
D02 Birmingham Division 08/1967 M
D08 Liverpool Division 03/1972 M
D09 Manchester Division 03/1973 M
LO Longsight 05/1973 M
BS Bescot 08/1973 M
Renumbered 25145 02/1974 M
CD Crewe Diesel 08/1980 M
KD Kingmoor Diesel 11/1980 M
LO Longsight 01/1981 M
CW Cricklewood East 11/1981 M
BS Bescot 01/1984 M
KD Kingmoor Diesel 09/1985 M
Withdrawn 02/01/1986 E
Stored at Crewe Diesel. Sold to Vic Berry, Leicester in 12/86, moved to Knighton

D5295 contd.
Sidings, Leicester 23/01/87 and into Berry's Yard 26/01/87, where it was cut up by 02/05/87. Cabs still there on 02/11/87.

D5296
16A Toton 18/09/1964 E
16C Derby 09/1964 M
16D Nottingham 10/1964 M
D16 Nottingham Division 16/01/1965 E
40E Colwick 01/1965 M
D16 Nottingham Division 04/1965 M
LMML LM Midland Lines 03/1967 M
D02 Birmingham Division 08/1967 M
D09 Manchester Division 03/1972 M
LO Longsight 05/1973 M
Renumbered 25146 06/11/1973 E
KM Kingmoor Diesel 03/1974 M
Allocation recoded KM to KD 01/1975 M
Withdrawn 07/08/1983 E
Moved to ZE Derby Works by 22/10/83 and remained stored there until moved to ZL Swindon Works 04/02/85 and scrapped by 17/04/85.

D5297
16A Toton 18/09/1964 E
16C Derby 09/1964 M
16D Nottingham 10/1964 M
D16 Nottingham Division 16/01/1965 E
LMML LM Midland Lines 09/1967 M
D16 Nottingham Division 17/06/1968 E
D10 Preston Division 07/1969 M
KM Kingmoor Diesel 05/1973 M
BS Bescot 09/1973 M
LO Longsight 12/1973 M
KM Kingmoor Diesel 01/1974 M
LO Longsight 03/1974 M
Renumbered 25147 18/03/1974 E
CD Crewe Diesel 10/1976 M
SP Springs Branch 05/1977 M
BS Bescot 08/1977 M
KD Kingmoor Diesel 01/1980 M
Withdrawn 30/03/1980 E
Stored at Toton. Moved to ZL Swindon Works 20/06/80 and cut up by 10/09/80.

D5298
16A Toton 28/09/1964 E
16D Nottingham 10/1964 M
D16 Nottingham Division 16/01/1965 E
2E Saltley 03/1965 M
D02 Birmingham Division 04/1966 M
LMML LM Midland Lines 04/1966 M
D16 Nottingham Division 17/06/1968 E

D5298 contd.
D10 Preston Division 07/1969 M
KM Kingmoor Diesel 05/1973 M
Renumbered 25148 02/1974 M
LO Longsight 06/1974 M
CD Crewe Diesel 10/1976 M
LO Longsight 05/1977 M
CD Crewe Diesel 10/1977 M
KD Kingmoor Diesel 03/1980 M
CD Crewe Diesel 02/1981 M
CW Cricklewood East 03/1981 M
Withdrawn 07/09/1981 E
Withdrawn due to collision damage. Moved to ZE Derby Works 10/81 and stored until 18/03/82 when it moved to ZL Swindon Works and was broken up by 12/05/82.

D5299
D16 Nottingham Division 16/10/1965 E
LMML LM Midland Lines 09/1967 M
D16 Nottingham Division 17/06/1968 E
D10 Preston Division 11/1969 M
KM Kingmoor Diesel 05/1973 M
This locomotive, when still D5299 or 5299, was selected to be a testbed for an uprated Sulzer 1,750hp Type 3 engine, but the project was cancelled (date not reported).
Renumbered 25149 14/09/1973 E
Allocation recoded KM to KD 01/1975 M
Withdrawn 10/01/1982 E
Stored at Toton. Moved to ZL Swindon Works 26/04/82 and was dismantled by 24/05/83.

D7500
16A Toton 02/10/1964 E
16F Burton-on-Trent 12/1964 M
D16 Nottingham Division 16/01/1965 E
LMML LM Midland Lines 02/1968 M
D16 Nottingham Division 17/06/1968 E
64B Haymarket 10/1972 M
Allocation recoded 64B to HA 05/1973 M
TI Tinsley 05/1973 M
Renumbered 25150 02/1974 M
ED Eastfield 07/1975 M
LO Longsight 08/1975 M
CD Crewe Diesel 10/1976 M
BS Bescot 07/1977 M
LO Longsight 01/1980 M
Withdrawn 13/06/1982 E
Involved in a collision at Kilby Bridge on 06/06/82. Stored in damaged condition at ZE Derby Works 10/06/82 and remained

D7500 contd.
there until sent to ZL Swindon Works on 05/02/85 and was cut up by 12/06/85.

D7501
16A Toton 06/10/1964 E
16F Burton-on-Trent 12/1964 M
D16 Nottingham Division 16/01/1965 E
LMML LM Midland Lines 02/1968 M
D16 Nottingham Division 17/06/1968 E
64B Haymarket 11/1972 M
Allocation recoded 64B to HA 05/1973 M
TI Tinsley 05/1973 M
Renumbered 25151 02/1974 M
ED Eastfield 07/1975 M
LO Longsight 08/1975 M
CD Crewe Diesel 10/1976 M
BS Bescot 07/1977 M
LO Longsight 01/1980 M
Ran out of control with a train of hopper wagons through Slaithwaite and Huddersfield stations on 03/9/82, diverted into Hillhouse Goods Yard where a collision caused extensive damage. Moved to Healey Mills 06/09/82.
Withdrawn 12/09/1982 E
Stored at Healey Mills, then moved to Toton 01/83 for further storage and was used several times for rerailing exercises until at least 24/06/87. Sold to Vic Berry, Leicester and was broken up on site at Coton Hill, Toton by staff from Berrys between 15/12/87 and 20/01/88.

D7502
16A Toton 08/10/1964 E
16F Burton-on-Trent 12/1964 M
D16 Nottingham Division 16/01/1965 E
D01 London Division (WCML) 02/1967 M
D05 Stoke Division 08/1967 M
8F Springs Branch 11/1967 M
D08 Liverpool Division 17/06/1968 E
D16 Nottingham Division 05/1969 M
84A Laira 01/1972 M
82A Bristol Bath Road 10/1972 M
86A Cardiff (Canton) 12/1972 M
Allocation recoded 86A to CF 05/1973 M
Renumbered 25152 04/1974 M
BR Bristol Bath Road 10/1974 M
CD Crewe Diesel 02/1976 M
TO Toton 09/1977 M
CW Cricklewood East 03/1983 M
Withdrawn 26/01/1984 E
Moved to ZL Swindon Works 16/02/84 and dismantled by 31/01/85.

D7503
16A Toton 14/10/1964 E
16F Burton-on-Trent 12/1964 M
D16 Nottingham Division 16/01/1965 E
D14 London (Midland) Division 10/1965 M
LMML LM Midland Lines 02/1968 M
D16 Nottingham Division 17/06/1968 E
84A Laira 01/1972 M
82A Bristol Bath Road 11/1972 M
86A Cardiff (Canton) 12/1972 M
Allocation recoded 86A to CF 05/1973 M
Renumbered 25153 04/1974 M
BR Bristol Bath Road 10/1974 M
CD Crewe Diesel 02/1976 M
SP Springs Branch 03/1980 M
CD Crewe Diesel 02/1981 M
CW Cricklewood East 04/1981 M
TO Toton 11/1982 M
CD Crewe Diesel 03/1983 M
Withdrawn 03/04/1983 E
Moved to Swindon Transfer Yard 12/07/84 and on to ZL Swindon Works 23/07/84. Finally cut up by 27/02/87, the cabs were moved to Vic Berry, Leicester and were still there on 02/11/87.

D7504
16A Toton 17/10/1964 E
16F Burton-on-Trent 12/1964 M
D16 Nottingham Division 16/01/1965 E
D14 London (Midland) Division 01/1968 M
LMML LM Midland Lines 02/1968 M
D16 Nottingham Division 17/06/1968 E
84A Laira 01/1972 M
82A Bristol Bath Road 11/1972 M
86A Cardiff (Canton) 12/1972 M
Allocation recoded 86A to CF 05/1973 M
Renumbered 25154 03/1974 M
CD Crewe Diesel 12/1976 M
LO Longsight 03/1978 M
BS Bescot 01/1980 M
CD Crewe Diesel 09/1981 M
KM Kingmoor New Yard 04/1982 M
CW Cricklewood East 11/1982 M
BS Bescot 01/1984 M
Withdrawn 27/03/1985 E
Stored at Tyseley, moved to Bescot 30/03/87, then to Basford Hall Yard 31/03/87, both for further storage. Moved to Humberstone Road, Leicester 09/07/87 and then to Vic Berry, Leicester next day. Partly dismantled, it was put in the 'pyramid' by 10/10/87 and was quickly retrieved and cut up by 13/11/87.

A blue livery variation to appear later in the life of some of the Class 25s was for the number to moved from the cabside to the bodyside as here on 25202 at Manchester Victoria on 28th September 1983. *(John E. Henderson/Colour-Rail.com*

D7505
16A Toton 22/10/1964 E
16F Burton-on-Trent 12/1964 M
D16 Nottingham Division 16/01/1965 E
LMML LM Midland Lines 02/1968 M
D16 Nottingham Division 17/06/1968 E
84A Laira 01/1972 M
86A Cardiff (Canton) 12/1972 M
Allocation recoded 86A to CF 05/1973 M
Renumbered 25155 04/1974 M
BR Bristol Bath Road 10/1974 M
CF Cardiff (Canton) 11/1975 M
LA Laira 05/1977 M
SP Springs Branch 10/1980 M
Store 15/11/1980 E
Stored at ZL Swindon Works 15/11/80
Withdrawn 01/12/1980 E
Cut up at Swindon Works by 29/09/81.

D7506
16A Toton 23/10/1964 E
D16 Nottingham Division 16/01/1965 E
8F Springs Branch 10/1967 M
D08 Liverpool Division 17/06/1968 E
D16 Nottingham Division 05/1969 M
84A Laira 01/1972 M
Allocation recoded 84A to LA 05/1973 M

D7506 contd.
CF Cardiff (Canton) 09/1973 M
Renumbered 25156 03/07/1974 E
BR Bristol Bath Road 09/1974 M
LO Longsight 02/1976 M
CD Crewe Diesel 02/1976 M
Withdrawn 20/12/1981 E
Stored at Tyseley. Moved to ZL Swindon Works 16/03/82 and cut up by 27/05/82.

D7507
16A Toton 29/10/1964 E
D16 Nottingham Division 16/01/1965 E
LMML LM Midland Lines 02/1968 M
D16 Nottingham Division 17/06/1968 E
84A Laira 01/1972 M
82A Bristol Bath Road 12/1972 M
Allocation recoded 82A to BR 05/1973 M
CF Cardiff (Canton) 09/1973 M
BR Bristol Bath Road 11/1973 M
CF Cardiff (Canton) 05/1974 M
Renumbered 25157 31/05/1974 E
BR Bristol Bath Road 05/1975 M
BS Bescot 02/1976 M
CD Crewe Diesel 02/1976 M
SP Springs Branch 07/1980 M
Unofficially named *City of Stoke on Trent,*

D7507 contd.
date unknown but thought to be between 07/80 and 10/82.
CD Crewe Diesel 10/1982 M
Withdrawn 30/10/1982 E
Stored at Kingmoor Diesel. Moved to Ashburys, Manchester 14/06/84, to Bescot 15/06/84, to Swindon Cocklebury Yard 11/07/84 and into ZL Swindon Works on 25/07/84. It remained in derelict condition until finally broken up by 13/03/87, the last main line locomotive cut up at the works before closure.

D7508
16A Toton 05/11/1964 E
D16 Nottingham Division 16/01/1965 E
2E Saltley 01/1965 M
D02 Birmingham Division 04/1966 M
LMML LM Midland Lines 04/1966 M
D16 Nottingham Division 01/1967 M
LMWL LM Western Lines 03/1967 M
LMML LM Midland Lines 03/1967 M
D16 Nottingham Division 12/1967 M
LMML LM Midland Lines 02/1968 M
D16 Nottingham Division 17/06/1968 E
84A Laira 01/1972 M
86B Ebbw Junction 12/1972 M
Allocation recoded 86B to EJ 05/1973 M
BR Bristol Bath Road 05/1973 M
CF Cardiff (Canton) 07/1973 M
Renumbered 25158 05/1974 M
BR Bristol Bath Road 10/1974 M
CF Cardiff (Canton) 12/1974 M
BR Bristol Bath Road 05/1975 M
TO Toton 02/1976 M
CD Crewe Diesel 02/1976 M
Withdrawn 22/05/1983 E
Stored at Newton Heath by 03/84. Moved to ZL Swindon Works 26/06/84 and stored awaiting scrap, but due to Swindon Works impending closure, the locomotive was sold to Vic Berry, Leicester. Moved to Swindon Cocklebury Yard on 26/05/87 and then Oxford Hinksey Yard 02/06/87 and to Berry's Yard 11/06/87. Cutting started by 25/06/87 and was completed by 02/07/87, with only the cabs still left on 02/11/87.

D7509
16A Toton 05/11/1964 E
D16 Nottingham Division 16/01/1965 E
LMML LM Midland Lines 04/1968 M
D16 Nottingham Division 17/06/1968 E

D7509 contd.
84A Laira 01/1972 M
86B Ebbw Junction 07/1972 M
Allocation recoded 86B to EJ 05/1973 M
Renumbered 25159 03/1974 M
CF Cardiff (Canton) 05/1974 M
BR Bristol Bath Road 05/1975 M
TO Toton 02/1976 M
CD Crewe Diesel 02/1976 M
Withdrawn 12/11/1980 E
Moved to ZL Swindon Works 19/12/80 and broken up by 18/03/81.

D7510
16A Toton 10/11/1964 E
D16 Nottingham Division 16/01/1965 E
LMML LM Midland Lines 04/1968 M
D16 Nottingham Division 17/06/1968 E
86B Ebbw Junction 01/1972 M
Allocation recoded 86B to EJ 05/1973 M
Renumbered 25160 04/1974 M
CF Cardiff (Canton) 05/1974 M
BR Bristol Bath Road 05/1975 M
CD Crewe Diesel 02/1976 M
Withdrawn 10/10/1982 E
Stored at Polmadie 10/82, then moved across the main line to Shawfield Sidings by 27/11/83 and stored there until sold for scrap to Vic Berry, Leicester. Moved to Thornton Junction 04/87 for cutting on site, but then rescinded and locomotive was prepared for movement to Berry's Yard. Moved to Mossend Yard 10/06/87, to Carlisle 11/06/87, to Basford Hall Yard 22/06/87, and to Humberstone Road, Leicester 23/06/87 and into Berry's Yard the same day. Cutting started and only the cabs and underframe were left by 15/07/87, the cabs still extant on 02/11/87.

D7511
16A Toton 17/11/1964 E
16D Nottingham 11/1964 M
D16 Nottingham Division 16/01/1965 E
LMML LM Midland Lines 04/1968 M
D16 Nottingham Division 17/06/1968 E
86B Ebbw Junction 01/1972 M
Allocation recoded 86B to EJ 05/1973 M
Renumbered 25161 04/1974 M
CF Cardiff (Canton) 05/1974 M
BR Bristol Bath Road 05/1975 M
CD Crewe Diesel 01/1976 M
Withdrawn 28/11/1984 E

D7511 contd.

Stored at Toton. Moved to Gloucester on 21/02/85 and arrived at ZL Swindon Works 25/02/85. Remained at Swindon Works, but as the works was due to close the locomotive was sold to Vic Berry, Leicester 05/87. Moved to Swindon Cocklebury Yard 03/06/87, to Humberstone Road, Leicester 04/06/87 and into Berry's Yard 05/06/87, where it was put in the 'pyramid' by 08/87, cutting started in 03/88 and was completed by 24/03/88.

D7512

16A Toton 20/11/1964 E
D16 Nottingham Division 16/01/1965 E
D15 Leicester Division 10/1965 M
D16 Nottingham Division 08/1967 M
LMML LM Midland Lines 04/1968 M
D16 Nottingham Division 17/06/1968 E
86B Ebbw Junction 01/1972 M
Allocation recoded 86B to EJ 05/1973 M
Renumbered 25162 04/1974 M
CF Cardiff (Canton) 05/1974 M
BR Bristol Bath Road 05/1975 M
CD Crewe Diesel 01/1976 M
Withdrawn 31/05/1981 E
Moved to ZL Swindon Works 03/08/81 and broken up by 23/06/82.

D7513

16A Toton 25/11/1964 E
D16 Nottingham Division 16/01/1965 E
D01 London Division (WCML) 02/1967 M
D05 Stoke Division 08/1967 M
9A Longsight 03/1968 M
D09 Manchester Division 17/06/1968 E
D02 Birmingham Division 01/1969 M
D16 Nottingham Division 11/1970 M
86B Ebbw Junction 01/1972 M
Allocation recoded 86B to EJ 05/1973 M
Renumbered 25163 03/1974 M
CF Cardiff (Canton) 05/1974 M
BR Bristol Bath Road 11/1975 M
CD Crewe Diesel 01/1976 M
Withdrawn 10/11/1980 E
Moved to ZL Swindon Works 19/12/80 and scrapped by 16/03/83.

D7514

16A Toton 25/11/1964 E
D16 Nottingham Division 16/01/1965 E
D15 Leicester Division 10/1965 M
D16 Nottingham Division 08/1967 M
LMML LM Midland Lines 04/1968 M

D7514 contd.

D16 Nottingham Division 17/06/1968 E
86B Ebbw Junction 01/1972 M
Allocation recoded 86B to EJ 05/1973 M
Renumbered 25164 04/1974 M
CF Cardiff (Canton) 05/1974 M
BR Bristol Bath Road 11/1975 M
CD Crewe Diesel 01/1976 M
Withdrawn 21/08/1983 E
Moved to ZE Derby Works by 04/10/83 and stored there, then sent to ZL Swindon Works on 24/07/85 and awaited scrap. However, due to Swindon Works closing in 1987, the locomotive was sold to Vic Berry, Leicester about 04/87 and left for Swindon Cocklebury Yard 03/06/87, to Humberstone Road, Leicester 05/06/87, into Berry's Yard on 08/06/87 and put in the 'pyramid'. Taken off in 11/87 and last noted intact on 15/11/87, it was cut completely by 11/12/87.

D7515

16A Toton 02/12/1964 E
14B Cricklewood West 12/1964 M
D14 London (Midland) Division 16/01/1965 E
LMML LM Midland Lines 09/1965 M
D16 Nottingham Division 08/1966 M
LMML LM Midland Lines 04/1968 M
D16 Nottingham Division 17/06/1968 E
86B Ebbw Junction 01/1972 M
Allocation recoded 86B to EJ 05/1973 M
Renumbered 25165 04/1974 M
CF Cardiff (Canton) 05/1974 M
CD Crewe Diesel 01/1976 M
Withdrawn 03/11/1978 E
Moved to ZE Derby Works early 1979 and cut in two by 10/79. Cutting was completed by 14/05/81, but one of the cabs was still there on 10/07/86. Derby Works official cutting up list gave 03/11/78 but that was its withdrawal date.

D7516

16A Toton 04/12/1964 E
14B Cricklewood West 12/1964 M
D14 London (Midland) Division 16/01/1965 E
LMML LM Midland Lines 09/1965 M
D16 Nottingham Division 02/1966 M
LMML LM Midland Lines 05/1968 M
D16 Nottingham Division 17/06/1968 E
86B Ebbw Junction 01/1972 M
Allocation recoded 86B to EJ 05/1973 M
Renumbered 25166 04/1974 M
CF Cardiff (Canton) 05/1974 M

D7516 contd.
CD Crewe Diesel 05/1976 M
Withdrawn 14/11/1980 E
Moved to ZL Swindon Works 03/03/81 and was dismantled by 01/07/81.

D7517
16A Toton 09/12/1964 E
14B Cricklewood West 12/1964 M
D14 London (Midland) Division 16/01/1965 E
LMML LM Midland Lines 09/1965 M
D16 Nottingham Division 08/1966 M
LMML LM Midland Lines 05/1968 M
D16 Nottingham Division 17/06/1968 E
86B Ebbw Junction 07/1972 M
Allocation recoded 86B to EJ 05/1973 M
CF Cardiff (Canton) 08/1973 M
Renumbered 25167 02/1974 M
BR Bristol Bath Road 01/1976 M
CD Crewe Diesel 02/1976 M
Withdrawn 29/05/1983 E
Stored at Crewe Diesel. Moved to ZL Swindon Works 16/02/84 and quickly cut up by 17/04/84.

D7518
16A Toton 12/12/1964 E
D16 Nottingham Division 16/01/1965 E
2E Saltley 01/1965 M
D02 Birmingham Division 04/1966 M
LMML LM Midland Lines 04/1966 M
D16 Nottingham Division 12/1967 M
LMML LM Midland Lines 05/1968 M
D16 Nottingham Division 17/06/1968 E
86B Ebbw Junction 07/1972 M
Allocation recoded 86B to EJ 05/1973 M
CF Cardiff (Canton) 05/1973 M
Renumbered 25168 03/1974 M
LA Laira 11/1975 M
BR Bristol Bath Road 01/1976 M
CD Crewe Diesel 02/1976 M
Officially withdrawn 31/05/81, but continued in traffic; withdrawal officially cancelled.
Withdrawn 22/05/1983 E
Moved to ZL Swindon Works 16/02/84 and cut up by 09/04/84.

D7519
16A Toton 09/01/1965 E
D16 Nottingham Division 16/01/1965 E
2E Saltley 03/1965 M
D16 Nottingham Division 03/1965 M
2E Saltley 07/1965 M
D02 Birmingham Division 04/1966 M
LMML LM Midland Lines 04/1966 M

D7519 contd.
D16 Nottingham Division 12/1967 M
LMML LM Midland Lines 05/1968 M
D16 Nottingham Division 17/06/1968 E
86A Cardiff (Canton) 07/1972 M
Allocation recoded 86A to CF 05/1973 M
Renumbered 25169 09/1973 M
LA Laira 10/1975 M
SP Springs Branch 07/1976 M
CD Crewe Diesel 08/1976 M
Withdrawn 08/09/1981 E
Stored at Bescot 10/81. Moved to ZL Swindon Works 24/12/81 and was cut up by 17/02/82.

D7520
16A Toton 22/12/1964 E
D16 Nottingham Division 16/01/1965 E
2E Saltley 03/1965 M
D02 Birmingham Division 04/1966 M
LMML LM Midland Lines 04/1966 M
D16 Nottingham Division 12/1967 M
LMML LM Midland Lines 05/1968 M
D16 Nottingham Division 17/06/1968 E
86A Cardiff (Canton) 07/1972 M
Allocation recoded 86A to CF 05/1973 M
Renumbered 25170 04/07/1974 E
LA Laira 10/1975 M
CD Crewe Diesel 05/1978 M
Withdrawn 18/04/1982 E
Stored at Reddish. Officially reinstated to Crewe Diesel 20/06/82 but was still stored at Reddish 04/07/82.
CD Crewe Diesel 20/06/1982 E
Reinstated 20/06/1982 E
Store 20/06/1982 E
Withdrawn 02/08/1982 E
Moved to ZE Derby Works on 01/08/82, was withdrawn the next day and was broken up by 06/04/83.

D7521
16A Toton 09/01/1965 E
D16 Nottingham Division 16/01/1965 E
LMML LM Midland Lines 05/1968 M
D16 Nottingham Division 17/06/1968 E
86A Cardiff (Canton) 07/1972 M
Allocation recoded 86A to CF 05/1973 M
Renumbered 25171 12/06/1974 E
LA Laira 10/1974 M
BR Bristol Bath Road 05/1975 M
CF Cardiff (Canton) 06/1975 M
HA Haymarket 10/1975 M
Withdrawn 15/10/1978 E

D7521 contd.

Withdrawn due to severe collision damage at Arbroath Goods Yard when a runaway train was diverted into the yard on 22/09/78. It was cut up on site by BR staff in 01/79. Wagons containing remains were still on site 14/02/79 and were later taken to ZH Glasgow Works for disposal.

D7522

16A Toton 09/01/1965 E
D16 Nottingham Division 16/01/1965 E
D15 Leicester Division 10/1965 M
D16 Nottingham Division 08/1967 M
LMML LM Midland Lines 05/1968 M
D16 Nottingham Division 17/06/1968 E
D01 London Division 08/1972 M
D10 Preston Division 09/1972 M
D01 London Division 12/1972 M
WN Willesden 05/1973 M
CD Cricklewood East 06/1973 M
Allocation recoded CD to CW 12/1973 M
WN Willesden 01/1974 M
CF Cardiff (Canton) 05/1974 M
Renumbered 25172 20/05/1974 E
LA Laira 10/1974 M
BR Bristol Bath Road 05/1975 M
CF Cardiff (Canton) 06/1975 M
HA Haymarket 10/1975 M
SP Springs Branch 12/1976 M
Withdrawn 01/02/1981 E
Stored at Carlisle Kingmoor by 03/02/81. Moved to ZL Swindon Works 06/04/81 and dismantled by 07/05/83.

D7523

D16 Nottingham Division 16/01/1965 E
LMML LM Midland Lines 05/1968 M
D16 Nottingham Division 17/06/1968 E
D01 London Division 08/1972 M
D09 Manchester Division 10/1972 M
LO Longsight 05/1973 M
WN Willesden 05/1973 M
Renumbered 25173 20/04/1974 E
CW Cricklewood East 06/1975 M
TO Toton 10/1976 M
CW Cricklewood East 05/1977 M
TO Toton 10/1977 M
CW Cricklewood East 03/1978 M
CD Crewe Diesel 01/1984 M
Withdrawn 19/03/1987 E
Stored at Crewe Gresty Lane until 07/87. Sold to Vic Berry, Leicester for scrap and moved from Basford Hall Yard, then to

D7523 contd.

Humberstone Road, Leicester on 29/07/87 and into Berry's Yard the next day. Stored intact at Berry's Yard. Reportedly sold for preservation to the Dean Forest Railway and moved to Humberstone Road, Leicester on 24/09/87, then to Basford Hall Yard 25/09/87 and to ZC Crewe Works on 01/10/87. However, the locomotive contained asbestos and was due to go back to Berry's Yard for its removal, but did not move from Crewe Works to Leicester stabling point until 21/06/88 and into Berry's Yard on 28/06/88. After asbestos removal it left Berrys on 19/01/89 and was moved to Leicester stabling point and held until moved once again to Basford Hall on 12/05/89. It was named *John F Kennedy* at BREL Crewe Works on 21/07/90 and is painted as D7523. Kept at Crewe until moved to the premises of Rail & Marine Engineering, Thingley Junction, Wiltshire on 08/07/95.

For preservation

Moved by road from there to the West Somerset Railway 01/05/96, then to the Epping Ongar Railway on 06-07/09/11. The nameplates were removed in 2011 before it left the WSR. To Shackerstone, Battlefield Line 11/10/14 for overhaul and service there.
HQ Headquarters Pool 04/02/2005 E
Reregistered as 89223 to allow rail movement to galas on other heritage railways.

D7524

D16 Nottingham Division 23/01/1965 E
D01 London Division 08/1972 M
WN Willesden 05/1973 M
Renumbered 25174 04/03/1974 E
CW Cricklewood East 06/1975 M
Withdrawn 20/09/1976 E
Collided with 25030 at Aylesbury 05/08/76. Moved to ZE Derby Works 09/08/76 and scrapped by 08/78. However, Derby Works official scrapping list reported that it was cut up 12/78.

D7525

D16 Nottingham Division 30/01/1965 E
D01 London Division 10/1971 M
WN Willesden 05/1973 M
Renumbered 25175 03/1974 M
CW Cricklewood East 06/1975 M
Store 04/1982 M

D7525 contd.
Stored at Toton, then moved to ZE Derby Works about 08/82, and restored to service after being repaired.
CW Cricklewood East 1982 Y
Returned to service 1982 Y
CD Crewe Diesel 01/1984 M
Withdrawn 05/12/1985 E
Stored at Crewe Diesel until sold to Vic Berry, Leicester 12/86 for scrap. Moved to Knighton Sidings, Leicester 23/01/87 and into Berry's Yard on 26/01/87, was still intact on 08/04/87, but had been cut up by 05/05/87, except the cabs still there 07/87.

D7526
D16 Nottingham Division 30/01/1965 E
31B March 02/1965 M
34G Finsbury Park 05/1965 M
D16 Nottingham Division 06/1965 M
D01 London Division 10/1971 M
WN Willesden 05/1973 M
Renumbered 25176 04/1974 M
CW Cricklewood East 06/1975 M
KD Kingmoor Diesel 11/1984 M

D7526 contd.
CD Crewe Diesel 03/1986 M
Withdrawn 09/03/1987 E
Stored at Longsight, moved to Ashburys, Manchester on 27/07/87, then back to Longsight on 01/08/87. Moved to Crewe South on 26/11/87, to Basford Hall Yard 09/12/87, to Bescot on 11/12/87, to Humberstone Road, Leicester 17/12/87, and on to Leicester stabling point on 18/12/87. Sent to Toton on 06/01/88, then back to Leicester stabling point on 08/01/88, to Humberstone Road on 21/01/88, and finally into Vic Berry, Leicester on 25/01/88 for scrap. Cut up in 07/88. There were unconfirmed reports that this locomotive had been sold for preservation but, if so, that never happened.

D7527
D16 Nottingham Division 30/01/1965 E
D01 London Division 10/1971 M
WN Willesden 05/1973 M
Renumbered 25177 03/1974 M
CW Cricklewood East 06/1975 M

The renumbering of a small number of the Class 25s to the 259xx series saw both bodyside and cabside numbers used at random throughout the sub-class probably being applied in the same position as the previously carried number. 25903 is at Crewe Diesel depot on 15th October 1986.
(P. M. Dunkley/Colour-Rail.com

D7527 contd.

Withdrawn 28/11/1982 E

Stored at Stratford and used for derailing/rerailing exercises at Stratford open day on 09/07/83. It was then moved to Temple Mills Yard and used in rerailing exercises on 26/03/84, then returned to Stratford. To Temple Mills again on 05/06/84 for breakdown tests, returned to Stratford and moved to Reading the same day. Moved to ZL Swindon Works 14/06/84 and was cut up by 07/05/86.

D7528

D16 Nottingham Division 06/02/1965 E
D01 London Division 10/1971 M
WN Willesden 05/1973 M
Renumbered 25178 19/03/1974 E
CW Cricklewood East 06/1975 M
BS Bescot 05/1981 M
CD Crewe Diesel 10/1981 M
Withdrawn 01/04/1985 E

Stored at Kingmoor Diesel then moved to Kingmoor New Yard 10/85 for further storage. Moved to Carlisle Upperby 04/08/88 for inspection prior to movement south and returned to Kingmoor New Yard a few days later. Moved again to Upperby on 10/11/88 and held there until moved to Crewe Basford Hall Yard on 30/11/88, then to Toton and on to Leicester stabling point on 15/12/88 and into Vic Berry, Leicester on 19/12/88. Cutting up had started by 04/03/89 and was completed by 17/03/89.

D7529

D16 Nottingham Division 13/02/1965 E
D01 London Division 08/1969 M
WN Willesden 05/1973 M
Renumbered 25179 04/1974 M
CW Cricklewood East 06/1975 M
Withdrawn 28/11/1982 E

Stored at Springs Branch. Moved to ZL Swindon Works 27/06/84 and broken up by 13/02/87.

D7530

D16 Nottingham Division 13/02/1965 E
D01 London Division 08/1969 M
WN Willesden 05/1973 M
Renumbered 25180 20/04/1974 E
CW Cricklewood East 06/1975 M
Withdrawn 28/11/1982 E

Stored at Saltley, then moved to Tyseley

D7530 contd.

about 05/83 for further storage. Moved to ZL Swindon Works on 25/03/85 and remained until being sold for scrap about 04/87 to Vic Berry, Leicester. Departed Swindon Works for Cocklebury Yard 03/06/87 and to Humberstone Road, Leicester the same day, and into Vic Berry, Leicester 04/06/87. Put into the 'pyramid' by 08/87 and remained thus until last noted intact on 17/02/88, but had been cut by 04/03/88 except for the cabs which were still in evidence on 06/06/90.

D7531

D16 Nottingham Division 20/02/1965 E
D01 London Division 08/1969 M
WN Willesden 05/1973 M
Renumbered 25181 04/1974 M
CW Cricklewood East 06/1975 M
CD Crewe Diesel 01/1984 M
Withdrawn 11/08/1986 E

Withdrawn due to failure at Andover on 27/07/86 whilst hauling "The Coastway Crusader" rail tour. Moved to Eastleigh on 19/08/86 and held awaiting further movement. However, it was reported sold to Energy Consultants & Control, Marton, Blackpool in 08/87 for scrapping on site, which handed the job over to staff from Vic Berry, Leicester, who cut it at Eastleigh in three days at the end of 07/88.

D7532

D16 Nottingham Division 20/02/1965 E
D01 London Division 08/1969 M
D02 Birmingham Division 04/1972 M
D01 London Division 08/1972 M
WN Willesden 05/1973 M
Renumbered 25182 02/1974 M
CW Cricklewood East 06/1975 M
CD Crewe Diesel 01/1976 M
CW Cricklewood East 08/1976 M
CD Crewe Diesel 01/1984 M
Withdrawn 21/01/1985 E

Moved to ZL Swindon Works on 27/03/85 and scrapped by 13/08/85.

D7533

D16 Nottingham Division 27/02/1965 E
D01 London Division 08/1969 M
D02 Birmingham Division 04/1972 M
D01 London Division 08/1972 M
WN Willesden 05/1973 M
Renumbered 25183 02/1974 M

D7533 contd.
CW Cricklewood East 06/1975 M
CD Crewe Diesel 01/1976 M
CW Cricklewood East 08/1976 M
Store 23/10/1980 E
Stored at Toton by 23/10/80
Withdrawn 01/12/1980 E
Moved to ZL Swindon Works on 15/11/80 and dismantled by 30/09/81.

D7534
D16 Nottingham Division 06/03/1965 E
D01 London Division 07/1969 M
D02 Birmingham Division 12/1971 M
BS Bescot 05/1973 M
WN Willesden 07/1973 M
Renumbered 25184 13/07/1974 E
KM Kingmoor Diesel 11/1974 M
Allocation recoded KM to KD 01/1975 M
BS Bescot 02/1975 M
WN Willesden 05/1975 M
CW Cricklewood East 06/1975 M
LO Longsight 01/1976 M
CD Crewe Diesel 10/1976 M
LO Longsight 03/1978 M
BS Bescot 01/1980 M
LO Longsight 10/1981 M
Store 04/1982 M
LO Longsight 05/1982 M
Returned to Service 05/1982 M
Withdrawn 28/08/1983 E
Moved to ZL Swindon Works on 21/09/83 and cut up by 06/02/84.

D7535
D16 Nottingham Division 06/03/1965 E
D01 London Division 07/1969 M
D02 Birmingham Division 05/1970 M
D01 London Division 06/1970 M
D02 Birmingham Division 12/1971 M
BS Bescot 05/1973 M
WN Willesden 07/1973 M
Renumbered 25185 28/02/1974 E
TO Toton 10/1974 M
WN Willesden 03/1975 M
CW Cricklewood East 06/1975 M
LO Longsight 01/1976 M
CD Crewe Diesel 10/1976 M
KD Kingmoor Diesel 05/1977 M
SP Springs Branch 02/1981 M
Store 04/1981 M
SP Springs Branch 05/1981 M
Returned to Service 05/1981 M
CD Crewe Diesel 10/1982 M

D7535 contd.
Withdrawn 05/11/1984 E
For preservation
Stored at Crewe until sold for preservation to the Dart Valley Railway, for use on the Torbay Railway, later the Paignton & Dartmouth Railway, and was moved to its site on 15/03/86. It was painted as D7535 and in 1987 was named *Mercury*. The name was removed and, instead, was given the name *Hercules*, was freshly painted in 06/04. Has also carried the name *BOCO*. Returned to the South Devon Railway, previously the Dart Valley Railway, on 10/10/18, remaining there apart from visiting galas on other heritage railways.

D7536
D16 Nottingham Division 13/03/1965 E
D15 Leicester Division 09/1965 M
D16 Nottingham Division 08/1967 M
D01 London Division 07/1969 M
D09 Manchester Division 07/1971 M
D08 Liverpool Division 08/1971 M
D01 London Division 01/1972 M
D09 Manchester Division 02/1972 M
D02 Birmingham Division 03/1972 M
BS Bescot 05/1973 M
WN Willesden 03/1974 M
Renumbered 25186 04/1974 M
SP Springs Branch 10/1974 M
LO Longsight 07/1975 M
CD Crewe Diesel 10/1977 M
KD Kingmoor Diesel 01/1978 M
CD Crewe Diesel 01/1979 M
KD Kingmoor Diesel 05/1980 M
TO Toton 11/1980 M
Withdrawn 28/11/1982 E
Stored at Crewe Diesel. Moved to ZL Swindon Works 10/02/84 and was finally broken up by 23/01/87.

D7537
D16 Nottingham Division 13/03/1965 E
D15 Leicester Division 10/1965 M
D16 Nottingham Division 08/1967 M
D01 London Division 07/1969 M
D02 Birmingham Division 01/1971 M
BS Bescot 05/1973 M
WN Willesden 03/1974 M
BS Bescot 03/1974 M
Renumbered 25187 04/1974 M
LO Longsight 01/1980 M
Withdrawn 28/11/1982 E

D7537 contd.
Stored at Saltley, then to Bescot 02/83 for further storage. Moved to Swindon Cocklebury Yard 11/07/84 and into ZL Swindon Works 25/07/84 and cutting up was completed by 30/01/87.

D7538
D16 Nottingham Division 20/03/1965 E
9A Longsight 05/1968 M
D09 Manchester Division 17/06/1968 E
D01 London Division 10/1969 M
D02 Birmingham Division 01/1971 M
BS Bescot 05/1973 M
Renumbered 25188 04/1974 M
LO Longsight 01/1980 M
Withdrawn 15/08/1982 E
Stored at Springs Branch. Moved to ZL Swindon Works on 27/06/84 and scrapped by 06/02/87.

D7539
D16 Nottingham Division 27/03/1965 E
9A Longsight 05/1968 M
D09 Manchester Division 17/06/1968 E
D01 London Division 10/1969 M
D02 Birmingham Division 01/1971 M
D09 Manchester Division 07/1971 M
D08 Liverpool Division 10/1971 M
D02 Birmingham Division 04/1972 M
D09 Manchester Division 10/1972 M
D16 Nottingham Division 12/1972 M
TO Toton 05/1973 M
BS Bescot 11/1973 M
Renumbered 25189 02/1974 M
WN Willesden 03/1974 M
LO Longsight 08/1974 M
CW Cricklewood East 02/1976 M
TO Toton 10/1976 M
CW Cricklewood East 04/1977 M
CD Crewe Diesel 01/1984 M
Withdrawn 12/07/1985 E
Stored at Crewe Gresty Lane. Moved to ZF Doncaster Works about 29/01/86 and was cut up by 31/05/86, leaving just the cabs which were still there on 06/07/86.

D7540
D16 Nottingham Division 03/04/1965 E
9A Longsight 05/1968 M
D09 Manchester Division 17/06/1968 E
D08 Liverpool Division 01/1971 M
D09 Manchester Division 07/1971 M
D08 Liverpool Division 10/1971 M
D02 Birmingham Division 10/1972 M

D7540 contd.
D09 Manchester Division 10/1972 M
D16 Nottingham Division 12/1972 M
TO Toton 05/1973 M
KM Kingmoor Diesel 05/1973 M
Renumbered 25190 08/06/1974 E
SP Springs Branch 09/1974 M
KM Kingmoor Diesel 11/1974 M
Allocation recoded KM to KD 01/1975 M
TO Toton 02/1975 M
WN Willesden 03/1975 M
CW Cricklewood East 06/1975 M
CD Crewe Diesel 12/1976 M
CW Cricklewood East 05/1977 M
TO Toton 09/1981 M
CD Crewe Diesel 03/1983 M
Withdrawn 28/01/1987 E
Stored at Basford Hall Yard, then moved direct to Vic Berry, Leicester on 29/05/87, scrapping started immediately, with just the cabs left by 14/06/87, still extant on 02/11/87.

D7541
D16 Nottingham Division 10/04/1965 E
D14 London (Midland) Division 10/1965 M
9A Longsight 05/1968 M
D09 Manchester Division 17/06/1968 E
D08 Liverpool Division 10/1971 M
SP Springs Branch 05/1973 M
KM Kingmoor Diesel 05/1973 M
Renumbered 25191 04/1974 M
Allocation recoded KM to KD 01/1975 M
CD Crewe Diesel 05/1986 M
Withdrawn 18/03/1987 E
Stored at Basford Hall Yard. Sold to Vic Berry, Leicester and moved to Humberstone Road, Leicester on 08/07/87, and into Berrys Yard the next day where it remained intact.

For preservation

Sold for preservation to the North Yorkshire Moors Railway about 11/87. Left Berry for Humberstone Road on 25/01/88 and on to Toton the same day, moved to Tinsley and then York 26/01/88, to Tees Yard on 27/01/88 and to the NYMR at Grosmont on 29/01/88. Later renumbered back to D7541 and named *The Diana* 23/04/89 at Grosmont station.
HQ Headquarters Pool 01/2005 M
Offered for sale by HNRC but only to heritage railways 05/10, moved to the South Devon Railway 14/04/11.

D7542
D16 Nottingham Division 10/04/1965 E
9A Longsight 05/1968 M
D09 Manchester Division 17/06/1968 E
D08 Liverpool Division 05/1971 M
D10 Preston Division 07/1971 M
KM Kingmoor Diesel 05/1973 M
SP Springs Branch 08/1973 M
Renumbered 25192 02/1974 M
KD Kingmoor Diesel 04/1975 M
SP Springs Branch 05/1976 M
LO Longsight 04/1977 M
CD Crewe Diesel 10/1977 M
SP Springs Branch 07/1980 M
CD Crewe Diesel 10/1982 M
Withdrawn 09/05/1986 E
Stored at Tyseley. Moved to Bescot 30/03/87 and on to Basford Hall 01/04/87 and held there until sent to Humberstone Road, Leicester on 09/07/87 and into Vic Berry, Leicester 10/07/87. Consigned to the 'pyramid' by 10/87, taken off on 03/11/87 and broken up by 13/11/87.

D7543
D16 Nottingham Division 17/04/1965 E
9A Longsight 05/1968 M
D09 Manchester Division 17/06/1968 E
D02 Birmingham Division 02/1971 M
D10 Preston Division 05/1971 M
KM Kingmoor Diesel 05/1973 M
SP Springs Branch 08/1973 M
Renumbered 25193 02/1974 M
KD Kingmoor Diesel 04/1975 M
WN Willesden 05/1975 M
CW Cricklewood East 06/1975 M
TO Toton 10/1975 M
CW Cricklewood East 04/1976 M
TO Toton 10/1976 M
CW Cricklewood East 05/1977 M
TO Toton 11/1977 M
CW Cricklewood East 07/1978 M
CD Crewe Diesel 01/1984 M
Withdrawn 12/11/1984 E
Stored at Toton. Moved to Gloucester on 21/02/85 and to ZL Swindon Works on 25/02/85. Sold to Vic Berry, Leicester about 04/87 and moved to Swindon Cocklebury Yard and on to Humberstone Road, Leicester 03/06/87, then into Berry's Yard the next day. Put on the 'pyramid' by 10/87, taken off by 01/11/87 and dismantled by 13/11/87.

D7544
D16 Nottingham Division 15/05/1965 E
9A Longsight 05/1968 M
D09 Manchester Division 17/06/1968 E
D02 Birmingham Division 01/1971 M
D10 Preston Division 05/1971 M
KM Kingmoor Diesel 05/1973 M
SP Springs Branch 08/1973 M
Renumbered 25194 02/1974 M
LO Longsight 06/1974 M
BS Bescot 01/1980 M
CD Crewe Diesel 03/1983 M
Withdrawn 17/06/1985 E
Stored at Shrewsbury Coton Hill Yard, then moved to Bescot 29/08/86 where it was stored in derelict condition. Sold to MC Metal Processing, Glasgow in 09/93 but remained at Bescot until moved by road to MC Metals arriving on 28/03/94 and was cut up on 06/05/94.

D7545
D16 Nottingham Division 08/05/1965 E
9A Longsight 05/1968 M
D09 Manchester Division 17/06/1968 E
D10 Preston Division 01/1969 M
D09 Manchester Division 07/1970 M
D08 Liverpool Division 11/1970 M
D10 Preston Division 07/1971 M
KM Kingmoor Diesel 05/1973 M
SP Springs Branch 08/1973 M
Renumbered 25195 27/02/1974 E
LO Longsight 06/1974 M
CD Crewe Diesel 05/1978 M
SP Springs Branch 05/1980 M
CD Crewe Diesel 10/1982 M
Withdrawn 14/06/1985 E
Stored at Toton, moved to ZF Doncaster Works 03/03/86 and then to Goole Docks on 15/08/86, both for further storage. Sold to Vic Berry, Leicester in 10/86. Moved to Humberstone Road, Leicester on 29/10/86 and into Berry's Yard the next day. It was cut up during 12/86, the cabs still in evidence on 02/11/87.

D7546
D16 Nottingham Division 08/05/1965 E
8F Springs Branch 11/1967 M
8J Allerton 05/1968 M
D08 Liverpool Division 17/06/1968 E
D10 Preston Division 10/1968 M
KM Kingmoor Diesel 05/1973 M
Renumbered 25196 02/1974 M

D7546 contd.
LO Longsight 03/1974 M
KM Kingmoor Diesel 09/1974 M
Allocation recoded KM to KD 01/1975 M
TO Toton 08/1975 M
LO Longsight 10/1975 M
KD Kingmoor Diesel 05/1984 M
Withdrawn 17/03/1986 E
Stored at Crewe Diesel, then moved to Gresty Lane 03/87 for further storage. Moved to Basford Hall 07/87, then to Humberstone Road, Leicester on 15/07/87 and into Vic Berry, Leicester on 20/07/87. Noted partly cut up 26/07/87 and completed by 06/08/87.

D7547
D16 Nottingham Division 15/05/1965 E
8F Springs Branch 11/1967 M
8J Allerton 05/1968 M
D08 Liverpool Division 17/06/1968 E
D10 Preston Division 10/1968 M
KM Kingmoor Diesel 05/1973 M
Renumbered 25197 02/1974 M
SP Springs Branch 01/1975 M
LO Longsight 05/1975 M
BS Bescot 01/1980 M
Store 11/1980 M

D7547 contd.
Stored at ZL Swindon Works 11/80
Withdrawn 01/12/1980 E
Used with 25116 to start stored locomotives at Swindon Works, then broken up by 11/03/83.

D7548
D16 Nottingham Division 22/05/1965 E
8F Springs Branch 11/1967 M
8J Allerton 05/1968 M
D08 Liverpool Division 17/06/1968 E
D10 Preston Division 10/1968 M
KM Kingmoor Diesel 05/1973 M
Renumbered 25198 19/03/1974 E
Allocation recoded KM to KD 01/1975 M
LO Longsight 10/1975 M
KD Kingmoor Diesel 05/1984 M
Withdrawn 24/02/1986 E
Stored at Crewe Diesel. Sold to Vic Berry, Leicester 12/86 for scrap and moved to its yard on 12/01/87. It was still there on 01/02/87 partly cut up, completed by 20/02/87.

D7549
D16 Nottingham Division 29/05/1965 E
8F Springs Branch 10/1967 M
12A Kingmoor 11/1967 M
D10 Preston Division 17/06/1968 E

After the withdrawal of all of the Class 25s, a survivor acquired celebrity status, this being 25912 which had been retained in departmental use. It was reinstated in 1990 as D7672 carrying the name *Tamworth Castle* and is here in two-tone green with full yellow ends, a livery not carried in its earlier life; at Bescot in 1990. *(Ray Reed/RCTS Photo Archive*

D7549 contd.
KM Kingmoor Diesel 05/1973 M
Renumbered 25199 21/03/1974 E
Allocation recoded KM to KD 01/1975 M
LO Longsight 10/1975 M
KD Kingmoor Diesel 05/1984 M
CD Crewe Diesel 05/1986 M
Withdrawn 09/02/1987 E
Stored at Basford Hall Yard. Sold to Berry of Leicester about 04/87. Moved to Humberstone Road, Leicester 02/06/87 and into Berry's Yard on 03/06/87 and noted in the 'pyramid' by 10/87 and was seen partly cut up by 08/04/89, with scrapping completed by 28/04/89.

D7550
D16 Nottingham Division 05/06/1965 E
D15 Leicester Division 10/1965 M
D16 Nottingham Division 10/1965 M
12A Kingmoor 10/1967 M
D10 Preston Division 17/06/1968 E
KM Kingmoor Diesel 05/1973 M
Renumbered 25200 04/1974 M
Went to ZE Derby Works 12/85 for overhaul but was condemned instead.
Withdrawn 10/02/1986 E
Sold to Vic Berry, Leicester 01/87 and moved to Humberstone Road, Leicester on 19/01/87 and into Berry's Yard on 27/01/87. It was still intact on 14/02/87, but had been dismantled by 20/02/87, with just the cabs remaining by 07/04/87.

D7551
D16 Nottingham Division 19/06/1965 E
D15 Leicester Division 10/1965 M
D16 Nottingham Division 08/1967 M
12A Kingmoor 10/1967 M
8F Springs Branch 01/1968 M
8J Allerton 05/1968 M
D08 Liverpool Division 17/06/1968 E
D10 Preston Division 09/1968 M
KM Kingmoor Diesel 05/1973 M
Renumbered 25201 03/1974 M
Allocation recoded KM to KD 01/1975 M
CD Crewe Diesel 05/1986 M
Unofficially named *Castell-y-Bere,* date unknown but probably in mid-1986.
Withdrawn 28/01/1987 E
Stored at Basford Hall until sent to Humberstone Road, Leicester 29/07/87 and into Vic Berry, Leicester on 30/07/87. Cutting up started about 11/12/87, then ceased for

D7551 contd.
the Christmas holiday and was finally completed by 20/01/88.

D7552
D16 Nottingham Division 26/06/1965 E
8F Springs Branch 10/1967 M
8J Allerton 05/1968 M
D08 Liverpool Division 17/06/1968 E
D10 Preston Division 09/1968 M
KM Kingmoor Diesel 05/1973 M
Renumbered 25202 27/02/1974 E
Allocation recoded KM to KD 01/1975 M
CD Crewe Diesel 05/1986 M
Withdrawn 28/07/1986 E
Stored at Etches Park until moved to Stratford in 07/87, then to Peterborough West Yard 31/07/87 and to March TMD 10/09/87 for further storage. Sent to Doncaster about 20/03/88 and again stored. It was then moved to Humberstone Road, Leicester on 17/03/89 spending two or three days at Toton en route and into Vic Berry, Leicester on 22/03/89. Cutting started about 06/04/89 and continued slowly, until completed by 16/06/89.

D7553
D16 Nottingham Division 26/06/1965 E
12A Kingmoor 10/1967 M
D10 Preston Division 17/06/1968 E
KM Kingmoor Diesel 05/1973 M
Renumbered 25203 26/02/1974 E
Allocation recoded KM to KD 01/1975 M
CW Cricklewood East 01/1976 M
Store 03/11/1980 E
Stored at Toton by 03/11/80, then moved to ZL Swindon Works on 15/11/80.
Withdrawn 01/12/1980 E
Cut up at Swindon Works by 03/03/82.

D7554
D16 Nottingham Division 03/07/1965 E
8F Springs Branch 09/1967 M
12A Kingmoor 11/1967 M
D10 Preston Division 17/06/1968 E
D01 London Division 12/1971 M
D08 Liverpool Division 03/1972 M
SP Springs Branch 05/1973 M
KD Kingmoor New Yard 05/1973 M
Renumbered 25204 17/05/1974 E
Allocation recoded KD to KM 01/1975 M
CW Cricklewood East 01/1976 M
Store 05/1980 M
Stored at Willesden from 05/80 due to

D7554 contd.
collision damage, then moved to Crewe Diesel about 06/80.
Withdrawn 06/07/1980 E
Moved to ZL Swindon Works 14/08/80 and scrapped by 15/10/80.

D7555
D16 Nottingham Division 10/07/1965 E
D15 Leicester Division 10/1965 M
LMML LM Midland Lines 01/1966 M
D05 Stoke Division 05/1966 M
LMML LM Midland Lines 09/1966 M
D16 Nottingham Division 09/1966 M
8F Springs Branch 09/1967 M
12A Kingmoor 11/1967 M
D10 Preston Division 17/06/1968 E
D01 London Division 12/1971 M
WN Willesden 05/1973 M
Renumbered 25205 04/1974 M
CW Cricklewood East 05/1974 M
SP Springs Branch 08/1974 M
TO Toton 08/1975 M
CW Cricklewood East 11/1977 M
LO Longsight 11/1981 M
BS Bescot 05/1984 M
KD Kingmoor Diesel 09/1985 M
Withdrawn 12/05/1986 E
Moved to Bescot for storage and remained in derelict condition, then sold for spares to the Railway Age, Crewe 09/93, but the sale was cancelled, the loco remaining at Bescot. It was eventually moved to MC Metal Processing, Glasgow, arriving on 17/06/95, and was broken up 29/06/95.

D7556
D16 Nottingham Division 10/07/1965 E
8F Springs Branch 09/1967 M
12A Kingmoor 11/1967 M
D10 Preston Division 17/06/1968 E
D16 Nottingham Division 11/1970 M
D10 Preston Division 04/1971 M
D16 Nottingham Division 10/1972 M
TO Toton 05/1973 M
Renumbered 25206 05/1974 M
BS Bescot 06/1974 M
TO Toton 03/1975 M
LO Longsight 08/1977 M
LA Laira 03/1978 M
SP Springs Branch 10/1980 M
CD Crewe Diesel 10/1982 M
Withdrawn 21/03/1986 E

D7556 contd.
Stored at Bescot. Moved on 20/03/90 being required at BRML Doncaster Works for spares for D7672, and remained until sent by road to MC Metal Processing, Glasgow on 17/03/95 and was scrapped on 21/06/95.

D7557
D16 Nottingham Division 07/08/1965 E
8F Springs Branch 09/1967 M
D08 Liverpool Division 17/06/1968 E
D10 Preston Division 09/1968 M
D02 Birmingham Division 05/1970 M
D16 Nottingham Division 11/1970 M
D10 Preston Division 10/1971 M
D16 Nottingham Division 10/1972 M
TO Toton 05/1973 M
Renumbered 25207 02/1974 M
BS Bescot 06/1974 M
TO Toton 03/1975 M
LO Longsight 08/1977 M
LA Laira 03/1978 M
BS Bescot 10/1980 M
Withdrawn 12/11/1984 E
Stored at Toton. Moved to Gloucester 21/02/85 and to ZL Swindon Works 25/02/85. Sold to Vic Berry, Leicester about 04/87, it left for Swindon Cocklebury Yard 03/06/87, to Humberstone Road, Leicester 04/06/87 and into Berry's Yard on 05/06/87. It was put in the 'pyramid' by 08/87 and remained until cutting up started about 20/02/88 and was completed by 08/03/88.

D7558
D16 Nottingham Division 14/08/1965 E
D02 Birmingham Division 05/1967 M
9A Longsight 01/1968 M
D09 Manchester Division 17/06/1968 E
D10 Preston Division 10/1968 M
D02 Birmingham Division 05/1970 M
D16 Nottingham Division 11/1970 M
TO Toton 05/1973 M
Renumbered 25208 01/09/1973 E
LO Longsight 08/1974 M
BS Bescot 01/1980 M
LO Longsight 01/1983 M
Withdrawn 04/05/1984 E
Stored at Newton Heath by 02/06/84. Moved to ZL Swindon Works 25/06/84 and sold to Vic Berry, Leicester about 04/87. Departed for Swindon Cocklebury Yard 03/06/87, to Humberstone Road, Leicester 04/06/87 and to Berry's Yard on 05/06/87.

D7558 contd.
Cutting was underway by 04/07/87, and only the cabs left by 19/07/87, with these being scrapped by 17/09/87.

D7559
D16 Nottingham Division 28/08/1965 E
D02 Birmingham Division 05/1967 M
D05 Stoke Division 06/1967 M
D02 Birmingham Division 08/1967 M
To the Derby Research Centre in 01/68 returning to D02 in 02/68.
D10 Preston Division 02/1970 M
D02 Birmingham Division 05/1970 M
D16 Nottingham Division 11/1970 M
TO Toton 05/1973 M
Renumbered 25209 04/1974 M
LO Longsight 08/1974 M
BS Bescot 01/1980 M
LO Longsight 01/1983 M
BS Bescot 05/1984 M
CD Crewe Diesel 07/1985 M
Withdrawn 17/12/1985 E
Stored at Toton in bad condition but was still moved by rail 13-16/02/92 to BRML Glasgow Works, then moved next door to MC Metal Processing on 19/02/92 and was broken up on 06/03/92.

D7560
D16 Nottingham Division 18/09/1965 E
D01 London Division (WCML) 04/1967 M
8F Springs Branch 11/1967 M
D08 Liverpool Division 17/06/1968 E
D02 Birmingham Division 01/1969 M
D16 Nottingham Division 11/1970 M
TO Toton 05/1973 M
Renumbered 25210 19/12/1973 E
CW Cricklewood East 11/1978 M
CD Crewe Diesel 01/1984 M
Withdrawn 30/04/1985 E
Stored at Crewe Gresty Lane. Moved to ZF Doncaster Works about 29/01/86, cutting started 14/03/86, with just cabs and bogies left 17/03/86. The cabs were still intact on 06/07/86, but were disposed of by 01/08/86.

D7561
D16 Nottingham Division 23/10/1965 E
D01 London Division (WCML) 04/1967 M
D02 Birmingham Division 03/1968 M
D16 Nottingham Division 11/1970 M
TO Toton 05/1973 M
Renumbered 25211 24/11/1973 E
LO Longsight 03/1979 M

D7561 contd.
BS Bescot 07/1984 M
CD Crewe Diesel 07/1985 M
Withdrawn 27/06/1986 E
Stored at Crewe Diesel, then moved to Bescot Yard about 10/86 for further storage. Sold to MC Metal Processing, Glasgow about 09/93. Remained at Bescot until moved by road arriving there on 14/06/95 and was consigned to history on 04/07/95 as the last BR-owned Class 25 to be cut up.

D7562
D16 Nottingham Division 04/12/1965 E
D01 London Division (WCML) 04/1967 M
D02 Birmingham Division 03/1968 M
D16 Nottingham Division 12/1970 M
TO Toton 05/1973 M
Renumbered 25212 28/02/1974 E
BS Bescot 05/1980 M
CD Crewe Diesel 10/1981 M
Withdrawn 12/05/1985 E
Stored at Basford Hall. Moved to Humberstone Road, Leicester on 08/07/87 and on to Vic Berry, Leicester the following day. Put in the 'pyramid' by 10/87, and taken off again when cutting was underway on 24/10/87 and completed by 13/11/87.

D7563
D16 Nottingham Division 13/11/1965 E
D01 London Division (WCML) 04/1967 M
D01 London Division 17/06/1968 E
D10 Preston Division 07/1968 M
D02 Birmingham Division 10/1969 M
D16 Nottingham Division 05/1971 M
TO Toton 05/1973 M
TI Tinsley 10/1973 M
Renumbered 25213 04/11/1973 E
ED Eastfield 07/1975 M
TO Toton 10/1976 M
CW Cricklewood East 10/1978 M
CD Crewe Diesel 01/1984 M
Withdrawn 19/03/1987 E
Stored at Kingmoor Diesel until moved to Upperby Depot on 09/08/88 for inspection, returned to Kingmoor Diesel a few days later prior to moving to Vic Berry, Leicester for scrap. Moved to Upperby again on 10/11/88, to Crewe Basford Hall 30/11/88, then Toton and on to Leicester stabling point 15/12/88 and into Berry's Yard on 19/12/88. It remained intact right up to 12/90, when cutting started and was noted

D7563 contd.
in pieces 30/12/90, believed to be the last whole locomotive cut at Berry's Yard. One cab was still in existence on 13/01/91.

D7564
D16 Nottingham Division 18/12/1965 E
D01 London Division (WCML) 04/1967 M
D01 London Division 17/06/1968 E
D10 Preston Division 07/1968 M
D02 Birmingham Division 10/1969 M
D16 Nottingham Division 05/1971 M
TO Toton 05/1973 M
WN Willesden 05/1973 M
CW Cricklewood East 05/1974 M
TO Toton 05/1974 M
Renumbered 25214 28/05/1974 E
CW Cricklewood East 04/1976 M
TO Toton 10/1976 M
SP Springs Branch 05/1981 M
CD Crewe Diesel 10/1982 M
Withdrawn 28/11/1982 E
Stored at Stratford, then to Healey Mills 19-21/02/83 for further storage. Sent to ZF Doncaster Works on 14/05/85, where it was again stored. Moved to Gloucester 20/03/86 and on to Swindon next day. Shunted into ZL Swindon Works on 24/03/86 and was cut up by 30/09/86, the cabs going to Vic Berry, Leicester by road and noted still there 11/87.

D7565
D16 Nottingham Division 04/12/1965 E
D02 Birmingham Division 05/1967 M
D16 Nottingham Division 01/1972 M
D01 London Division 08/1972 M
64B Haymarket 10/1972 M
Allocation recoded 64B to HA 05/1973 M
Renumbered 25215 12/1973 M
CF Cardiff (Canton) 08/1975 M
LA Laira 10/1975 M
CD Crewe Diesel 05/1978 M
Withdrawn 19/06/1983 E
Departed for ZL Swindon Works on 27/08/83, but did not arrive until 08/09/83, and was quickly scrapped by 28/10/83.

D7566
D16 Nottingham Division 19/01/1966 E
D02 Birmingham Division 05/1967 M
D16 Nottingham Division 01/1972 M
D01 London Division 08/1972 M
WN Willesden 05/1973 M
ED Eastfield 01/1974 M
Renumbered 25216 04/1974 M

D7566 contd.
HA Haymarket 05/1974 M
CF Cardiff (Canton) 08/1975 M
LA Laira 10/1975 M
CD Crewe Diesel 03/1978 M
Withdrawn 28/12/1980 E
Moved to ZL Swindon Works 20/02/81, then to ZE Derby Works 13/10/81 and dismantled by 05/03/83, with the remains noted being loaded onto a wagon there on 08/03/83 and then disposed of.

D7567
D16 Nottingham Division 20/01/1966 E
D02 Birmingham Division 05/1967 M
D16 Nottingham Division 01/1972 M
D01 London Division 08/1972 M
WN Willesden 05/1973 M
LO Longsight 11/1973 M
ED Eastfield 01/1974 M
Renumbered 25217 04/1974 M
HA Haymarket 05/1974 M
CF Cardiff (Canton) 08/1975 M
LA Laira 10/1975 M
CD Crewe Diesel 03/1978 M
Withdrawn 01/02/1981 E
Stored at Crewe Diesel. Moved to ZE Derby Works 04/81 and held until scrapped by 22/01/82.

D7568
16A Toton 28/09/1963 E
16D Nottingham 02/1964 M
16C Derby 10/1964 M
14B Cricklewood West 12/1964 M
LMML LM Midland Lines 16/01/1965 E
55A Leeds Holbeck 08/1967 M
D16 Nottingham Division 08/1972 M
TO Toton 05/1973 M
Renumbered 25218 07/03/1974 E
CW Cricklewood East 11/1977 M
Suffered collision damage at Stonebridge Park 19/03/80, moved to ZE Derby Works and then ZL Swindon Works by 16/08/80, repaired and returned to service by 10/80.
KD Kingmoor Diesel 08/1980 M
Caught fire at Gretton, near Corby 07/06/83, later moved to Wellingborough stabling point; subsequently repaired and returned to service.
Withdrawn 28/01/1985 E
Stored at Bescot by 02/03/85. Moved to ZL Swindon Works 27/03/85 and was broken up by 31/05/85.

D7569
14B Cricklewood West 12/10/1963 E
16C Derby 10/1964 M
14B Cricklewood West 12/1964 M
LMML LM Midland Lines 16/01/1965 E
55A Leeds Holbeck 08/1967 M
LMML LM Midland Lines 03/1968 M
8J Allerton 04/1968 M
D05 Stoke Division 05/1968 M
D08 Liverpool Division 11/1968 M
D09 Manchester Division 05/1970 M
82A Bristol Bath Road 01/1972 M
86A Cardiff (Canton) 05/1972 M
Allocation recoded 86A to CF 05/1973 M
Renumbered 25219 05/1974 M
LA Laira 10/1974 M
BR Bristol Bath Road 05/1975 M
CF Cardiff (Canton) 11/1975 M
CD Crewe Diesel 11/1977 M
Store 03/1983 M
Withdrawn 06/04/1983 E
Stored at Cricklewood. Moved to Acton on 08/05/85, then to Swindon on 14/05/85 and into ZL Swindon Works the next day. It was cut up by 27/02/87.

D7570
16A Toton 05/10/1963 E
2E Saltley 04/1964 M
D02 Birmingham Division 04/1966 M
LMML LM Midland Lines 04/1966 M
D02 Birmingham Division 08/1967 M
55A Leeds Holbeck 08/1967 M
8F Springs Branch 05/1968 M
D08 Liverpool Division 17/06/1968 E
D09 Manchester Division 05/1970 M
D01 London Division 09/1972 M
D16 Nottingham Division 03/1973 M
TO Toton 05/1973 M
Renumbered 25220 02/1974 M
BR Bristol Bath Road 05/1974 M
LA Laira 07/1975 M
CF Cardiff (Canton) 12/1976 M
CD Crewe Diesel 11/1977 M
Withdrawn 13/06/1982 E
Moved to ZE Derby Works 08/82 and remained stored there until sent to ZL Swindon Works 04/02/85, where it was scrapped by 24/04/85.

D7571
14B Cricklewood West 12/10/1963 E
16C Derby 10/1964 M
D16 Nottingham Division 16/01/1965 E

D7571 contd.
D15 Leicester Division 06/1965 M
D16 Nottingham Division 07/1965 M
LMML LM Midland Lines 03/1967 M
55A Leeds Holbeck 08/1967 M
D16 Nottingham Division 08/1972 M
D01 London Division 03/1973 M
WN Willesden 05/1973 M
CD Cricklewood East 09/1973 M
Allocation recoded CD to CW 12/1973 M
Renumbered 25221 02/1974 M
WN Willesden 03/1974 M
CW Cricklewood East 06/1975 M
CD Crewe Diesel 05/1977 M
LO Longsight 08/1981 M
Withdrawn 31/01/1984 E
Stored at Springs Branch. Moved to ZL Swindon Works 21/02/85 and broken up by 19/12/86.

D7572
14B Cricklewood West 19/10/1963 E
16C Derby 10/1964 M
14B Cricklewood West 12/1964 M
LMML LM Midland Lines 16/01/1965 E
55A Leeds Holbeck 08/1967 M
D16 Nottingham Division 08/1972 M
D01 London Division 03/1973 M
WN Willesden 05/1973 M
CD Cricklewood East 09/1973 M
Allocation recoded CD to CW 12/1973 M
Renumbered 25222 22/03/1974 E
WN Willesden 03/1974 M
CW Cricklewood East 06/1975 M
CD Crewe Diesel 05/1977 M
CW Cricklewood East 04/1979 M
LO Longsight 08/1980 M
Store 24/10/1980 E
Stored by 24/10/80, then moved to ZL Swindon Works on 30/10/80.
Withdrawn 14/12/1980 E
Cut up at Swindon Works by 24/12/81.

D7573
14B Cricklewood West 26/10/1963 E
16C Derby 10/1964 M
14B Cricklewood West 12/1964 M
LMML LM Midland Lines 16/01/1965 E
55A Leeds Holbeck 08/1967 M
9A Longsight 05/1968 M
D09 Manchester Division 17/06/1968 E
84A Laira 10/1971 M
Allocation recoded 84A to LA 05/1973 M
Renumbered 25223 04/1974 M

D7573 contd.
Withdrawn 05/10/1980 E
Moved to ZL Swindon Works on 07/10/80 and broken up by 05/11/80.

D7574
14B Cricklewood West 26/10/1963 E
16C Derby 10/1964 M
14B Cricklewood West 12/1964 M
LMML LM Midland Lines 16/01/1965 E
D16 Nottingham Division 04/1966 M
LMML LM Midland Lines 09/1966 M
D02 Birmingham Division 08/1967 M
LMML LM Midland Lines 09/1967 M
8J Allerton 04/1968 M
D08 Liverpool Division 17/06/1968 E
D09 Manchester Division 05/1970 M
84A Laira 10/1971 M
Allocation recoded 84A to LA 05/1973 M
Renumbered 25224 02/1974 M
CD Crewe Diesel 05/1978 M
Withdrawn 23/01/1983 E
CD Crewe Diesel 02/1983 M
Reinstated 02/1983 M
Withdrawn 08/05/1986 E
Stored at Crewe Diesel. Sold to Vic Berry, Leicester 12/86 and moved to Berry's Yard 12/01/87. Noted still intact on 12/02/87, but was scrapped by the end of the month. Only the cabs remained by 02/11/87.

D7575
16A Toton 09/11/1963 E
14B Cricklewood West 11/1963 M
16C Derby 10/1964 M
14B Cricklewood West 12/1964 M
LMML LM Midland Lines 16/01/1965 E
8J Allerton 04/1968 M
D08 Liverpool Division 17/06/1968 E
D09 Manchester Division 05/1970 M
84A Laira 10/1971 M
Allocation recoded 84A to LA 05/1973 M
Renumbered 25225 06/02/1974 E
Withdrawn 08/10/1980 E
Moved to ZL Swindon Works 08/10/80 and cut up by 26/11/80.

D7576
16A Toton 09/11/1963 E
14B Cricklewood West 11/1963 M
16C Derby 10/1964 M
LMML LM Midland Lines 16/01/1965 E
65A Eastfield 09/1967 M
64B Haymarket 06/1969 M
65A Eastfield 02/1970 M

D7576 contd.
Allocation recoded 65A to ED 05/1973 M
HA Haymarket 09/1973 M
Renumbered 25226 09/1974 M
IS Inverness 05/1977 M
ED Eastfield 05/1978 M
HA Haymarket 02/1981 M
ED Eastfield 08/1981 M
HA Haymarket 09/1982 M
CD Crewe Diesel 10/1982 M
Withdrawn 10/06/1985 E
Stored at Basford Hall Yard from 06/10/85. Moved to ZF Doncaster Works on 16/04/86 and was cut up by 23/08/86.

D7577
16A Toton 16/11/1963 E
14B Cricklewood West 11/1963 M
16C Derby 10/1964 M
D16 Nottingham Division 16/01/1965 E
LMML LM Midland Lines 03/1967 M
8J Allerton 04/1968 M
D08 Liverpool Division 17/06/1968 E
D09 Manchester Division 10/1969 M
84A Laira 10/1971 M
82A Bristol Bath Road 10/1972 M
Allocation recoded 82A to BR 05/1973 M
Renumbered 25227 24/06/1974 E
LA Laira 05/1976 M
ED Eastfield 10/1976 M
Store 01/1982 M
ED Eastfield 01/1982 M
Returned to Service 01/1982 M
CD Crewe Diesel 10/1982 M
Withdrawn 26/06/1983 E
Moved from Acton Yard to ZL Swindon Works 23/08/83 and broken up by 23/12/83.

D7578
16A Toton 30/11/1963 E
50A York 12/1963 M
55H Neville Hill 01/1964 M
50A York 06/1964 M
16A Toton 10/1964 M
16C Derby 11/1964 M
D16 Nottingham Division 16/01/1965 E
40E Colwick 04/1965 M
D16 Nottingham Division 05/1965 M
LMML LM Midland Lines 03/1967 M
65A Eastfield 09/1967 M
64B Haymarket 06/1969 M
Allocation recoded 64B to HA 05/1973 M
Renumbered 25228 04/1974 M
IS Inverness 05/1977 M

Loathed by steam photographers, the ETHEL train heating units spent many hours being towed around the country sandwiched between a steam engine and the train stock. BR did try to make them blend in by painting them in coaching stock look-alike liveries and 97251 carried Rail Blue and grey when pictured in 1987 having started life as D7655 and later 25305.

(Ken Fairey/Colour-Rail.com

D7578 contd.

ED Eastfield 05/1978 M
HA Haymarket 03/1982 M
LO Longsight 09/1982 M
Moved to ZE Derby Works on 25/01/84 for repairs, but these were cancelled and it was withdrawn instead.
Withdrawn 20/03/1984 E
Moved to ZL Swindon Works 05/02/85 for scrap but when the works was due to close it was sold to Vic Berry, Leicester. Moved to Swindon Cocklebury Yard on 26/05/87, to Oxford Hinksey Yard on 02/06/87 and into Berry's Yard on 11/06/87. Cutting up started 20/06/87 and was completed by 25/06/87, except the cabs which were still there on 02/11/87.

D7579

16A Toton 14/12/1963 E
16C Derby 01/1964 M
15A Leicester (Midland) 02/1964 M
LMML LM Midland Lines 16/01/1965 E
65A Eastfield 09/1967 M

D7579 contd.

64B Haymarket 06/1969 M
65A Eastfield 02/1970 M
Allocation recoded 65A to ED 05/1973 M
HA Haymarket 09/1973 M
Renumbered 25229 04/1974 M
IS Inverness 05/1977 M
ED Eastfield 05/1978 M
HA Haymarket 09/1982 M
LO Longsight 10/1982 M
CD Crewe Diesel 05/1984 M
Withdrawn 12/05/1985 E
Stored at Crewe Gresty Lane. Moved to ZF Doncaster Works 24/01/86 and on to ZL Swindon Works 10/03/86, where it was scrapped by 13/09/86 with some parts remaining on 30/11/86, but were disposed of soon afterwards.

D7580

16A Toton 14/12/1963 E
16D Nottingham 02/1964 M
LMML LM Midland Lines 16/01/1965 E
D14 London (Midland) Division 01/1967 M

D7580 contd.
8J Allerton 04/1968 M
D08 Liverpool Division 17/06/1968 E
65A Eastfield 06/1968 M
64B Haymarket 06/1969 M
Allocation recoded 64B to HA 05/1973 M
Renumbered 25230 03/1974 M
ED Eastfield 05/1975 M
HA Haymarket 03/1982 M
LO Longsight 10/1982 M
CD Crewe Diesel 05/1984 M
Withdrawn 06/06/1986 E
Stored at Crewe Diesel, then moved to Basford Hall by 03/87 for further storage. Moved to Humberstone Road, Leicester on 15/07/87 and to Vic Berry, Leicester on 20/07/87. It was put in the 'pyramid' by 10/87, but was taken off by 16/10/87, when cutting up started, and was completed by 24/10/87.

D7581
16A Toton 28/12/1963 E
12A Kingmoor 01/1964 M
16A Toton 07/1964 M
14B Cricklewood West 09/1964 M
16C Derby 10/1964 M
D16 Nottingham Division 16/01/1965 E
LMML LM Midland Lines 03/1967 M
65A Eastfield 09/1967 M
64B Haymarket 06/1969 M
Allocation recoded 64B to HA 05/1973 M
Renumbered 25231 09/1974 M
ED Eastfield 05/1976 M
IS Inverness 05/1977 M
ED Eastfield 05/1978 M
LO Longsight 10/1982 M
CD Crewe Diesel 05/1984 M
Withdrawn 23/08/1985 E
Stored at Basford Hall by 10/85, then to Crewe Diesel by 27/04/86 for further storage. Sold to Vic Berry, Leicester in 12/86 for scrap. Moved to Knighton sidings, Leicester on 23/01/87 and into Berry's Yard on 26/01/87, where it was scrapped by 03/05/87, except the cabs which remained on 07/06/87, but had gone by 03/09/87.

D7582
16A Toton 07/01/1964 E
2E Saltley 04/1964 M
D02 Birmingham Division 04/1966 M
LMML LM Midland Lines 04/1966 M
D02 Birmingham Division 08/1967 M

D7582 contd.
LMML LM Midland Lines 09/1967 M
8J Allerton 04/1968 M
D08 Liverpool Division 17/06/1968 E
65A Eastfield 08/1968 M
64B Haymarket 06/1969 M
Allocation recoded 64B to HA 05/1973 M
SP Springs Branch 09/1973 M
Renumbered 25232 02/1974 M
HA Haymarket 01/1975 M
ED Eastfield 05/1975 M
Withdrawn 01/12/1980 E
Moved to ZL Swindon Works 02/01/81 and was cut up by 18/05/83.

D7583
16A Toton 21/01/1964 E
16C Derby 08/1964 M
D16 Nottingham Division 16/01/1965 E
LMML LM Midland Lines 03/1967 M
65A Eastfield 09/1967 M
Allocation recoded 65A to ED 05/1973 M
SP Springs Branch 08/1973 M
Renumbered 25233 03/1974 M
HA Haymarket 01/1975 M
ED Eastfield 05/1975 M
IS Inverness 05/1977 M
ED Eastfield 05/1978 M
LO Longsight 10/1982 M
Withdrawn 13/03/1983 E
Stored at Etches Park 07/83, then moved to ZE Derby Works about 11/83 for further storage. Moved to ZL Swindon Works on 04/02/85 and dismantled by 08/05/85.

D7584
16A Toton 01/02/1964 E
15A Leicester (Midland) 02/1964 M
LMML LM Midland Lines 16/01/1965 E
65A Eastfield 09/1967 M
Allocation recoded 65A to ED 05/1973 M
SP Springs Branch 08/1973 M
Renumbered 25234 02/1974 M
HA Haymarket 01/1975 M
ED Eastfield 05/1975 M
IS Inverness 05/1977 M
ED Eastfield 05/1978 M
HA Haymarket 03/1982 M
LO Longsight 10/1982 M
CD Crewe Diesel 05/1984 M
Went to ZE Derby Works on 08/11/84 for repairs but was withdrawn instead.
Withdrawn 28/02/1985 E

D7584 contd.

Moved to ZL Swindon Works on 24/07/85 and was awaiting scrap. However, due to the impending closure of Swindon Works, it was sold to Vic Berry, Leicester. Moved to Swindon Cocklebury Yard on 26/05/87, to Oxford Hinksey Yard on 02/06/87 and to Berry's Yard on 11/06/87. It was noted partly cut on 27/06/87 and was completed by 01/07/87, with cabs only on 04/07/87.

D7585

16A Toton 13/02/1964 E
16D Nottingham 02/1964 M
16C Derby 10/1964 M
D16 Nottingham Division 16/01/1965 E
2E Saltley 06/1965 M
D02 Birmingham Division 04/1966 M
LMML LM Midland Lines 04/1966 M
8J Allerton 04/1968 M
D08 Liverpool Division 17/06/1968 E
D10 Preston Division 09/1968 M
D09 Manchester Division 11/1968 M
LO Longsight 05/1973 M
Renumbered 25235 12/11/1973 E
ED Eastfield 07/1975 M
HA Haymarket 02/1978 M
ED Eastfield 05/1978 M
TO Toton 02/1981 M
SP Springs Branch 05/1982 M
CD Crewe Diesel 10/1982 M
Withdrawn 13/03/1985 E
Stored in Bescot Yard in deteriorating condition. Despite this, it was moved by rail to Basford Hall Yard on 11/07/90, to Carnforth 13/07/90, to Workington 14/07/90, then to Carlisle 17/07/90, on to Mossend Yard on 01/08/90 and finally to ZH Glasgow Works on 04/08/90 for asbestos removal by next door MC Metal Processing, as the locomotive had been sold for preservation to the Bo'ness & Kinneil Railway.

For preservation

Moved by road to the Bo'ness and Kinneil Railway about 18/10/90 for further use.
HQ Headquarters Pool 28/02/2009 E
Reregistered 28/02/09 to allow it to be moved by rail to gala events on other heritage railways.

D7586

16A Toton 25/02/1964 E
9E Trafford Park 03/1964 M
D16 Nottingham Division 16/01/1965 E

D7586 contd.

9E Trafford Park 01/1965 M
9A Longsight 10/1967 M
55A Leeds Holbeck 05/1968 M
52A Gateshead 09/1968 M
55A Leeds Holbeck 10/1971 M
52A Gateshead 01/1972 M
55A Leeds Holbeck 02/1972 M
D01 London Division 07/1972 M
WN Willesden 05/1973 M
CD Cricklewood East 09/1973 M
Allocation recoded CD to CW 12/1973 M
Renumbered 25236 09/03/1974 E
WN Willesden 05/1974 M
CW Cricklewood East 06/1975 M
KD Kingmoor Diesel 11/1980 M
Withdrawn 05/12/1984 E
Moved to ZL Swindon Works on 21/02/85 and was cut up by 22/11/86. The cabs were taken to Vic Berry, Leicester and were still in evidence on 02/11/87.

D7587

16A Toton 09/03/1964 E
2E Saltley 04/1964 M
D02 Birmingham Division 04/1966 M
LMML LM Midland Lines 04/1966 M
8J Allerton 04/1968 M
D05 Stoke Division 05/1968 M
D16 Nottingham Division 11/1968 M
D09 Manchester Division 10/1971 M
LO Longsight 05/1973 M
Renumbered 25237 26/11/1973 E
HA Haymarket 11/1974 M
ED Eastfield 05/1975 M
HA Haymarket 02/1976 M
ED Eastfield 12/1978 M
HA Haymarket 03/1982 M
KD Kingmoor Diesel 10/1982 M
CD Crewe Diesel 05/1983 M
Store 08/01/1984 E
CD Crewe Diesel 22/01/1984 E
Returned to Service 22/01/1984 E
Withdrawn 10/06/1985 E
Stored at Crewe Gresty Lane. Moved to ZF Doncaster Works about 29/01/86 and was cut up by 06/05/86, except for the cabs which were disposed of about 09/86.

D7588

16A Toton 10/03/1964 E
15A Leicester (Midland) 05/1964 M
LMML LM Midland Lines 16/01/1965 E
9A Longsight 05/1968 M

D7588 contd.
D09 Manchester Division 17/06/1968 E
D16 Nottingham Division 10/1969 M
D09 Manchester Division 10/1971 M
82A Bristol Bath Road 01/1972 M
86A Cardiff (Canton) 05/1972 M
Allocation recoded 86A to CF 05/1973 M
LA Laira 03/1974 M
CF Cardiff (Canton) 05/1974 M
Renumbered 25238 05/1974 M
LA Laira 10/1974 M
CF Cardiff (Canton) 06/1975 M
HA Haymarket 08/1975 M
IS Inverness 05/1977 M
ED Eastfield 05/1978 M
Withdrawn 14/10/1980 E
Withdrawn at Ayr. Moved to ZL Swindon Works on 27/10/80 and finally scrapped by 23/07/83.

D7589
16A Toton 13/04/1964 E
15A Leicester (Midland) 05/1964 M
LMML LM Midland Lines 16/01/1965 E
9A Longsight 05/1968 M
D09 Manchester Division 17/06/1968 E
D16 Nottingham Division 10/1969 M
D09 Manchester Division 11/1970 M
LO Longsight 05/1973 M
Renumbered 25239 04/1974 M
CD Crewe Diesel 10/1975 M
TO Toton 11/1975 M
ED Eastfield 06/1976 M
KD Kingmoor Diesel 10/1982 M
CD Crewe Diesel 10/1982 M
Withdrawn 05/11/1984 E
Moved to ZL Swindon Works 03/04/85 and was broken up by 16/09/86, with the cabs being taken to Vic Berry, Leicester, and noted there in 11/86.

D7590
16A Toton 15/04/1964 E
16D Nottingham 05/1964 M
LMML LM Midland Lines 16/01/1965 E
9A Longsight 05/1968 M
D09 Manchester Division 17/06/1968 E
65A Eastfield 08/1968 M
64B Haymarket 10/1968 M
Allocation recoded 64B to HA 05/1973 M
SP Springs Branch 09/1973 M
Renumbered 25240 02/1974 M
HA Haymarket 11/1974 M
ED Eastfield 05/1975 M

D7590 contd.
Store 01/1982 M
ED Eastfield 01/1982 M
Returned to Service 01/1982 M
SP Springs Branch 09/1982 M
CD Crewe Diesel 10/1982 M
Withdrawn 28/08/1983 E
Moved to ZL Swindon Works 22/09/83 and was cut up by 08/12/83.

D7591
16A Toton 25/04/1964 E
16D Nottingham 05/1964 M
LMML LM Midland Lines 16/01/1965 E
9A Longsight 05/1968 M
D09 Manchester Division 17/06/1968 E
65A Eastfield 08/1968 M
64B Haymarket 10/1968 M
Allocation recoded 64B to HA 05/1973 M
Renumbered 25241 04/1974 M
ED Eastfield 05/1975 M
Withdrawn 06/05/1981 E
Moved to ZL Swindon Works 06/07/81 and was scrapped by 09/09/81.

D7592
16A Toton 13/05/1964 E
15B Wellingborough 05/1964 M
15A Leicester (Midland) 07/1964 M
LMML LM Midland Lines 16/01/1965 E
9A Longsight 06/1968 M
D09 Manchester Division 17/06/1968 E
LO Longsight 05/1973 M
WN Willesden 08/1973 M
Renumbered 25242 02/1974 M
LO Longsight 10/1974 M
BS Bescot 01/1980 M
CD Crewe Diesel 03/1983 M
Withdrawn 04/05/1984 E
Moved to Swindon Cocklebury Yard 07/07/84, into ZL Swindon Works 23/07/84 and was cut up by 15/11/84.

D7593
16A Toton 27/05/1964 E
15B Wellingborough 06/1964 M
15A Leicester (Midland) 07/1964 M
LMML LM Midland Lines 16/01/1965 E
55A Leeds Holbeck 03/1968 M
52A Gateshead 09/1968 M
55A Leeds Holbeck 10/1971 M
52A Gateshead 01/1972 M
D16 Nottingham Division 04/1972 M
D01 London Division 04/1972 M
CD Cricklewood East 05/1973 M

D7593 contd.
Allocation recoded CD to CW 12/1973 M
Renumbered 25243 03/1974 M
WN Willesden 05/1974 M
CW Cricklewood East 06/1974 M
Withdrawn 11/09/1983 E
Withdrawn due to catching fire at Bletchley on 17/08/83. Stored at Bletchley, then moved to Acton on 30/10/83, on to ZL Swindon Works on 08/11/83 and dismantled by 13/01/84.

D7594
16A Toton 03/06/1964 E
16C Derby 07/1964 M
D16 Nottingham Division 16/01/1965 E
LMML LM Midland Lines 03/1967 M
9A Longsight 06/1968 M
D09 Manchester Division 17/06/1968 E
LO Longsight 05/1973 M
Renumbered 25244 30/10/1973 E
ED Eastfield 08/1975 M
Store 01/1982 M
ED Eastfield 01/1982 M
Returned to Service 01/1982 M
LO Longsight 10/1982 M
CW Cricklewood East 05/1984 M
CD Crewe Diesel 11/1984 M
Withdrawn 28/07/1986 E
Stored at Crewe Diesel, then moved to Basford Hall by 03/87 for further storage. Sold to Vic Berry, Leicester about 04/87. Moved to Humberstone Road, Leicester on 02/06/87 and into Berry's Yard 03/06/87, where it remained intact.

For preservation

Sold for preservation to Swanage Railway Society on 07/07/87, then reported to Swanage Railway Diesel Group on 21/09/87. Moved at slow speed to Basingstoke on 25/09/87 for an open day, then to Eastleigh depot on 27/09/87, and later moved into Eastleigh Works where it was physically renumbered as D7594. Finally, moved to the Swanage Railway on 26/05/89,and remained there until moved to the Nene Valley Railway in 06/92.

Moved to the Kent & East Sussex Railway in 03/95 and was marked as 7594 and 25244. Restoration work was due to start in 2006 but hadn't been completed by 2013; still in stored condition at the K&ESR in 2024.

D7595
16A Toton 20/06/1964 E
15B Wellingborough 07/1964 M
15A Leicester (Midland) 07/1964 M
LMML LM Midland Lines 16/01/1965 E
9A Longsight 06/1968 M
D09 Manchester Division 17/06/1968 E
LO Longsight 05/1973 M
TO Toton 05/1973 M
Renumbered 25245 01/03/1974 E
BS Bescot 10/1976 M
CD Crewe Diesel 04/1979 M
Withdrawn 25/06/1985 E
Stored at Basford Hall Yard by 10/85. Moved to ZF Doncaster Works on 16/04/86 and was cut up by 23/08/86.

D7596
16A Toton 07/07/1964 E
14B Cricklewood West 07/1964 M
16C Derby 10/1964 M
D16 Nottingham Division 16/01/1965 E
2E Saltley 06/1965 M
D02 Birmingham Division 04/1966 M
LMML LM Midland Lines 04/1966 M
55A Leeds Holbeck 05/1968 M
52A Gateshead 09/1968 M
55A Leeds Holbeck 10/1971 M
52A Gateshead 01/1972 M
D16 Nottingham Division 04/1972 M
D01 London Division 04/1972 M
WN Willesden 05/1973 M
Renumbered 25246 02/1974 M
HA Haymarket 11/1974 M
ED Eastfield 05/1975 M
Store 04/1981 M
Withdrawn 09/04/1981 E
Moved to ZL Swindon Works 25/06/81 and broken up by 05/03/83.

D7597
16A Toton 12/08/1964 E
16D Nottingham 08/1964 M
LMML LM Midland Lines 16/01/1965 E
9A Longsight 06/1968 M
D09 Manchester Division 17/06/1968 E
LO Longsight 05/1973 M
SP Springs Branch 09/1973 M
Renumbered 25247 06/03/1974 E
ED Eastfield 10/1976 M
KD Kingmoor Diesel 09/1982 M
Withdrawn 24/07/1983 E
Stored at Crewe Diesel until moved to ZL Swindon Works 27/08/83 and cut up by

D7597 contd.

29/11/83. One cab, possibly from this locomotive, was painted as D7597 and in use as a shed at an unknown location in 12/83.

D7598

41A Tinsley 05/02/1966 E
65A Eastfield 10/1966 M
LMML LM Midland Lines 09/1967 M
D02 Birmingham Division 09/1967 M
D01 London Division 01/1971 M
D16 Nottingham Division 02/1971 M
D09 Manchester Division 10/1971 M
D16 Nottingham Division 10/1972 M
D09 Manchester Division 11/1972 M
LO Longsight 05/1973 M
KM Kingmoor Diesel 05/1973 M
SP Springs Branch 08/1973 M
Renumbered 25248 02/1974 M
CD Crewe Diesel 01/1976 M
SP Springs Branch 05/1976 M
TO Toton 10/1978 M
Withdrawn 28/11/1982 E
Stored at Crewe Diesel. Moved to ZE Derby Works 03/02/83 and later stored at Etches Park. Sent to ZL Swindon Works 24/07/85 and was scrapped by 24/04/86.

D7599

41A Tinsley 05/02/1966 E
65A Eastfield 10/1966 M
LMML LM Midland Lines 09/1967 M
D16 Nottingham Division 17/06/1968 E
D02 Birmingham Division 12/1969 M
D09 Manchester Division 10/1971 M
D08 Liverpool Division 03/1972 M
D10 Preston Division 11/1972 M
KM Kingmoor Diesel 05/1973 M
SP Springs Branch 07/1973 M
Renumbered 25249 02/1974 M
KD Kingmoor New Yard 09/1974 M
SP Springs Branch 01/1975 M
LO Longsight 10/1975 M
TO Toton 08/1977 M
SP Springs Branch 11/1980 M
CD Crewe Diesel 10/1982 M
Withdrawn 29/01/1987 E
Stored at Basford Hall by 03/87. Sold to Vic Berry, Leicester, left for Humberstone Road, Leicester on 02/06/87 and was moved into Berry's Yard 03/06/87. It was put in the 'pyramid' by 10/87, taken off 02/89 and last noted intact 05/03/89, but had been cut up completely by 25/03/89.

D7600

41A Tinsley 15/02/1966 E
41E Staveley (Barrow Hill) 06/1966 M
34G Finsbury Park 08/1966 M
65A Eastfield 10/1966 M
LMML LM Midland Lines 09/1967 M
D16 Nottingham Division 17/06/1968 E
D02 Birmingham Division 12/1969 M
D08 Liverpool Division 05/1970 M
D09 Manchester Division 10/1971 M
D01 London Division 03/1973 M
WN Willesden 05/1973 M
Renumbered 25250 02/1974 M
CW Cricklewood East 06/1975 M
CD Crewe Diesel 01/1984 M
Withdrawn 13/05/1984 E
Moved to Swindon Cocklebury Yard 07/07/84 and into ZL Swindon Works on 23/07/84,where it was noted being cut up on 21/01/85 and was completed by 03/02/85.

D7601

41A Tinsley 16/02/1966 E
41E Staveley (Barrow Hill) 06/1966 M
65A Eastfield 10/1966 M
LMML LM Midland Lines 09/1967 M
D16 Nottingham Division 17/06/1968 E
D08 Liverpool Division 05/1970 M
D09 Manchester Division 10/1971 M
D08 Liverpool Division 03/1973 M
SP Springs Branch 05/1973 M
BS Bescot 08/1973 M
Renumbered 25251 04/1974 M
CW Cricklewood East 05/1976 M
CD Crewe Diesel 01/1984 M
Withdrawn 16/01/1985 E
Moved to ZL Swindon Works on 02/04/85 and was dismantled by 14/11/86. The cabs were sent to Vic Berry, Leicester and were noted there on 17/06/87.

D7602

41A Tinsley 21/02/1966 E
41E Staveley (Barrow Hill) 06/1966 M
64B Haymarket 12/1966 M
D16 Nottingham Division 06/1969 M
D02 Birmingham Division 12/1969 M
BS Bescot 05/1973 M
Renumbered 25252 20/03/1974 E
Withdrawn 30/03/1980 E
Stored at Toton. Moved to ZL Swindon Works 15/08/80 and was broken up by 24/09/80.

With the advent of InterCity livery and with that sector providing the stock for excursions, the ETHELs were some of the few small locomotives to receive that livery treatment and here is 97252 at Derby on 21st March 1987. It was withdrawn in 1993 and cut up the next year.
(S. R. Lee/Colour-Rail.com

D7603
41A Tinsley 25/02/1966 E
41E Staveley (Barrow Hill) 06/1966 M
64B Haymarket 12/1966 M
D16 Nottingham Division 06/1969 M
D02 Birmingham Division 12/1969 M
BS Bescot 05/1973 M
Renumbered 25253 21/03/1974 E
CD Crewe Diesel 02/1981 M
Withdrawn 25/09/1983 E
Moved immediately after withdrawal to ZE Derby Works for scrap but stored and then sent to ZL Swindon Works on 05/02/85 and was broken up by 18/10/85.

D7604
41A Tinsley 11/03/1966 E
41E Staveley (Barrow Hill) 06/1966 M
64B Haymarket 12/1966 M
D16 Nottingham Division 06/1969 M
TO Toton 05/1973 M
Renumbered 25254 20/04/1974 E
SP Springs Branch 11/1980 M
CD Crewe Diesel 10/1982 M
Withdrawn 04/09/1986 E
Stored in derelict condition at Springs Branch. Sent to Leicester Humberstone Road on 24/05/89, and into Vic Berry, Leicester on 25/05/89 where it was noted

D7604 contd.
intact on 17/06/89, but had been completely broken up by 24/06/89.

D7605
41A Tinsley 12/03/1966 E
41E Staveley (Barrow Hill) 06/1966 M
64B Haymarket 12/1966 M
D16 Nottingham Division 06/1969 M
Severely damaged in a collision with D8142+ D8115 at Lenton, near Nottingham on 16/12/71, then stabled between Nottingham and Trent Junction, covered with a tarpaulin. Moved to ZE Derby Works for assessment on 06/02/72. D8142 was also badly damaged but later repaired.
Withdrawn 03/1972 M
Cut up by 11/06/72 at Derby Works. The works official list reported cut up in 1974.

D7606
41A Tinsley 19/03/1966 E
41E Staveley (Barrow Hill) 06/1966 M
64B Haymarket 12/1966 M
D16 Nottingham Division 06/1969 M
D02 Birmingham Division 11/1970 M
D01 London Division 01/1971 M
D16 Nottingham Division 10/1971 M
D02 Birmingham Division 04/1972 M
D16 Nottingham Division 07/1972 M

D7606 contd.
D08 Liverpool Division 02/1973 M
SP Springs Branch 05/1973 M
WN Willesden 09/1973 M
TO Toton 10/1973 M
BS Bescot 03/1974 M
Renumbered 25256 03/1974 M
CW Cricklewood East 05/1976 M
CD Crewe Diesel 07/1983 M
Withdrawn 01/04/1985 E
Stored at Crewe Gresty Lane by 10/85. Moved to ZF Doncaster Works on 24/01/86, then moved to Gloucester on 20/03/86, to Swindon 21/03/86 and into ZL Swindon Works 24/03/86 and was cut up by 10/10/86.

D7607
41A Tinsley 24/03/1966 E
41E Staveley (Barrow Hill) 06/1966 M
64B Haymarket 12/1966 M
D16 Nottingham Division 06/1969 M
D02 Birmingham Division 12/1970 M
D01 London Division 01/1971 M
D16 Nottingham Division 10/1971 M
D02 Birmingham Division 04/1972 M
D16 Nottingham Division 07/1972 M
D08 Liverpool Division 02/1973 M
SP Springs Branch 05/1973 M
WN Willesden 09/1973 M
TO Toton 10/1973 M
BS Bescot 03/1974 M
Renumbered 25257 20/04/1974 E
HA Haymarket 10/1974 M
LO Longsight 11/1974 M
TO Toton 08/1977 M
SP Springs Branch 11/1980 M
CD Crewe Diesel 10/1982 M
Withdrawn 21/12/1983 E
CD Crewe Diesel 24/01/1984 E
Reinstated 24/01/1984 E
Withdrawn 06/02/1984 E
CD Crewe Diesel 09/07/1984 E
Reinstated 09/07/1984 E
Store 10/1985 M
Withdrawn 03/12/1985 E
Stored at Toton. Moved to ZF Doncaster Works on 03/03/86 then to Goole Docks on 15/08/86 for further storage and was sold to Vic Berry, Leicester for scrap in 10/86.
Moved to Humberstone Road, Leicester on 29/10/86 and into Berry's Yard on 30/10/86 where it was cut up in 01/87 and only a few bits remained on 01/02/87.

D7608
41A Tinsley 02/04/1966 E
41E Staveley (Barrow Hill) 06/1966 M
64B Haymarket 12/1966 M
D16 Nottingham Division 06/1969 M
TO Toton 05/1973 M
Renumbered 25258 04/1974 M
SP Springs Branch 05/1981 M
CD Crewe Diesel 10/1982 M
Withdrawn 21/12/1984 E
Stored at Kingmoor Diesel. Moved to ZL Swindon Works 03/04/85 and broken up by 05/02/86.

D7609
41A Tinsley 02/04/1966 E
41E Staveley (Barrow Hill) 12/1966 M
8F Springs Branch 10/1967 M
D08 Liverpool Division 17/06/1968 E
D02 Birmingham Division 01/1969 M
BS Bescot 05/1973 M
Renumbered 25259 01/03/1974 E
CD Crewe Diesel 11/1982 M
KD Kingmoor Diesel 07/1985 M
CD Crewe Diesel 05/1986 M
Withdrawn 21/08/1986 E
Stored in Bescot Yard in derelict condition. Moved by road 15/06/95 to MC Metal Processing, Glasgow and consigned to scrap metal on 27/06/95.

D7610
41A Tinsley 07/04/1966 E
41E Staveley (Barrow Hill) 12/1966 M
8F Springs Branch 10/1967 M
D08 Liverpool Division 17/06/1968 E
D02 Birmingham Division 01/1969 M
D01 London Division 01/1971 M
D02 Birmingham Division 05/1971 M
BS Bescot 05/1973 M
Renumbered 25260 01/03/1974 E
Withdrawn 13/12/1982 E
Stored at Derby Etches Park. Moved to ZL Swindon Works on 24/07/85 for scrap, but due to large number of other locomotives being cut up, it was still there in 04/87 when it was sold to Vic Berry, Leicester, as Swindon Works was due to close. Left to Cocklebury Yard 03/06/87, on to Humberstone Road, Leicester 05/06/87 and into Berry's Yard on 08/06/87 where it was noted intact on 15/11/87, but had been cut up completely by 12/12/87.

D7611
65A Eastfield 16/04/1966 E
LMML LM Midland Lines 09/1967 M
D16 Nottingham Division 17/06/1968 E
D02 Birmingham Division 09/1968 M
BS Bescot 05/1973 M
Renumbered 25261 20/04/1974 E
Withdrawn 04/01/1981 E
Stored at Tyseley. Moved to ZE Derby Works on 04/03/82 for scrap, where cutting up started 06/04/83 but, due to a dispute at Derby, cutting ceased about 05/83, and the locomotive lay half cut up until at least 14/11/85, but only small parts remained by 27/11/85. It is believed the final breaking up of this loco at Derby Works was carried out by staff working for Vic Berry, Leicester.

D7612
65A Eastfield 23/04/1966 E
LMML LM Midland Lines 09/1967 M
D16 Nottingham Division 17/06/1968 E
D02 Birmingham Division 09/1968 M
D16 Nottingham Division 01/1972 M
D02 Birmingham Division 11/1972 M
BS Bescot 05/1973 M
Renumbered 25262 06/03/1974 E
Store 04/1982 M
BS Bescot 05/1982 M
Returned to Service 05/1982 M
KD Kingmoor Diesel 09/1985 M
KM Kingmoor New Yard 11/1985 M
Renumbered 25901 20/12/1985 E
Withdrawn 16/03/1987 E
Stored at Kingmoor Diesel, moved to Upperby depot on 09/08/88 for inspection prior to movement south, then returned to Carlisle to Kingmoor New Yard, again towed to Upperby on 10/11/88 and stored. Moved to Crewe South Yard on 31/05/89 and was scheduled to go to Vic Berry, Leicester for scrap but, before further movement, it was discovered that it had not been sold so it was towed back to Carlisle Yard on 07/06/89, on to Mossend Yard on 08/06/89 and then to ZH Glasgow Works and moved next door to MC Metal Processing the same day for asbestos removal.
Sold to Harry Needle but instead of going to the South Yorkshire Railway Preservation Society, Meadowhall was moved by road to the East Lancashire Railway on 17/09/89 for further use.

D7612 contd.
For preservation
Sold to South Devon Diesel Traction, Dart Valley Railway (subsequently renamed as the South Devon Railway) and moved there on 30/03/99. Repainted as 25901 in BR small logo blue about 09/02, subsequently repainted in BR two-tone green as D7612.
HQ Headquarters Pool 07/03/2002 E
Reregistered on TOPS as 89262 on 07/03/02 to allow movement by rail to galas at other heritage railways.
Renumbered 25262 03/2016 M
Officially renumbered from 25901 back to 25262 by 03/16 but still 89262 on TOPS.
Repainted in BR small logo blue livery as 25262 by 23/08/24.
Moved from the South Devon Railway to the Severn Valley Railway 09/24.

D7613
65A Eastfield 30/04/1966 E
D09 Manchester Division 08/1968 M
D02 Birmingham Division 09/1968 M
D16 Nottingham Division 01/1972 M
D02 Birmingham Division 11/1972 M
BS Bescot 05/1973 M
Renumbered 25263 15/05/1974 E
Withdrawn 17/11/1980 E
Moved to ZL Swindon Works 03/03/81 and was cut up by 18/05/83.

D7614
65A Eastfield 07/05/1966 E
D09 Manchester Division 07/1968 M
D02 Birmingham Division 09/1968 M
D16 Nottingham Division 01/1972 M
D02 Birmingham Division 02/1973 M
BS Bescot 05/1973 M
TO Toton 09/1973 M
BS Bescot 09/1973 M
Renumbered 25264 22/03/1974 E
TO Toton 05/1974 M
CD Crewe Diesel 01/1976 M
TO Toton 12/1976 M
Withdrawn 14/12/1980 E
Moved to ZL Swindon Works 27/03/81 and was scrapped during 06/83.

D7615
65A Eastfield 12/05/1966 E
D08 Liverpool Division 08/1968 M
D10 Preston Division 09/1968 M
D02 Birmingham Division 11/1968 M
D16 Nottingham Division 12/1970 M

D7615 contd.
D02 Birmingham Division 10/1971 M
D16 Nottingham Division 01/1972 M
D02 Birmingham Division 02/1973 M
D16 Nottingham Division 03/1973 M
TO Toton 05/1973 M
Renumbered 25265 02/03/1974 E
CW Cricklewood East 05/1974 M
WN Willesden 06/1974 M
CW Cricklewood East 06/1975 M
CD Crewe Diesel 01/1984 M
Unofficially named *Castell Harlech/Harlech Castle*, date unknown but possibly in 1985.
Withdrawn 18/03/1987 E
Stored at Basford Hall Yard. Moved to Humberstone Road, Leicester on 14/07/87 and held there until finally moved to Vic Berry, Leicester on 11/09/87 for scrap but remained intact.

For preservation

Sold for preservation to Peak Rail, left by road from Berry's Yard on 07/07/88 and arrived at Matlock on 16/07/88. It was named *Harlech Castle* at Darley Dale on 17/10/92. It was later sold, name removed and moved by road to the Battlefield Line, Shackerstone 27/11/94 where it remained until moved to the Great Central Railway, Loughborough about 05/99.
Moved to Nemesis Rail, Burton-upon-Trent by 2017 but arrival date unknown.

D7616
65A Eastfield 19/05/1966 E
D08 Liverpool Division 06/1968 M
D10 Preston Division 09/1968 M
D16 Nottingham Division 11/1968 M
D02 Birmingham Division 10/1971 M
D16 Nottingham Division 01/1972 M
TO Toton 05/1973 M
Renumbered 25266 05/12/1973 E
LO Longsight 01/1974 M
SP Springs Branch 08/1974 M
LO Longsight 10/1975 M
SP Springs Branch 01/1976 M
CW Cricklewood East 05/1976 M
CD Crewe Diesel 01/1984 M
Withdrawn 19/09/1986 E
Stored at Kingmoor Diesel, moved to Carlisle Upperby depot on 14/07/88 for inspection prior to movement south, then towed back to Kingmoor Diesel. Moved to Workington on 07/12/88, to Carnforth and on to Basford Hall 08/12/88, then to

D7616 contd.
Leicester stabling point on 16/12/88 and into Vic Berry, Leicester on 20/12/88, cutting started about 20/01/89 and was completed by 18/02/89.

D7617
65A Eastfield 12/08/1966 E
D10 Preston Division 08/1968 M
D16 Nottingham Division 11/1968 M
D02 Birmingham Division 10/1971 M
D16 Nottingham Division 01/1972 M
TO Toton 05/1973 M
Renumbered 25267 27/02/1974 E
Withdrawn 01/02/1981 E
Stored at Leicester. Moved to ZE Derby Works about 07/81 and was broken up by 18/02/82.

D7618
65A Eastfield 18/08/1966 E
D10 Preston Division 07/1968 M
D16 Nottingham Division 11/1968 M
D02 Birmingham Division 11/1970 M
D16 Nottingham Division 01/1972 M
TO Toton 05/1973 M
Renumbered 25268 25/05/1974 E
KD Kingmoor Diesel 05/1981 M
SP Springs Branch 09/1981 M
CD Crewe Diesel 10/1982 M
KM Kingmoor New Yard 11/1985 M
Renumbered 25902 11/12/1985 E
Withdrawn 02/03/1987 E
Stored at Basford Hal. Moved to Humberstone Road, Leicester on 03/07/87 and into Vic Berry, Leicester 06/07/87, where it was put in the 'pyramid' in 10/87, but was taken off about 03/11/87 and cut up by 13/11/87.

D7619
65A Eastfield 20/08/1966 E
D10 Preston Division 01/07/1968 E
D16 Nottingham Division 11/1968 M
D02 Birmingham Division 11/1970 M
D16 Nottingham Division 01/1972 M
TO Toton 05/1973 M
Renumbered 25269 20/04/1974 E
BS Bescot 08/1981 M
KD Kingmoor Diesel 09/1985 M
Withdrawn 03/04/1986 E
Stored at Crewe Diesel. Sold for scrap to Vic Berry, Leicester in 12/86, moved to Berry's Yard on 12/01/87 where it was noted being dismantled on 15/03/87 and this was completed by 20/03/87.

D7620
65A Eastfield 26/08/1966 E
D10 Preston Division 07/1968 M
D16 Nottingham Division 11/1968 M
TO Toton 05/1973 M
BS Bescot 11/1973 M
Renumbered 25270 15/06/1974 E
TO Toton 06/1974 M
Withdrawn 28/11/1982 E
Stored at Newton Heath. Moved to ZL Swindon Works 19/02/85 and was scrapped by 03/06/86. At least one of the cabs went by road to Vic Berry, Leicester on 04/06/86.

D7621
65A Eastfield 29/08/1966 E
D10 Preston Division 07/1968 M
D16 Nottingham Division 11/1968 M
D02 Birmingham Division 11/1970 M
D01 London Division 01/1971 M
D02 Birmingham Division 07/1971 M
BS Bescot 05/1973 M
Renumbered 25271 20/04/1974 E
Withdrawn 13/10/1981 E
Stored at Crewe Diesel. Moved to ZE Derby Works 19/02/82 and scrapped by 22/09/82.

D7622
65A Eastfield 02/09/1966 E
D10 Preston Division 07/1968 M
D16 Nottingham Division 11/1968 M
D02 Birmingham Division 11/1970 M
BS Bescot 05/1973 M
Renumbered 25272 14/05/1974 E
Withdrawn 16/07/1981 E
Moved to ZE Derby Works on 04/03/82 and cut up by 06/08/82.

D7623
65A Eastfield 08/09/1966 E
D10 Preston Division 07/1968 M
D16 Nottingham Division 11/1968 M
D02 Birmingham Division 11/1970 M
BS Bescot 05/1973 M
Renumbered 25273 03/1974 M
Withdrawn 01/02/1981 E
Moved to ZL Swindon Works on 23/03/81 and was dismantled by 05/04/82.

D7624
41A Tinsley 30/07/1965 E
41C Wath 04/1966 M
55A Leeds Holbeck 08/1967 M
86B Ebbw Junction 11/1970 M
84A Laira 12/1972 M

D7624 contd.
Allocation recoded 84A to LA 05/1973 M
BR Bristol Bath Road 09/1973 M
LA Laira 03/1974 M
Renumbered 25274 05/1974 M
BS Bescot 08/1975 M
Withdrawn 02/05/1982 E
Moved to ZE Derby Works during 05/82 and remained there until sent to ZL Swindon Works on 04/02/85 and was broken up by 24/04/85.

D7625
41A Tinsley 30/07/1965 E
41C Wath 04/1966 M
55A Leeds Holbeck 08/1967 M
86B Ebbw Junction 11/1970 M
82A Bristol Bath Road 01/1972 M
86A Cardiff (Canton) 05/1972 M
84A Laira 12/1972 M
Allocation recoded 84A to LA 05/1973 M
BR Bristol Bath Road 09/1973 M
LA Laira 03/1974 M
Renumbered 25275 04/1974 M
BS Bescot 08/1975 M
Withdrawn 18/04/1982 E
Stored at Tyseley. Moved to ZL Swindon Works 25/03/85 and was cut up by 24/07/85.

D7626
41A Tinsley 05/08/1965 E
41C Wath 04/1966 M
55A Leeds Holbeck 08/1967 M
D09 Manchester Division 07/1968 M
D02 Birmingham Division 11/1968 M
D10 Preston Division 05/1970 M
D01 London Division 05/1971 M
D16 Nottingham Division 10/1971 M
D01 London Division 04/1972 M
D16 Nottingham Division 08/1972 M
D10 Preston Division 10/1972 M
KM Kingmoor Diesel 05/1973 M
SP Springs Branch 05/1973 M
BS Bescot 09/1973 M
Renumbered 25276 04/1974 M
CD Crewe Diesel 09/1985 M
KM Kingmoor New Yard 11/1985 M
Renumbered 25903 02/01/1986 E
Withdrawn 18/03/1987 E
Stored at Kingmoor Diesel. Moved to Upperby depot 09/08/88 for inspection prior to being moved south, then back to Carlisle to Kingmoor New Yard. Towed again to Upperby on 10/11/88 and held until sent to

D7626 contd.
Crewe South Yard on 31/05/89, to Nuneaton 02/06/89, then to Humberstone Road, Leicester on 03/06/89 and into Vic Berry, Leicester on 05/06/89. It was still intact on 18/06/89, but had been completely dismantled by 24/06/89.

D7627
41A Tinsley 12/08/1965 E
41C Wath 04/1966 M
LMML LM Midland Lines 08/1967 M
D02 Birmingham Division 09/1967 M
LMML LM Midland Lines 09/1967 M
D16 Nottingham Division 17/06/1968 E
D02 Birmingham Division 01/1969 M
BS Bescot 05/1973 M
Renumbered 25277 01/02/1974 E
While a train was being shunted at Euston station on 25/11/83, it ran away, colliding with 25277 and derailing it.
Withdrawn 15/04/1984 E
Moved to ZE Derby Works on 25/01/84 for repairs, but these were cancelled and the locomotive was withdrawn. Then moved to ZL Swindon Works on 05/02/85 and was cut up by 26/09/85. The damaged cab was still at Derby Works in 10/86.

D7628
41A Tinsley 12/08/1965 E
41C Wath 04/1966 M
LMML LM Midland Lines 08/1967 M
D16 Nottingham Division 17/06/1968 E
D02 Birmingham Division 01/1969 M
BS Bescot 05/1973 M
Renumbered 25278 29/01/1974 E
LO Longsight 05/1974 M
SP Springs Branch 12/1974 M
CW Cricklewood East 05/1976 M
KD Kingmoor Diesel 01/1984 M
CD Crewe Diesel 03/1986 M
Unofficially named *Castell Powys/Powis Castle*, date unknown but probably after 03/86.
Withdrawn 17/03/1987 E
Stored at Basford Hall Yard. Moved to Humberstone Road, Leicester on 08/07/87 and to Vic Berry next day where it remained intact.
For preservation
Sold for preservation on the North Yorkshire Moors Railway and moved to Humberstone Road and on to Toton 25/01/88, then to

D7628 contd.
Tinsley and on to York on 26/01/88, to Tees Yard 27/01/88 and finally to the NYMR on 29/01/88. It was named *Sybilla* and externally renumbered back to D7628 in 03/89. Reregistered in order for it to work services to Whitby.
GT North Yorkshire Moors Railway Grosmont 11/1998 M
Allocation recoded GT to NY 12/2000 M
HQ Headquarters Pool 06/01/2001 E

D7629
41A Tinsley 07/09/1965 E
41C Wath 04/1966 M
LMML LM Midland Lines 08/1967 M
D02 Birmingham Division 09/1967 M
LMML LM Midland Lines 09/1967 M
9A Longsight 06/1968 M
D09 Manchester Division 17/06/1968 E
D10 Preston Division 11/1968 M
D02 Birmingham Division 01/1969 M
D01 London Division 01/1971 M
D02 Birmingham Division 10/1972 M
D08 Liverpool Division 02/1973 M
SP Springs Branch 05/1973 M
Renumbered 25279 30/01/1974 E
CW Cricklewood East 05/1976 M
TO Toton 11/1978 M
SP Springs Branch 05/1981 M
CD Crewe Diesel 10/1982 M
Store 13/03/1987 E
Withdrawn 18/03/1987 E
Stored at Crewe Diesel, then Basford Hall. Moved to Humberstone Road, Leicester on 10/07/87 and to Vic Berry, Leicester on 28/07/87 for scrap but remained intact.
For preservation
Sold for preservation on the Llangollen Railway and moved there by road on 19/03/88. Moved to Gloucestershire Warwickshire Railway about 01/93, and was painted as D7629. Moved to the Northampton & Lamport Railway in 04/99, sold and moved to the Great Central Railway, Loughborough in 08/00, later to the Great Central Railway (Nottingham). Re-registered on 23/06/09 to allow movement by rail to galas on other heritage railways.
HQ Headquarters Pool 23/06/2009 E
Moved to the Ecclesbourne Valley Railway 14/10/15, returned to the Great Central Railway (Nottingham) in 12/16, then moved

D7629 contd.

to the East Lancashire Railway in 07/17 for a planned long stay.

Repainted into BR small logo blue livery carrying the number 25279 instead of the previous D7629.

D7630

41A Tinsley 16/09/1965 E
41C Wath 04/1966 M
Loaned to the LM region 07/67, shed not recorded and back to 41C the same month.
LMML LM Midland Lines 08/1967 M
9A Longsight 06/1968 M
D09 Manchester Division 17/06/1968 E
D10 Preston Division 11/1968 M
D02 Birmingham Division 01/1969 M
BS Bescot 05/1973 M
Renumbered 25280 20/04/1974 E
CD Crewe Diesel 10/1975 M
BS Bescot 11/1975 M
TO Toton 08/1976 M
Withdrawn 08/11/1981 E
Moved to ZL Swindon Works 18/03/82 and was cut up by 30/07/83.

D7631

41A Tinsley 29/09/1965 E
41C Wath 04/1966 M
LMML LM Midland Lines 08/1967 M
9A Longsight 06/1968 M
D09 Manchester Division 17/06/1968 E
D02 Birmingham Division 01/1969 M
BS Bescot 05/1973 M
Renumbered 25281 04/1974 M
SP Springs Branch 10/1976 M
Withdrawn 01/02/1981 E
Stored at Reddish. Moved to ZL Swindon Works 27/02/81 and broken up by 13/05/81.

D7632

41A Tinsley 08/10/1965 E
41C Wath 04/1966 M
LMML LM Midland Lines 08/1967 M
D02 Birmingham Division 09/1967 M
8F Springs Branch 06/1968 M
D08 Liverpool Division 17/06/1968 E
SP Springs Branch 05/1973 M
Renumbered 25282 12/09/1973 E
BS Bescot 10/1976 M
CD Crewe Diesel 09/1985 M
Withdrawn 10/03/1986 E
Stored at Crewe Diesel, then moved to Kingmoor New Yard by 10/86 for further storage. Moved to Upperby depot on

D7632 contd.

10/11/88 for inspection, prior to movement south, then back to Kingmoor a few days later. Sent to Workington 07/12/88, to Carnforth and on to Basford Hall Yard 08/12/88, then to Leicester stabling point on 16/12/88 and into Vic Berry, Leicester on 20/12/88. It was noted partly cut up on 29/02/89 and 06/03/89, but had gone completely by 24/03/89.

D7633

41A Tinsley 30/10/1965 E
41C Wath 04/1966 M
8F Springs Branch 10/1967 M
D08 Liverpool Division 17/06/1968 E
D02 Birmingham Division 08/1972 M
D01 London Division 12/1972 M
D08 Liverpool Division 02/1973 M
SP Springs Branch 05/1973 M
Renumbered 25283 27/02/1974 E
CD Crewe Diesel 10/1982 M
KM Kingmoor New Yard 11/1985 M
Renumbered 25904 12/11/1985 E
Withdrawn 23/03/1987 E
Stored at Basford Hall Yard. Moved to Humberstone Road, Leicester on 03/07/87 and into Vic Berry, Leicester on 06/07/87 and remained intact.

For preservation

Sold for preservation for use on the Severn Valley Railway and was moved to Birmingham Railway Museum, Tyseley on 16/12/87, then moved to the SVR on 11/01/88 and was externally renumbered back to D7633. Moved to the Dean Forest Railway on 30/10/03 for further restoration. At times painted as 25283, dates not currently known.
HQ Headquarters Pool 04/02/2005 E
Reregistered as 89233 on 04/02/05 to allow rail movement to galas on other heritage railways.
Acquired by HNRC. Moved from the Dean Forest Railway to Reids Freight Yard, Longton on 21/03/19, remaining there until 03/02/23 when it was moved to Worksop.

D7634

41A Tinsley 19/10/1965 E
41C Wath 04/1966 M
8F Springs Branch 10/1967 M
D08 Liverpool Division 17/06/1968 E
SP Springs Branch 05/1973 M

D7634 contd.
TI Tinsley 08/1973 M
SP Springs Branch 10/1973 M
Renumbered 25284 20/10/1973 E
CD Crewe Diesel 10/1982 M
Withdrawn 21/01/1985 E
Moved to ZL Swindon Works 02/04/85 and was scrapped by 03/11/86. The cabs were taken by road to Vic Berry, Leicester and noted there on 26/04/87, but gone by 09/87.

D7635
41A Tinsley 05/11/1965 E
41C Wath 04/1966 M
8F Springs Branch 10/1967 M
D08 Liverpool Division 17/06/1968 E
D10 Preston Division 01/1970 M
D08 Liverpool Division 05/1971 M
SP Springs Branch 05/1973 M
Renumbered 25285 20/04/1974 E
CD Crewe Diesel 10/1982 M
Withdrawn 17/03/1986 E
Stored at Crewe Diesel, moved to Gresty Lane 03/87 and later Basford Hall, both for further storage. Moved to Humberstone Road, Leicester on 16/07/87 and into Vic Berry, Leicester on 24/07/87 for scrap. Last noted intact on 26/09/87, it was cut up by 04/10/87.

D7636
41A Tinsley 15/11/1965 E
41C Wath 04/1966 M
8F Springs Branch 10/1967 M
D08 Liverpool Division 17/06/1968 E
D10 Preston Division 01/1970 M
D08 Liverpool Division 05/1971 M
SP Springs Branch 05/1973 M
Renumbered 25286 20/04/1974 E
CD Crewe Diesel 10/1982 M
KM Kingmoor New Yard 11/1985 M
Renumbered 25905 25/11/1985 E
Store 19/08/1986 E
Withdrawn 13/09/1986 E
Stored at Kingmoor New Yard, towed to Upperby depot on 14/07/88 for inspection prior to movement south, then back to Kingmoor New Yard. Moved again to Upperby depot on 10/11/88, to Mossend Yard 25/11/88 and to BRML Glasgow Works the same day for component recovery for 97251. It remained at Glasgow Works until moved next door into MC Metal Processing in 10/89. It was still intact on 20/01/90, but had been cut up by 12/02/90 when only the cabs remained.

D7637
41A Tinsley 22/11/1965 E

A Class 25 that survived into preservation was D5185. It was withdrawn in 1987 and sold to Vic Berry, Leicester that year. In 1988 it was then purchased for preservation and moved to the Northampton & Lamport Railway before a move to the Great Central Railway where it was photographed on 17th May 2008. *(Ray Reed/RCTS Photo Archive*

D7637 contd.
41C Wath 04/1966 M
8F Springs Branch 10/1967 M
D08 Liverpool Division 17/06/1968 E
SP Springs Branch 05/1973 M
Renumbered 25287 04/03/1974 E
Withdrawn 04/07/1976 E
Withdrawn 04/07/76 due to collision damage. Moved to ZE Derby Works by 31/07/76 and repaired.
SP Springs Branch 20/09/1976 E
Reinstated 20/09/1976 E
CD Crewe Diesel 10/1982 M
Store 05/1985 M
Withdrawn 03/12/1985 E
Stored at Toton. Moved to ZF Doncaster Works 03/03/86 for store, then to Goole Docks 13/08/86 for further storage. Sold to Vic Berry, Leicester and moved to Humberstone Road, Leicester on 30/10/86 and into Berry's Yard on 04/11/8. Partly cut up 01/02/87, completely cut up by 20/02/87.

D7638
41A Tinsley 30/11/1965 E
41C Wath 04/1966 M
10A Carnforth 07/1967 M
LMWL LM Western Lines 07/1967 M
10A Carnforth 07/1967 M
8F Springs Branch 05/1968 M
D08 Liverpool Division 17/06/1968 E
SP Springs Branch 05/1973 M
Renumbered 25288 01/10/1973 E
CD Crewe Diesel 10/1982 M
Withdrawn 19/02/1987 E
Stored at Basford Hall. Moved to Humberstone Road, Leicester on 27/07/87 and into Vic Berry, Leicester on 30/07/87 and put in the 'pyramid' by 10/87. Later taken off, and last noted on 14/03/88, it had been completely cut up by 09/04/88.

D7639
41A Tinsley 23/12/1965 E
41C Wath 04/1966 M
D01 London Division (WCML) 03/1967 M
D16 Nottingham Division 04/1967 M
8F Springs Branch 07/1967 M
D08 Liverpool Division 17/06/1968 E
D01 London Division 03/1972 M
D16 Nottingham Division 08/1972 M
D10 Preston Division 10/1972 M
KM Kingmoor Diesel 05/1973 M
SP Springs Branch 05/1973 M

D7639 contd.
Renumbered 25289 25/02/1974 E
HA Haymarket 10/1974 M
SP Springs Branch 11/1974 M
BS Bescot 08/1977 M
Suffered cab damage at Preston station on 14/01/84 during shunting operations.
Withdrawn 17/01/1984 E
Moved to Toton, then to Bescot 08/02/84 for further storage. Moved to ZL Swindon Works 22/03/84 and was cut up by 29/10/84.

D7640
41A Tinsley 31/12/1965 E
41C Wath 04/1966 M
D01 London Division (WCML) 03/1967 M
D16 Nottingham Division 04/1967 M
8F Springs Branch 09/1967 M
D08 Liverpool Division 17/06/1968 E
D02 Birmingham Division 05/1970 M
BS Bescot 05/1973 M
Renumbered 25290 05/03/1974 E
SP Springs Branch 05/1974 M
LO Longsight 06/1974 M
CD Crewe Diesel 10/1975 M
BS Bescot 06/1977 M
CD Crewe Diesel 05/1978 M
Withdrawn 04/10/1981 E
Stored at Tyseley 01/82. Moved to ZL Swindon Works 16/03/82 by mistake and left again on 19/03/82 for ZE Derby Works, but stopped at Gloucester for storage, then to Crewe Diesel for further storage, and did not arrive at Derby Works until 08/82. It was noted being cut up 06/04/83, and was completed by 20/05/83.

D7641
41A Tinsley 14/01/1966 E
41C Wath 04/1966 M
D01 London Division (WCML) 03/1967 M
D16 Nottingham Division 04/1967 M
8F Springs Branch 09/1967 M
D08 Liverpool Division 17/06/1968 E
D02 Birmingham Division 05/1970 M
BS Bescot 05/1973 M
Renumbered 25291 28/02/1974 E
SP Springs Branch 05/1974 M
LO Longsight 06/1974 M
CD Crewe Diesel 10/1975 M
Withdrawn 31/05/1981 E
Stored at Gloucester 12/81. Moved to ZL Swindon Works 26/01/82 and was scrapped by 11/11/82.

D7642
41A Tinsley 28/01/1966 E
41C Wath 04/1966 M
D01 London Division (WCML) 03/1967 M
D16 Nottingham Division 04/1967 M
8F Springs Branch 09/1967 M
D08 Liverpool Division 17/06/1968 E
D02 Birmingham Division 05/1970 M
BS Bescot 05/1973 M
Renumbered 25292 02/1974 M
SP Springs Branch 05/1974 M
LO Longsight 06/1974 M
CD Crewe Diesel 10/1975 M
Withdrawn 19/10/1981 E
Stored at Springs Branch. Moved to ZL Swindon Works on 14/12/81 and was broken up by 02/03/83.

D7643
41A Tinsley 08/02/1966 E
41C Wath 04/1966 M
D01 London Division (WCML) 03/1967 M
D16 Nottingham Division 04/1967 M
8F Springs Branch 09/1967 M
D08 Liverpool Division 17/06/1968 E
D01 London Division 08/1969 M
D02 Birmingham Division 10/1969 M
D08 Liverpool Division 02/1970 M
D02 Birmingham Division 05/1970 M
BS Bescot 05/1973 M
Renumbered 25293 02/1974 M
LO Longsight 06/1974 M
CD Crewe Diesel 10/1975 M
Withdrawn 01/02/1981 E
Moved to ZL Swindon Works 03/03/81 and cut up by 25/08/81.

D7644
41A Tinsley 23/02/1966 E
41C Wath 04/1966 M
D01 London Division (WCML) 03/1967 M
D01 London Division 17/06/1968 E
D02 Birmingham Division 05/1970 M
BS Bescot 05/1973 M
Renumbered 25294 23/05/1974 E
LO Longsight 06/1974 M
CD Crewe Diesel 10/1975 M
Withdrawn 10/10/1982 E
Stored at Reddish, then moved to Ashburys Yard, Manchester 18/05/83 for further storage. Sent to ZE Derby Works about 03/07/83 and again stored. Moved to ZL Swindon Works on 04/02/85 and cut up by 08/05/85.

D7645
41A Tinsley 15/03/1966 E
41E Staveley (Barrow Hill) 12/1966 M
D01 London Division (WCML) 03/1967 M
D01 London Division 17/06/1968 E
D02 Birmingham Division 06/1970 M
D09 Manchester Division 01/1971 M
D01 London Division 03/1973 M
WN Willesden 05/1973 M
CW Cricklewood East 01/1974 M
Renumbered 25295 02/1974 M
Withdrawn 10/06/1978 E
Moved to ZE Derby Works 07/78, only the shell was left by 10/79, the remains were finally cut up by 30/10/81.

D7646
41A Tinsley 25/03/1966 E
41E Staveley (Barrow Hill) 12/1966 M
D01 London Division (WCML) 03/1967 M
D01 London Division 17/06/1968 E
D08 Liverpool Division 10/1969 M
D02 Birmingham Division 06/1970 M
D09 Manchester Division 01/1971 M
D10 Preston Division 10/1972 M
KM Kingmoor Diesel 05/1973 M
SP Springs Branch 05/1973 M
Renumbered 25296 02/1974 M
CD Crewe Diesel 10/1982 M
KM Kingmoor New Yard 11/1985 M
Renumbered 25906 13/12/1985 E
Withdrawn 01/11/1986 E
Stored at Basford Hall Yard. Sold to Vic Berry, Leicester about 04/87, moved to Humberstone Road Yard, Leicester on 02/06/87 and into Berry's Yard the next day. It was noted intact on 15/11/87 but had been broken up by 12/12/87.

D7647
41A Tinsley 30/03/1966 E
41E Staveley (Barrow Hill) 12/1966 M
D16 Nottingham Division 01/1967 M
D02 Birmingham Division 04/1967 M
9A Longsight 03/1968 M
D09 Manchester Division 17/06/1968 E
D16 Nottingham Division 10/1969 M
TO Toton 05/1973 M
Renumbered 25297 15/12/1973 E
LO Longsight 01/1974 M
SP Springs Branch 05/1974 M
CD Crewe Diesel 10/1982 M
Store 10/06/1985 E
CD Crewe Diesel 07/1985 M

D7647 contd.
Returned to Service 07/1985 M
KM Kingmoor New Yard 11/1985 M
Renumbered 25907 26/11/1985 E
Withdrawn 18/09/1986 E
Stored at Springs Branch in derelict condition. Moved to Humberstone Road, Leicester on 24/05/89 and into Vic Berry, Leicester the next day. Noted still intact on 17/06/89, partly cut up on 24/06/89 and scrapping completed by 14/07/89.

D7648
41A Tinsley 07/04/1966 E
41E Staveley (Barrow Hill) 12/1966 M
D16 Nottingham Division 01/1967 M
D02 Birmingham Division 04/1967 M
9A Longsight 03/1968 M
D09 Manchester Division 17/06/1968 E
D16 Nottingham Division 10/1969 M
D08 Liverpool Division 11/1970 M
SP Springs Branch 05/1973 M
Renumbered 25298 04/1974 M
CD Crewe Diesel 10/1982 M
Withdrawn 19/03/1985 E
Stored at Crewe Gresty Lane. Moved to ZF Doncaster Works about 29/01/86 and cut up by 27/09/86.

D7649
41A Tinsley 15/04/1966 E
41E Staveley (Barrow Hill) 12/1966 M
D16 Nottingham Division 01/1967 M
D02 Birmingham Division 04/1967 M
9A Longsight 03/1968 M
D09 Manchester Division 17/06/1968 E
D16 Nottingham Division 05/1969 M
TO Toton 05/1973 M
Renumbered 25299 02/1974 M
CD Crewe Diesel 10/1975 M
LO Longsight 05/1977 M
BS Bescot 06/1977 M
CW Cricklewood East 04/1981 M
Withdrawn 05/10/1981 E
Stored at Crewe Diesel. Moved to ZE Derby Works 19/02/82 and broken up by 10/06/82.

D7650
D16 Nottingham Division 07/05/1966 E
D01 London Division (WCML) 05/1966 M
D16 Nottingham Division 11/1966 M
D02 Birmingham Division 04/1967 M
9A Longsight 03/1968 M
D09 Manchester Division 17/06/1968 E
D16 Nottingham Division 05/1969 M

D7650 contd.
D08 Liverpool Division 05/1970 M
D01 London Division 03/1971 M
D08 Liverpool Division 10/1972 M
D01 London Division 12/1972 M
D08 Liverpool Division 02/1973 M
SP Springs Branch 05/1973 M
Renumbered 25300 30/11/1973 E
CD Crewe Diesel 10/1982 M
Store 05/1985 M
Withdrawn 03/12/1985 E
Stored at Kingmoor New Yard. Moved to ZF Doncaster Works in 03/86 and was scrapped by 28/06/86, with just the cabs remaining by 06/07/86.

D7651
D16 Nottingham Division 09/05/1966 E
D02 Birmingham Division 04/1967 M
9A Longsight 03/1968 M
D09 Manchester Division 17/06/1968 E
D16 Nottingham Division 05/1969 M
D10 Preston Division 10/1972 M
KM Kingmoor Diesel 05/1973 M
SP Springs Branch 05/1973 M
Renumbered 25301 02/03/1974 E
ED Eastfield 12/1976 M
TO Toton 02/1978 M
CW Cricklewood East 08/1981 M
CD Crewe Diesel 11/1983 M
Withdrawn 11/12/1983 E
Moved to ZL Swindon Works 17/04/84 and was cut up by 18/08/84.

D7652
D16 Nottingham Division 21/05/1966 E
D02 Birmingham Division 04/1967 M
D05 Stoke Division 05/1968 M
D16 Nottingham Division 11/1968 M
D08 Liverpool Division 11/1970 M
SP Springs Branch 05/1973 M
Renumbered 25302 02/1974 M
TI Tinsley 09/1974 M
BS Bescot 01/1975 M
WN Willesden 05/1975 M
TO Toton 06/1975 M
CD Crewe Diesel 10/1975 M
SP Springs Branch 11/1975 M
CW Cricklewood East 02/1977 M
TO Toton 11/1977 M
CD Crewe Diesel 03/1983 M
Withdrawn 14/06/1985 E
Stored at Kingmoor Diesel 10/85. Moved to ZF Doncaster Works 03/86 and was

D7652 contd.
dismantled by 28/06/86, with the cabs still extant on 06/07/86.

D7653
LMML LM Midland Lines 24/06/1966 E
D02 Birmingham Division 08/1967 M
D09 Manchester Division 17/06/1968 E
D16 Nottingham Division 05/1969 M
D08 Liverpool Division 11/1970 M
SP Springs Branch 05/1973 M
LO Longsight 09/1973 M
Renumbered 25303 02/1974 M
TO Toton 01/1976 M
CD Crewe Diesel 03/1983 M
Withdrawn 24/02/1986 E
Stored at Crewe Diesel. Sold to Vic Berry, Leicester in 12/86. Departed for Knighton Sidings, Leicester 23/01/87 and into Berry's Yard on 26/01/87 and was cut up by 10/05/87.

D7654
LMML LM Midland Lines 24/06/1966 E
D02 Birmingham Division 08/1967 M
D05 Stoke Division 06/1968 M
D16 Nottingham Division 11/1968 M
D08 Liverpool Division 11/1970 M
D09 Manchester Division 01/1971 M
LO Longsight 05/1973 M
Renumbered 25304 04/1974 M
CD Crewe Diesel 10/1975 M
Withdrawn 28/11/1982 E
Moved to ZE Derby Works by 03/83 for scrap, but then sent to ZL Swindon Works on 05/02/85 and was broken up by 19/06/85.

D7655
LMML LM Midland Lines 01/07/1966 E
D02 Birmingham Division 03/1967 M
LMML LM Midland Lines 04/1967 M
D16 Nottingham Division 17/06/1968 E
D01 London Division 02/1971 M
D02 Birmingham Division 07/1971 M
BS Bescot 05/1973 M
Renumbered 25305 03/1974 M
Store 12/04/1981 E
Stored 12/04/81, then moved to ZL Swindon Works 05/05/81.
Withdrawn 05/05/1981 E
BS Bescot 29/08/1982 E
Reinstated 29/08/1982 E
Reinstated to Bescot while still at Swindon Works, moved to Gloucester 17/09/72, then on to Bescot 22/09/82.
Withdrawn 31/07/1983 E

D7655 contd.
Withdrawn 31/07/83 although it had already gone from Mossend to Aberdeen for conversion to an ETHEL (Electric Train Heating Ex-Locomotive) on 26/07/83.
Renumbered 97251 08/83 M
While in Scotland the ETHELs were mainly used during the winter but 'out of use' in the summer although not always officially stored.
ED Eastfield 08/1983 M
Reinstated 08/1983 M
Named *ETHEL 2* in 08/83 at Ferryhill shed.
KM Kingmoor New Yard 01/1987 M
Noted stabled at Carlisle Kingmoor on 15/03/87, but was then moved to York and stabled at the back of Clifton Carriage Sidings on 16/03/87. Remained at York until towed back to Scotland and stored out of use at Fort William from 03/88. Reallocated to Carlisle Upperby Carriage Depot 24/07/88, but the locomotive remained at Fort William until 10/88.
CL Upperby Carriage Depot 24/07/1988 E
Withdrawn 18/03/1991 E
IS Inverness 16/01/1992 E
Reinstated 16/01/1992 E
Store 16/01/1992 E
Reinstated to Inverness 16/01/92 but remained in store.
Nameplates removed 11/93.
Withdrawn 18/11/1993 E
Remained at Inverness Yard until moved by road to MC Metal Processing, Glasgow on 07/06/94, arriving there on 10/6/94. It was cut up on 22/08/94. One cab was sold to Mel Thorley, moved by road to a lorry park in Stockport 29/11/94 and on to his home on 07/12/94 where it was craned over the house to the back garden. Sold to The South Wales Locomotive Cab Preservation Group, Bridgend, craned over his house 08/05/13 and moved by road to Bridgend.

D7656
LMML LM Midland Lines 05/07/1966 E
D01 London Division (WCML) 03/1967 M
D01 London Division 17/06/1968 E
D16 Nottingham Division 12/1968 M
D08 Liverpool Division 11/1970 M
84A Laira 10/1971 M
82A Bristol Bath Road 01/1972 M
86A Cardiff (Canton) 05/1972 M
84A Laira 12/1972 M
Allocation recoded 84A to LA 05/1973 M

D7656 contd.
Renumbered 25306 05/1974 M
CD Crewe Diesel 08/1975 M
Withdrawn 25/02/1985 E
Stored at Cricklewood. Moved to Acton Yard on 03/05/85, then to Swindon 14/05/85 and into ZL Swindon Works next day. Stored awaiting scrap, but due to impending closure of works, it was sold to Vic Berry, Leicester about 04/87. Moved to Swindon Cocklebury Yard, then to Humberstone Road, Leicester on 03/06/87 and into Berry's Yard the next day, where it was put in the 'pyramid' by 10/87. Taken off about 26/01/88 and was cut up by 13/02/88.

D7657
LMML LM Midland Lines 04/07/1966 E
D01 London Division (WCML) 03/1967 M
D01 London Division 17/06/1968 E
D16 Nottingham Division 12/1968 M
86B Ebbw Junction 09/1971 M
84A Laira 10/1971 M
82A Bristol Bath Road 01/1972 M
86A Cardiff (Canton) 05/1972 M
84A Laira 12/1972 M
Allocation recoded 84A to LA 05/1973 M
Renumbered 25307 05/1974 M
CD Crewe Diesel 08/1975 M
CW Cricklewood East 11/1980 M
KD Kingmoor Diesel 01/1984 M
KM Kingmoor New Yard 11/1985 M
Renumbered 25908 14/12/1985 E
Withdrawn 07/11/1986 E
Stored at Springs Branch, and then taken officially into Departmental service and supposedly renumbered ADB968026, based at Toton. However, it was still stabled at Springs Branch as 25908 on 06/04/87. Moved to Crewe on 07/04/87, to Bescot 08/04/87 and on to Toton on 10/04/87. It is believed to never have worked in departmental service, as it was stabled either at the TMD or the training compound and did not carry its departmental number. Moved to Toton 30/06/88 and to Vic Berry, Leicester on 05/07/88 where it was intact on 02/01/89 but had been cut up by 28/01/89.

D7658
LMML LM Midland Lines 19/07/1966 E
D01 London Division (WCML) 03/1967 M
D01 London Division 17/06/1968 E
D16 Nottingham Division 12/1968 M
D02 Birmingham Division 12/1970 M

D7658 contd.
D01 London Division 01/1971 M
D16 Nottingham Division 03/1973 M
TO Toton 05/1973 M
LO Longsight 07/1973 M
WN Willesden 08/1973 M
Renumbered 25308 20/04/1974 E
HA Haymarket 10/1974 M
SP Springs Branch 11/1974 M
CW Cricklewood East 05/1976 M
TO Toton 11/1977 M
CW Cricklewood East 07/1978 M
TO Toton 10/1978 M
Store 04/1982 M
TO Toton 05/1982 M
Returned to Service 05/1982 M
Store 09/1983 M
Withdrawn 16/10/1983 E
Moved to ZL Swindon Works 10/02/84 and was broken up by 26/11/84.

D7659
LMML LM Midland Lines 21/07/1966 E
D01 London Division (WCML) 03/1967 M
D01 London Division 17/06/1968 E
D16 Nottingham Division 12/1968 M
D08 Liverpool Division 05/1970 M
D09 Manchester Division 01/1971 M
D02 Birmingham Division 04/1972 M
D09 Manchester Division 07/1972 M
D02 Birmingham Division 08/1972 M
D10 Preston Division 10/1972 M
KM Kingmoor Diesel 05/1973 M
SP Springs Branch 05/1973 M
LO Longsight 07/1973 M
WN Willesden 08/1973 M
Renumbered 25309 04/1974 M
CW Cricklewood East 06/1975 M
TO Toton 11/1977 M
CW Cricklewood East 04/1979 M
TO Toton 09/1979 M
CW Cricklewood East 03/1980 M
KD Kingmoor Diesel 01/1984 M
KM Kingmoor New Yard 11/1985 M
Renumbered 25909 11/12/1985 E
Store 11/08/1986 E
Withdrawn 13/09/1986 E
Stored at Kingmoor New Yard. Moved to Crewe on 19/04/88, to Bescot 20/04/88 and to Humberstone Road, Leicester on 21/04/88. Taken into Vic Berry, Leicester on 22/04/88 for asbestos removal.
For preservation
After the work was completed, it moved

D7659 contd.
from Humberstone Road, Leicester on 02/06/88, to Coalville open day on 04/06/88 and to Manchester Red Bank Sidings on 06/06/88 and on to the East Lancashire Railway on 07/06/88. Moved to the Gloucestershire Warwickshire Railway arriving at Toddington on 18/07/96. It was sold to Rail Charter Services in 1996, but was sold back to Pete Waterman later in the year. Moved from store at L&NWR, Crewe to the Scottish Railway Preservation Society, Bo'ness on 24-25/11/04 for repairs to enable the locomotive to be used again. It was moved to Carnforth in 09/07 for further attention, then moved to Washwood Heath 01/07/13 for further work to be done.
HQ Headquarters Pool 04/02/2005 E
Reregistered as 89259 04/02/05 to allow movement by rail to galas on other heritage railways.
Moved to Peak Rail 13/07/17 to join Pete Waterman's other locomotives. Moved to North Norfolk Railway 09/06/22 initially to attend a gala but remained to replace steam locomotive workings during very hot weather; it had returned to Peak Rail by 18/09/22. It has attended several galas on other heritage lines. Moved again to the North Norfolk Railway 23/05/24 and on to the Churnet Valley Railway 31/10/24.

D7660
D01 London Division (WCML) 31/12/1966 E
D01 London Division 17/06/1968 E
WN Willesden 05/1973 M
Renumbered 25310 23/02/1974 E
CW Cricklewood East 06/1975 M
TO Toton 11/1977 M
CW Cricklewood East 04/1979 M
TO Toton 10/1979 M
CW Cricklewood East 03/1980 M
Withdrawn 10/10/1982 E
Stored at Tyseley. Moved to Mossend Yard 22/12/82 and then to ZH Glasgow Works 01/83 for conversion to an ETHEL (Electric Train Heating Ex-Locomotive). After the engine had been removed it was then moved to Aberdeen for conversion to ETHEL ADB97250.
Renumbered ADB97250 05/83 M
Moved to Inverness TMD on 10/05/83 and noted renumbered from 25310 into departmental stock, photographed there as ADB97250 on 11/05/83 although the official renumbering date was 03/07/83. While in Scotland, the ETHELs were mainly used during the winter but 'out of use' in the summer although not always officially stored.
Named *ETHEL 1* on 18/05/83 without ceremony at Aberdeen Ferryhill WRD.
ED Eastfield 06/1983 M
Renumbered 97250 1985 Y
The locomotive had the apparently erroneously applied ADB97250 number changed to just 97250 between 15/03/85 and 02/06/85.
Used at various places on the Scottish Region and upon a requirement being noted for an ETHEL, it was towed to York in 11/86 and then onto Tinsley on 01/12/86, where it was held, until moved to Derby on 04/12/86 for use at Litchurch Lane Works.
ZD Derby Litchurch Lane 12/1986 M
The nameplates were removed in 10/87.
Withdrawn 12/10/1987 E
Stored at Etches Park from 23/01/88 and kept there until a requirement was identified for an ETHEL to be utilised at Marylebone DMU depot, London. It was hauled towards Marylebone on 26/10/88, but the move was terminated at Oxford, and it was held there until moved to Old Oak Common on 06/11/88, mainly for static heating at Marylebone. Offered for sale 08/91 but not sold.
HQ Headquarters Pool 10/1991 M
Reinstated 10/1991 M
On 24/10/91, nearly three years after arriving at Old Oak Common, it was towed once again back to Scotland and noted at Inverness but the ETHEL was never put to work and instead was stored again and used as a spares source.
Withdrawn 18/11/1993 E
Remained in the yard at Inverness until moved by road to MC Metal Processing, Glasgow on 13/06/94 and was broken up on 24/08/94.

D7661
D01 London Division (WCML) 08/11/1966 E
D01 London Division 17/06/1968 E
WN Willesden 05/1973 M
Renumbered 25311 02/1974 M
CW Cricklewood East 06/1975 M
TO Toton 11/1977 M

D7661 contd.
CW Cricklewood East 04/1979 M
TO Toton 10/1979 M
CW Cricklewood East 03/1980 M
KD Kingmoor Diesel 11/1984 M
Withdrawn 28/02/1985 E
Stored at Toton
Reinstated 18/10/1985 E
CD Crewe Diesel 18/10/1985 E
Withdrawn 19/03/1986 E
Stored at Crewe Diesel, then moved to Kingmoor New Yard by 30/10/86 for further storage. Moved to Upperby depot on 14/07/88 for inspection prior to movement south, then back to Kingmoor New Yard. Moved again to Upperby depot on 10/11/88 and was held there until moved to Crewe Basford Hall on 12/12/88, then to Toton and Leicester stabling point on 15/12/88, and to Vic Berry, Leicester on 19/12/88. It was intact during 02/89, but partly cut by 04/03/89, with only bits remaining on 15/03/89, and these had gone by 25/03/89.

D7662
D01 London Division (WCML) 17/11/1966 E
D01 London Division 17/06/1968 E
D02 Birmingham Division 12/1968 M
D01 London Division 05/1970 M
CD Cricklewood East 05/1973 M
WN Willesden 06/1973 M
CW Cricklewood East 03/1974 M
Renumbered 25312 04/1974 M
WN Willesden 05/1974 M
CW Cricklewood East 06/1975 M
TO Toton 11/1977 M
CW Cricklewood East 04/1979 M
TO Toton 10/1979 M
CW Cricklewood East 03/1980 M
Sustained collision damage at Northampton in 05/82 and was stored at Bletchley. Moved to ZE Derby Works 25/05/82 for assessment.
Withdrawn 13/06/1982 E
Remained at ZE Derby Works in damaged state until finally moved to ZL Swindon Works on 24/07/85 and was cut up by 22/08/85.

D7663
D01 London Division (WCML) 23/11/1966 E
D01 London Division 17/06/1968 E
D02 Birmingham Division 12/1968 M
D01 London Division 05/1971 M
CD Cricklewood East 05/1973 M

D7663 contd.
Allocation recoded CD to CW 12/1973 M
Renumbered 25313 07/03/1974 E
TO Toton 11/1977 M
SP Springs Branch 02/1978 M
CW Cricklewood East 07/1978 M
LO Longsight 01/1984 M
BS Bescot 07/1984 M
CD Crewe Diesel 09/1985 M
Was noted carrying the unofficial name *Chirk Castle/Castell - y - Waun* in 1986.
Store 03/1987 M
Withdrawn 18/03/1987 E
Stored at Basford Hall. Moved to Humberstone Road, Leicester on 08/07/87, stored again, and then into Vic Berry, Leicester on 11/09/87 for scrap. However, it was reported sold to Hazet Tools, Gloucestershire, but this sale may have been cancelled.
For preservation
Sold for use on the Llangollen Railway and moved by road arriving there on 01/06/88. Eventually restored, and by 06/95 was painted as 25213. It carried the painted name *Chirk Castle/Castell - y - Waun* at the Llangollen diesel gala on 20/10/95, although the naming ceremony was postponed until 29/06/96 by which time it had been repainted back to the correct 25313.
Sold to the Wensleydale Railway due to corrosion damage, and was moved there by road on 07/09/09. Sold to HNRC and moved to Worksop 28/06/20.

D7664
D01 London Division (WCML) 23/11/1966 E
D01 London Division 17/06/1968 E
D02 Birmingham Division 12/1968 M
D01 London Division 05/1971 M
CD Cricklewood East 05/1973 M
Allocation recoded CD to CW 12/1973 M
Renumbered 25314 03/1974 M
Withdrawn 20/03/1983 E
Stored at Crewe Diesel. Moved to ZE Derby Works on 20/06/83 for attention.
Renumbered 97252 07/83M
Converted to an ETHEL (Electric Train Heating Ex-Locomotive) and transferred to Departmental stock. While in Scotland the ETHELs were mainly used during the winter but 'out of use' in the summer although not always officially stored.

D7664 contd.
ED Eastfield 07/1983 M
Named *ETHEL 3* without ceremony in 07/83.
BY Bletchley 19/10/1986 E
OC Old Oak Common 11/1987 M
Reallocated to Old Oak Common but remained at Marylebone to provide heat for coaching stock that was used on steam specials at the time.
Withdrawn 18/03/1991 E
IS Inverness 16/01/1992 E
Reinstated 16/01/1992 E
At Carlisle Upperby in 07/90. Offered for sale 08/91 while there but not sold. Moved to Inverness by the end of 1991.
Store 16/01/1992 E
The nameplates were removed in 11/93.
Withdrawn 18/11/1993 E
Remained in derelict condition at Inverness until it was collected by road transport and moved to MC Metal Processing, Glasgow arriving there on 14/06/94 and became the last of the three ETHELs to be cut up, when it was scrapped on 29/08/94.

D7665
D01 London Division (WCML) 07/12/1966 E
D01 London Division 17/06/1968 E
D02 Birmingham Division 12/1968 M
D01 London Division 07/1971 M
CD Cricklewood East 05/1973 M
Allocation recoded CD to CW 12/1973 M
WN Willesden 01/1974 M
Renumbered 25315 03/1974 M
CW Cricklewood East 03/1974 M
WN Willesden 05/1974 M
CW Cricklewood East 06/1975 M
TO Toton 11/1981 M
SP Springs Branch 06/1982 M
CD Crewe Diesel 07/1983 M
KM Kingmoor New Yard 11/1985 M
Renumbered 25910 04/12/1985 E
Withdrawn 18/03/1987 E
Moved to Humberstone Road,, Leicester on 16/07/87, and to Vic Berry, Leicester on 24/07/87. Noted being cut up 18/09/87 and was completed by 21/09/87.

D7666
D01 London Division (WCML) 16/12/1966 E
D01 London Division 17/06/1968 E
D02 Birmingham Division 01/1971 M
D01 London Division 07/1971 M

D7666 contd.
CD Cricklewood East 05/1973 M
Allocation recoded CD to CW 12/1973 M
Renumbered 25316 16/03/1974 E
LO Longsight 01/1984 M
Withdrawn 31/01/1984 E
Failed at Keighley on 27/01/84 and was withdrawn on 31/01/84. Stabled at York by 02/02/84, then moved to Toton by 02/04/84.
Reinstated 12/04/1984 E
LO Longsight 12/04/1984 E
CD Crewe Diesel 05/1985 M
KM Kingmoor New Yard 11/1985 M
Renumbered 25911 16/12/1985 E
Store 11/08/1986 E
Withdrawn 13/09/1986 E
Stored at Kingmoor New Yard. Moved to Upperby depot on 14/07/88 for inspection prior to movement south, then back to Kingmoor New Yard. Towed again to Upperby depot on 10/11/88 and moved to Crewe Basford Hall on 30/11/88, then Toton and onto Leicester stabling point on 15/12/88. Shunted into Vic Berry, Leicester on 20/12/88 where it was still intact on 19/02/89, noted partly cut up on 04/03/89 and was completely scrapped by 23/03/89.

D7667
D01 London Division (WCML) 07/01/1967 E
Carried a plaque on the non-driving cabside "D7667. This is the 1000th diesel locomotive to be built at Derby Locomotive Works".
D01 London Division 17/06/1968 E
D02 Birmingham Division 01/1971 M
D08 Liverpool Division 02/1973 M
SP Springs Branch 05/1973 M
Renumbered 25317 02/1974 M
CD Crewe Diesel 10/1982 M
Store 10/1982 M
Withdrawn 25/04/1983 E
Stored at Crewe Diesel. Moved to Toton 28/06/83, to Etches Park on 03/07/83 and into ZE Derby Works 28/07/83 where it remained until moved to ZL Swindon Works on 05/02/85 and was scrapped by 22/04/86.

D7668
D01 London Division (WCML) 21/01/1967 E
D01 London Division 17/06/1968 E
D02 Birmingham Division 01/1971 M
D08 Liverpool Division 07/1972 M
SP Springs Branch 05/1973 M
Renumbered 25318 08/03/1974 E

D7668 contd.
Withdrawn 25/07/1982 E
Stored at Toton 07/82. Moved in error to Bescot on 03/02/83, so moved on to Warrington 09/02/83, to Blackburn 18/02/83, then to Kingmoor New Yard 21/02/83. Finally moved to ZH Glasgow Works on 22/02/83. It remained there in deteriorating condition at Glasgow until sold to Vic Berry, Leicester in 01/87.
It was moved to Thornton Junction on 29/01/87 to be cut up on site, but that decision was changed and it was moved instead to Mossend Yard 03/06/87, to Carlisle Yard 04/06/87, to Basford Hall 05/06/87, to Humberstone Road, Leicester 08/06/87, and into Berry's Yard on 09/06/87 and was dismantled by 16/06/87, except for the cabs still there on 02/11/87.

D7669
D01 London Division (WCML) 04/03/1967 E
D01 London Division 17/06/1968 E
D02 Birmingham Division 01/1971 M
D08 Liverpool Division 07/1972 M
SP Springs Branch 05/1973 M
Renumbered 25319 05/03/1974 E
CD Crewe Diesel 10/1982 M
Withdrawn 20/03/1983 E
Moved to ZE Derby Works to be converted into an ETHEL but that was cancelled and 25305 converted instead. It remained there in decaying condition and was eventually moved to ZL Swindon Works on 21/02/85 for scrap and was cut up by 24/07/85.

D7670
D01 London Division (WCML) 28/01/1967 E
D16 Nottingham Division 03/1967 M
D02 Birmingham Division 04/1967 M
BS Bescot 05/1973 M
KM Kingmoor Diesel 05/1973 M
Renumbered 25320 20/03/1974 E
Allocation recoded KM to KD 01/1975 M
TO Toton 08/1977 M
LO Longsight 05/1981 M
Withdrawn 11/12/1983 E
Moved to ZE Derby Works by 22/10/83 and withdrawn while there. It remained for long-term storage, then was moved to ZL Swindon Works on 05/02/85 and broken up by 27/06/85.

D7671
D01 London Division (WCML) 04/02/1967 E
D16 Nottingham Division 03/1967 M

D7671 contd.
12B Upperby 07/1967 M
12A Kingmoor Diesel 02/1968 M
D10 Preston Division 17/06/1968 E
D08 Liverpool Division 05/1970 M
D02 Birmingham Division 07/1972 M
BS Bescot 05/1973 M
KM Kingmoor Diesel 05/1973 M
Renumbered 25321 14/05/1974 E
Allocation recoded KM to KD 01/1975 M
TO Toton 08/1977 M
CW Cricklewood East 11/1981 M
LO Longsight 01/1984 M
CD Crewe Diesel 05/1985 M
Withdrawn 29/09/1986 E
Stored at Etches Park 11/86. Moved to RTC, Derby 03/87 and sold for preservation to the City of Derby Museum and held supposedly in store at the RTC, but was frequently used for shunting at the RTC during 06/87 and was still there in 01/88.
For preservation
It was actually sold to the Derby Industrial Museum and was painted as D7671, but was to be kept in working order and was moved to the Midland Railway Centre, Butterley for safekeeping about 05/88. Reregistered 08/05/14 to allow movement by rail to galas on other heritage railways.
HQ Headquarters Pool 08/05/2014 E

D7672
D16 Nottingham Division 25/02/1967 E
12B Upperby 07/1967 M
12A Kingmoor Diesel 02/1968 M
D10 Preston Division 17/06/1968 E
D08 Liverpool Division 05/1970 M
D02 Birmingham Division 07/1972 M
BS Bescot 05/1973 M
KM Kingmoor Diesel 05/1973 M
Renumbered 25322 04/1974 M
Allocation recoded KM to KD 01/1975 M
CD Crewe Diesel 02/1976 M
SP Springs Branch 05/1978 M
KD Kingmoor Diesel 07/1978 M
Withdrawn 29/01/1984 E
Repainted 04/84, unofficially named *Tamworth Castle* and put on show at Tamworth from 12/05/84 to 20/05/84.
BS Bescot 17/05/1984 E
Reinstated 17/05/1984 E
CD Crewe Diesel 09/1985 M
KM Kingmoor New Yard 11/1985 M
Renumbered 25912 20/11/1985 E

D7672 contd.

Withdrawn 23/03/1987 E

Moved to Bescot 15/04/87 and on to Toton the same day, to Tinsley on 28/04/87 and on to Holbeck on 06/05/87 still painted as 25912. Allocated ADB 968027 for use as a training locomotive at Holbeck TMD, where it was noted numberless on 23/07/88 and had apparently not been used for training for many months. The departmental number was never applied to the loco. Repainted as D7672 by 26/03/89.

It was officially named *Tamworth Castle* at Leeds Holbeck Depot on 24/04/89.

Hauled legs of several rail tours in 1990 before being officially reinstated.

HQ Headquarters Pool 09/1990 M

Reinstated 09/1990 M

Store 09/1990 M

Officially reinstated in 09/90 but remained 'stored'.

HQ Headquarters Pool 23/11/1990 E

Returned to service 23/11/1990 E

Re-entered revenue stock on 23/11/90 which was the first time an extinct class had been 'revived' on TOPS.

Sold to the North Staffordshire Railway for preservation. Moved under its own power to MC Metal Processing, Glasgow 29/04/91 for asbestos removal. Upon completion, it arrived at the North Staffordshire Railway on 18/05/91 for further use whilst still in capital stock.

Withdrawn 26/09/1991 E

For preservation

Remained at the North Staffordshire Railway, which was later rebranded as the Churnet Valley Railway.

D7673

D16 Nottingham Division 18/03/1967 E

12B Upperby 07/1967 M

12A Kingmoor Diesel 02/1968 M

D10 Preston Division 17/06/1968 E

D08 Liverpool Division 05/1970 M

SP Springs Branch 05/1973 M

Renumbered 25323 13/11/1973 E

CD Crewe Diesel 01/1976 M

SP Springs Branch 08/1981 M

CD Crewe Diesel 10/1982 M

Received accident damage at Fazakerley Yard, Liverpool about 15/02/86 and was moved to Allerton depot on 19/02/86, repaired and returned to service.

D7673 contd.

Withdrawn 09/03/1987 E

Stored at Basford Hall Yard. Sent to Humberstone Road, Leicester on 03/07/87 and into Vic Berry, Leicester on 06/07/87, where it was placed on the 'pyramid' by 10/87, but was taken off by 20/10/87, noted being cut up 23/10/87 and the job was completed by 13/11/87.

D7674

D16 Nottingham Division 11/03/1967 E

12B Upperby 07/1967 M

12A Kingmoor Diesel 02/1968 M

9A Longsight 05/1968 M

D09 Manchester Division 17/06/1968 E

D08 Liverpool Division 01/1971 M

D01 London Division 03/1972 M

WN Willesden 05/1973 M

Renumbered 25324 04/1974 M

CW Cricklewood East 06/1975 M

LO Longsight 01/1984 M

CD Crewe Diesel 05/1985 M

Withdrawn 24/12/1985 E

Stored at Willesden, then moved to Crewe Diesel about 03/86 and to Gresty Lane by 03/87, both for further storage. Moved to Humberstone Road, Leicester on 15/07/87, into Vic Berry, Leicester on 20/07/87 and put in the 'pyramid' by 10/87. Taken off about 07/10/87, noted being scrapped on 10/10/87, and completed by 17/10/87.

D7675

D16 Nottingham Division 08/04/1967 E

12B Upperby 07/1967 M

12A Kingmoor Diesel 02/1968 M

9A Longsight 05/1968 M

D09 Manchester Division 17/06/1968 E

D08 Liverpool Division 11/1970 M

84A Laira 10/1971 M

86A Cardiff (Canton) 05/1972 M

84A Laira 12/1972 M

Allocation recoded 84A to LA 05/1973 M

Renumbered 25325 13/02/1974 E

CW Cricklewood East 05/1974 M

BS Bescot 10/1974 M

CD Crewe Diesel 09/1985 M

Withdrawn 24/12/1985 E

Stored at Kingmoor Diesel until moved to Upperby depot on 09/08/88 for inspection prior to movement south, then to Kingmoor Yard. Again moved to Upperby depot on 10/11/88, then to Mossend Yard on 25/11/88 and into BRML Glasgow Works the same day

D7675 contd.

or component recovery. It remained there until 10/89 when it was moved next door to MC Metal Processing and small amounts of cutting took place in 11/89, but otherwise remained intact until scrapped completely on 06/02/90.

D7676

D16 Nottingham Division 22/04/1967 E
12B Upperby 07/1967 M
12A Kingmoor Diesel 02/1968 M
9A Longsight 05/1968 M
D09 Manchester Division 17/06/1968 E
D08 Liverpool Division 11/1970 M
84A Laira 10/1971 M
82A Bristol Bath Road 01/1972 M
86A Cardiff (Canton) 05/1972 M
84A Laira 12/1972 M
Allocation recoded 84A to LA 05/1973 M
Renumbered 25326 04/02/1974 E
CD Crewe Diesel 08/1975 M
SP Springs Branch 05/1978 M
CW Cricklewood East 07/1978 M
CD Crewe Diesel 07/1983 M
Withdrawn 23/01/1985 E
Moved from Cricklewood to Acton Yard on 03/05/85, to Swindon 14/05/85 and into ZL Swindon Works 15/05/85 and dismantled by 26/02/86.

D7677

D16 Nottingham Division 29/04/1967 E
12B Upperby 07/1967 M
12A Kingmoor Diesel 02/1968 M
9A Longsight 05/1968 M
D09 Manchester Division 17/06/1968 E
D08 Liverpool Division 11/1970 M
86B Ebbw Junction 07/1971 M
84A Laira 10/1971 M
82A Bristol Bath Road 01/1972 M
86A Cardiff (Canton) 05/1972 M
84A Laira 12/1972 M
Allocation recoded 84A to LA 05/1973 M
Renumbered 25327 05/1974 M
CD Crewe Diesel 08/1975 M
BS Bescot 05/1978 M
Withdrawn 02/02/1984 E
Stored at Crewe Diesel. Moved to ZL Swindon Works on 02/04/85 and was to be scrapped, but because of the impending closure of the works it was sold to Vic Berry, Leicester 05/87. Departed for Swindon Cocklebury Yard 03/06/87, to Humberstone Road, Leicester 04/06/87, into Berry's Yard on 05/06/87, and put into the 'pyramid' by 08/87. It was still intact on 15/02/88 but had been broken up by 04/03/88, except for the cabs that were still extant on 06/05/90, but were disposed of by the end of the month.

Being saved for preservation does not always mean that a loco will be restored and kept in running order. The former D7672 at some point lost its green livery of the 1990s in favour of this unique version of BR blue but looks as though it had not been active for sometime when photographed at the Churnet Valley Railway in March 2024. *(Paul Chancellor/Colour-Rail.com*

CLASS 26

The Birmingham Railway Carriage & Wagon Co. (BRCW) were amongst the builders selected to supply a Type 2 design to BR under the Modernisation plan with D5300-19 being the trial batch of locos. These were fitted with a Sulzer 1,160 hp 6LDA28A diesel engine, being the same as the Class 24s, but they had Crompton Parkinson C17 traction motors and all were built in Birmingham. Before any evaluation could be carried out a further batch, D5320-46, were ordered and all were delivered in 1958-59. All of the first twenty were new to the Eastern Region at Hornsey whilst D5320-46 were received by the Scottish Region going new to Haymarket before rapidly moving north to their long term home of Inverness. Following the delivery of more Brush Type 2s to the Eastern Region, D5300-19 migrated north of the border in 1960 having been used mainly on commuter trains and empty stock movements whilst in the south. Haymarket, Eastfield and Inverness became the permanent home for the class where they provided the main motive power in the Highlands alongside the Class 27s whilst those allocated in the Central Belt of Scotland tended to cover freight duties and indeed the first seven were fitted with slow speed control apparatus for working MGR services to power stations. Of the various Type 2 classes the Class 26s outlived all but the Class 31s having been refurbished in the mid-1980s. Whilst the first normal service condemnations occurred back in 1977 it was to be 1993 before the final class members came out of traffic, completing around 35 years in service. Most were cut up in Scotland.

Renumbering into the TOPS series was reasonably straight forward with locos getting 26xxx numbers relating directly to the pre-TOPS number except for D5300 which became 26007, D5307 - 26020 and D5320 - 26028 as D5328 had already been condemned. The Class 26s had the greatest array of liveries of all the Type 2s except the Class 31s. Initially, they all carried BR green with cream window surrounds and a cream band all around the loco running just below the cab windows. Yellow panels were added later but the Scottish Region appeared reluctant to change those to full yellow ends with very few examples seen. Rail Blue with full yellow ends followed, soon modified to wrap around the cab windows and the top of the side doors. Some locomotives were later painted in large logo grey, Coal sector livery and engineers' livery whilst two reverted to green with yellow ends.

With many locomotives having been refurbished and being relatively later withdrawals, a disproportionate number compared to the class size were preserved with thirteen recorded as passing to the heritage sector.

For much of their lives the liveries applied to the Class 26s and 27s followed the same path with the delivery colour scheme being BR green with cream window surrounds and a cream band half way up the bodyside which went all around the locomotive. When less than a year old, Class 26 D5300 is at Kings Cross in that livery. *(Colour-Rail.com*

D5300
34B Hornsey 30/07/1958 E
64B Haymarket 13/04/1960 E
Allocation recoded 64B to HA 05/1973 M
Renumbered 26007 04/1974 M
ED Eastfield 05/1988 M
IS Inverness 08/1992 M
Store 02/10/1993 E
Stored at Inverness 02/10/93.
Withdrawn 04/10/1993 E
Sold to MC Metal Processing, Glasgow for preservation 05/95, moved there from Inverness on 02/08/95 for asbestos removal.

For preservation

Stored at MC Metal Processing as D5300 until sold to a private individual from the Manchester area about 05/97. It was moved to Barrow Hill Roundhouse Museum on 12/05/99. Reregistered on 07/05/09 to allow it to be moved to galas by rail.
HQ Headquarters Pool 07/05/2009 E

D5301
34B Hornsey 12/09/1958 E
64B Haymarket 04/1960 M
Allocation recoded 64B to HA 05/1973 M
Renumbered 26001 04/1974 M
ED Eastfield 05/1988 M
Store 08/1990 M
Suffered bad fire damage 08/90, was moved to Eastfield for store, moved to ZH Glasgow Works c.17/09/90 where it was repaired and returned to service c.03/91.
ED Eastfield 03/1991 M
Returned to service 03/1991 M
It was named *Eastfield* at Eastfield TMD on 26/07/91.
IS Inverness 08/1992 M
Store 02/10/1993 E
Stored at Inverness 02/10/93.
Withdrawn 04/10/1993 E

For preservation

Originally sold to Pete Waterman in 1994. Sale to him was cancelled and sold to MC Metal Processing, Glasgow 05/95 for preservation. Moved from Inverness arriving at MC Metals 02/08/95 for asbestos removal and storage.
Moved to the Bo'ness & Kinneil Railway as D5301 but only for its gala in 08/96. Then moved to the Lakeside & Haverthwaite Railway on 29/08/96 on permanent loan.

D5301 contd.
Moved from the Lakeside & Haverthwaite Railway to the Caledonian Railway, Brechin in 05/08, and to remain there.

D5302
34B Hornsey 02/10/1958 E
64B Haymarket 04/1960 M
Allocation recoded 64B to HA 05/1973 M
Renumbered 26002 04/1974 M
ED Eastfield 05/1988 M
Store 18/10/1991 E
Involved in a collision at Barassie permanent way depot on 18/10/91 and severely damaged, towed to Eastfield on 22/10/91. taken away for repair, returned to Eastfield by 04/92.
ED Eastfield 04/1992 M
Returned to service 04/1992 M
IS Inverness 08/1992 M
Store 09/10/1992 E
Stored at Inverness 9/10/92
Withdrawn 04/1993 M

For preservation

Sold for preservation to the Strathspey Railway in 09/93, and moved from Inverness to MC Metal Processing, Glasgow 06/09/94 for asbestos removal, returned to the Strathspey Railway on 22/11/94. Sold on to a private owner and moved to a private site at Port Elphinstone sidings, near Inverurie 11/09/23.

D5303
34B Hornsey 17/10/1958 E
60A Inverness 10/1958 M
65A Eastfield 11/1958 M
64H Leith Central 11/1958 M
34B Hornsey 12/1958 M
64B Haymarket 04/1960 M
Allocation recoded 64B to HA 05/1973 M
Renumbered 26003 05/1974 M
Store 09/1987 M
Stored at Toton 09/87
HA Haymarket 05/10/1987 E
Returned to Service 05/10/1987 E
ED Eastfield 05/1988 M
IS Inverness 08/1992 M
Store 02/10/1993 E
Stored at Inverness 02/10/93
Withdrawn 04/10/1993 E
Arrived at MC Metal Processing, Glasgow for scrap on 17/01/95 and was cut up on 25/01/95.

D5304

34B Hornsey 31/10/1958 E
34G Finsbury Park 04/1960 M
64B Haymarket 04/1960 M
Allocation recoded 64B to HA 05/1973 M
Renumbered 26004 04/1974 M
Reported that it was going to be named *Spirit of Springburn* about 1987, but not proceeded with.
ED Eastfield 05/1988 M
Store 20/07/1990 E
Suffered fire damage in 07/90 and moved to BRML Glasgow Works by 20/07/90 for assessment, repaired by 02/91 and returned to Eastfield.
ED Eastfield 01/02/1991 E
Returned to service 01/02/1991 E
IS Inverness 08/1992 M
Store 24/11/1992 E
Stored at Inverness 24/11/92.
Withdrawn 04/1993 M

For preservation

Sold for preservation to the Bo'ness & Kinneil Railway in 09/93. Moved from Inverness to MC Metal Processing, Glasgow on 06/09/94 for asbestos removal. Upon completion it was moved by road to Bo'ness on 23/11/94, and is owned by the 6LDA Society. Reregistered as TOPS 89204 to allow movement by rail to galas, officially renumbered back to 26004 in 02/09.
BT Bo'ness 18/06/2009 E

For preservation

The locomotive was last used in 2001, and was up for sale in 12/13, sale confirmed 07/14, moved to Nemesis Rail, Burton-upon-Trent 08-10/11/14.

D5305

34B Hornsey 14/11/1958 E
34G Finsbury Park 04/1960 M
64B Haymarket 28/04/1960 E
Allocation recoded 64B to HA 05/1973 M
Renumbered 26005 04/1974 M
ED Eastfield 05/1988 M
IS Inverness 08/1992 M
Store 02/10/1993 E
Stored at Inverness 02/10/93.
Withdrawn 04/10/1993 E
Moved to MC Metal Processing, Glasgow for scrap and arrived 17/01/95, with cutting up taking place on 13/02/95.

D5306

34B Hornsey 28/11/1958 E
34G Finsbury Park 04/1960 M
64B Haymarket 18/05/1960 E
Allocation recoded 64B to HA 05/1973 M
Renumbered 26006 12/1973 M
ED Eastfield 05/1988 M
Store 29/07/1991 E
ED Eastfield 08/1991 M
Returned to Service 02/08/1991 E
Store 05/08/1991 E
ED Eastfield 06/08/1991 E
Returned to Service 06/08/1991 E
Store 13/08/1991 E
ED Eastfield 16/08/1991 E
Returned to Service 16/08/1991 E
Store 26/08/1991 E
ED Eastfield 30/08/1991 E
Returned to Service 30/08/1991 E
Store 29/09/1991 E
ED Eastfield 06/09/1991 E
Returned to Service 06/09/1991 E
Store 10/09/1991 E
ED Eastfield 14/09/1991 E
Returned to Service 14/09/1991 E
Store 16/09/1991 E
ED Eastfield 20/09/1991 E
Returned to Service 20/09/1991 E
Store 23/09/1991 E
ED Eastfield 27/09/1991 E
Returned to Service 27/09/1991 E
Store 30/03/1991 E
ED Eastfield 01/10/1991 E
Returned to Service 01/10/1991 E
IS Inverness 08/1992 M
Store 05/06/1993 E
Stored at Inverness 05/06/93
Withdrawn 06/09/1993 E
Moved to MC Metal Processing, Glasgow on 03/04/95 and was broken up on 08/06/95.

D5307

34B Hornsey 05/12/1958 E
34G Finsbury Park 04/1960 M
64B Haymarket 05/1960 M
Allocation recoded 64B to HA 05/1973 M
Renumbered 26020 04/1974 M
IS Inverness 11/1975 M
Store 12/1976 M
Stored at Inverness Goods Yard 12/76.
Withdrawn 04/02/1977 E
Moved to ZH Glasgow Works by 06/08/77 and scrapped by 03/78.

Around the time of the introduction of TOPS numbering a livery variation appeared that would be applied across both Class 26 and 27 in due course, this being the extension of the yellow front to the cabside and windows and across the top half of the cab door along with the loco number being moved to the bodyside as seen on 26003 at Eastfield in October 1982.

(J. D. Jones/Colour-Rail.com

D5308

34B Hornsey 12/12/1958 E
34G Finsbury Park 04/1960 M
64B Haymarket 05/1960 M
Allocation recoded 64B to HA 05/1973 M
Renumbered 26008 04/1974 M
IS Inverness 10/1975 M
HA Haymarket 10/1978 M
IS Inverness 01/1985 M
HA Haymarket 03/1985 M
ED Eastfield 05/1987 M
IS Inverness 08/1992 M
Collided with a diesel rail crane at Kinclare viaduct, between Ayr and Girvan, on 25/02/93 and was extensively damaged.
Store 12/03/1993 E
Withdrawn 04/1993 M
Sold for scrap to MC Metal Processing, Glasgow in 09/93 and arrived there on 10/01/94, with scrapping taking place on 13/07/94.

D5309

34B Hornsey 19/12/1958 E
34G Finsbury Park 04/1960 M
64B Haymarket 05/1960 M

D5309 contd.

Allocation recoded 64B to HA 05/1973 M
Renumbered 26009 04/1974 M
IS Inverness 11/1975 M
Store 17/01/1977 E
Stored at Inverness 17/01/77.
Withdrawn 27/01/1977 E
Moved to ZH Glasgow Works by 31/05/77 and cut up by 25/03/78 except for the cabs which were still there 06/84 and disposed of later.

D5310

34B Hornsey 06/01/1959 E
34G Finsbury Park 04/1960 M
64B Haymarket 05/1960 M
Allocation recoded 64B to HA 05/1973 M
Renumbered 26010 04/1974 M
IS Inverness 11/1975 M
HA Haymarket 10/1978 M
ED Eastfield 05/1987 M
Store 05/10/1987 E
Stored at Toton 5/10/87, moved to moved to ZC Crewe Works on 14/10/87
ED Eastfield 11/1987 M
Returned to Service 08/11/1987 E

D5310 contd.
Store 01/10/1991 E
ED Eastfield 04/10/1991 E
Returned to Service 04/10/1991 E
Store 09/10/1991 E
ED Eastfield 12/10/1991 E
Returned to Service 12/10/1991 E
Store 14/10/1991 E
ED Eastfield 18/10/1991 E
Returned to Service 18/10/1991 E
Store 21/10/1991 E
ED Eastfield 21/10/1991 E
Returned to Service 21/10/1991 E
Store 26/10/1991 E
ED Eastfield 28/10/1991 E
Returned to Service 28/10/1991 E
Store 16/11/1991 E
ED Eastfield 18/11/1991 E
Returned to Service 18/11/1991 E
Store 23/11/1991 E
ED Eastfield 25/11/1991 E
Returned to Service 25/11/1991 E
Store 29/11/1991 E
ED Eastfield 02/12/1991 E
Returned to Service 02/12/1991 E
Store 07/12/1991 E
ED Eastfield 09/12/1991 E
Returned to Service 09/12/1991 E
Store 16/12/1991 E
ED Eastfield 21/12/1991 E
Returned to Service 21/12/1991 E
Store 23/12/1991 E
ED Eastfield 11/01/1992 E
Returned to Service 11/01/1992 E
Store 13/01/1992 E
ED Eastfield 17/01/1992 E
Returned to Service 17/01/1992 E
Store 20/01/1992 E
ED Eastfield 25/01/1992 E
Returned to Service 25/01/1992 E
IS Inverness 08/1992 M
Store 04/12/1992 E
Stored at Inverness 04/12/92.
Withdrawn 04/1993 M

For preservation

Sold for preservation to Peak Rail 09/93 and arrived at MC Metal Processing, Glasgow for asbestos removal on 06/09/94. However, upon completion, it did not leave until 24/01/95 and instead of Peak Rail, it moved to the Northampton & Lamport Railway for further use.

D5310 contd.

Sold to the Waverley Route Heritage Association by the Northampton & Lamport Railway, and to eventually move to Whitrope summit as its new base. However, it was first moved by road to Quorn, Great Central Railway on 27/01/06 for extensive repairs and repainting. Removed from Rothley Carriage Works on 28/11/06 and moved by rail to Quorn & Woodhouse, then by road to the Bo'ness & Kinneil Railway on 29/11/06. Moved by road from Bo'ness to the Llangollen Railway on 09/09/09. Re-registered 13/06/07 to allow movement by rail to galas.

HQ Headquarters Pool 13/06/2007 E
BT Bo'ness 09/01/2009 E

D5311

34B Hornsey 09/01/1959 E
34G Finsbury Park 04/1960 M
64B Haymarket 27/09/1960 E
Allocation recoded 64B to HA 05/1973 M
Renumbered 26011 04/1974 M
IS Inverness 10/1975 M
HA Haymarket 10/1978 M
ED Eastfield 05/1987 M
IS Inverness 08/1992 M
Store 24/11/1992 E
Stored at Inverness 24/11/92.
Withdrawn 04/1993 M

For preservation

Sold for preservation to Peak Rail 09/93. Moved from Inverness to MC Metal Processing, Glasgow for asbestos removal arriving on 16/09/94. Departed on 24/11/94 for Peak Rail. Moved to the Battlefield Line, Shackerstone on 24/04/96, then moved to Barrow Hill Roundhouse Museum on 01/07/99. Moved to Nemesis Rail, Burton-upon-Trent 25/08/11.

D5312

34B Hornsey 16/01/1959 E
34G Finsbury Park 04/1960 M
64B Haymarket 25/05/1960 E
Store 07/1971 M
Stored at ZH Glasgow Works 07/71.
64B Haymarket 09/1972 M
Returned to Service 09/1972 M
Allocation recoded 64B to HA 05/1973 M
Renumbered 26012 12/1973 M
IS Inverness 11/1975 M
HA Haymarket 10/1978 M

D5312 contd.

Moved to ZH Glasgow Works 28/11/81.
Withdrawn 31/01/1982 E
It was cut up at ZH Glasgow Works between 3rd and 12th August 1982.

D5313

34B Hornsey 23/01/1959 E
34G Finsbury Park 04/1960 M
64B Haymarket 25/05/1960 E
Allocation recoded 64B to HA 05/1973 M
Renumbered 26013 04/1974 M
IS Inverness 11/1975 M
Store 31/07/1979 E
Stored at Polmadie 31/07/79, then at ZC Crewe Works from 18/04/80. Reallocated to Haymarket 10/80 but remained at Crewe Works, moved to ZH Glasgow Works 15/01/81, and later returned to service.
HA Haymarket 10/1980 M
Store 10/1980 M
HA Haymarket 1981 Y
Returned to Service 1981 Y
Store 06/09/1982 E
Stored at Dundee 06/09/82, moved to Dunfermline Townhill by 15/08/83 and on to Thornton Junction in 12/84, both for further storage.
Withdrawn 18/03/1985 E
Moved to ZH Glasgow Works about 04/08/86 and was held there until returned to Thornton Junction on 04/04/87, having been sold to Vic Berry, Leicester 12/86 for scrapping on site. However, this decision was rescinded and the locomotive was got ready for movement south. Hauled to Mossend Yard 03/06/87, to Carlisle Yard 04/06/87, to Crewe Basford Hall Yard 05/06/87 and then to Leicester Humberstone Road Yard 08/06/87 and into Berry's yard next day. It was noted being scrapped on 16/06/87 and was completed by 08/07/87, except the cabs, still there on 02/11/87.

D5314

34B Hornsey 30/01/1959 E
34G Finsbury Park 04/1960 M
64B Haymarket 06/1960 M
Allocation recoded 64B to HA 05/1973 M
Renumbered 26014 04/1974 M
IS Inverness 11/1975 M
HA Haymarket 10/1980 M
Store 06/09/1982 E
Stored at Dundee 06/09/82, then moved to

D5314 contd.

Dunfermline Townhill by 15/08/83 for further storage.
HA Haymarket 09/06/1984 E
Returned to Service 09/06/1984 E
ED Eastfield 05/1987 M
Store 05/10/1987 E
Stored at Toton 5/10/87, then moved to ZH Glasgow Works 14/10/87.
ED Eastfield 06/11/1987 E
Returned to Service 06/11/1987 E
Store 01/10/1991 E
ED Eastfield 05/10/1991 E
Returned to Service 05/10/1991 E
Store 08/10/1991 E
ED Eastfield 12/10/1991 E
Returned to Service 12/10/1991 E
Store 14/10/1991 E
ED Eastfield 18/10/1991 E
Returned to Service 18/10/1991 E
Store 21/10/1991 E
ED Eastfield 26/10/1991 E
Returned to Service 26/10/1991 E
Store 28/10/1991 E
ED Eastfield 16/11/1991 E
Returned to Service 16/11/1991 E
Store 18/10/1991 E
ED Eastfield 22/11/1991 E
Returned to Service 22/11/1991 E
Store 25/10/1991 E
ED Eastfield 29/11/1991 E
Returned to Service 29/11/1991 E
Store 05/12/1991 E
ED Eastfield 11/12/1991 E
Returned to Service 11/12/1991 E
Store 16/12/1991 E
ED Eastfield 23/12/1991 E
Returned to Service 23/12/1991 E
Store 30/12/1991 E
ED Eastfield 11/01/1992 E
Returned to Service 11/01/1992 E
Store 13/01/1992 E
ED Eastfield 14/01/1992 E
Returned to Service 14/01/1992 E
Store 20/01/1992 E
ED Eastfield 24/01/1992 E
Returned to Service 24/01/1992 E
IS Inverness 08/1992 M
Store 09/10/1992 E
Stored at Perth 9/10/92
Withdrawn 04/1993 M
For preservation

D5314 contd.

Sold for preservation for use on the Caledonian Railway, Brechin in 09/93. Remained stored until moved to MC Metal Processing, Glasgow on 04/10/94 for asbestos removal; upon completion it arrived at Brechin on 29/11/94 for further use.

D5315

34B Hornsey 13/02/1959 E
34G Finsbury Park 04/1960 M
64B Haymarket 06/1960 M
Allocation recoded 64B to HA 05/1973 M
Renumbered 26015 04/1974 M
IS Inverness 10/1975 M
Store 06/1981 M
Stored at Millerhill 06/81.
HA Haymarket 05/1982 M
Returned to Service 05/1982 M
ED Eastfield 05/1987 M
Withdrawn 23/06/1991 E
Stored at Eastfield until moved to Perth in 07/92, then noted being hauled through Pitlochry on 17/08/92, possibly en route to Inverness for further storage. Sold for scrap 09/93 to MC Metal Processing, Glasgow where it arrived on 31/01/94 and was broken up on 31/08/94.

D5316

34B Hornsey 20/02/1959 E
34G Finsbury Park 04/1960 M
64B Haymarket 20/06/1960 E
60A Inverness 07/1967 M
64B Haymarket 01/1968 M
Allocation recoded 64B to HA 05/1973 M
Renumbered 26016 09/1974 M
Withdrawn 05/10/1975 E
Stored at Inverness 05/10/75. Moved to ZH Glasgow Works 06/03/76 and was being dismantled on 25/09/76, with only the frame and cabs left by 11/76. The frame was cut up in 11/76, but the cabs still remained until finally scrapped in 12/88.

D5317

34B Hornsey 27/02/1959 E
34G Finsbury Park 04/1960 M
64B Haymarket 20/06/1960 E
60A Inverness 07/1967 M
64B Haymarket 01/1968 M
Allocation recoded 64B to HA 05/1973 M
Renumbered 26017 11/1973 M
IS Inverness 11/1975 M
Store 16/08/1977 E
Stored at Inverness 16/08/77.
Withdrawn 29/08/1977 E

The mid-1980s saw a change in BR livery policy which resulted in some Class 26s being out shopped in large logo grey with wrap around yellow ends with a few such as 26035 which also gained the 'Scottie Dog' bodyside symbol. *(Geoff Dunster/RCTS Photo Archive*

D5317 contd.
Moved to ZH Glasgow Works 09/77 and broken up by 18/02/78, except the cabs which were cut up in 01/79.

D5318
34B Hornsey 06/03/1959 E
34G Finsbury Park 04/1960 M
64B Haymarket 21/09/1960 E
60A Inverness 04/1962 M
64B Haymarket 10/1965 M
60A Inverness 12/1966 M
64B Haymarket 04/1967 M
60A Inverness 07/1967 M
64B Haymarket 01/1968 M
60A Inverness 10/1968 M
64B Haymarket 11/1968 M
Allocation recoded 64B to HA 05/1973 M
Renumbered 26018 01/1974 M
IS Inverness 11/1975 M
HA Haymarket 10/1980 M
Store 23/11/1981 E
Caught fire while working a Dundee train in 11/81, moved to ZH Glasgow Works by 23/11/81.
Withdrawn 31/01/1982 E
Broken up at ZH Glasgow Works by 20/05/82, with the cabs cut about 09/82.

D5319
34B Hornsey 13/03/1959 E
34G Finsbury Park 04/1960 M
64B Haymarket 21/09/1960 E
60A Inverness 04/1962 M
64B Haymarket 10/1965 M
60A Inverness 12/1966 M
64B Haymarket 04/1967 M
60A Inverness 07/1967 M
64B Haymarket 11/1968 M
Allocation recoded 64B to HA 05/1973 M
Renumbered 26019 04/1974 M
IS Inverness 10/1975 M
HA Haymarket 11/1980 M
Store 07/02/1983 E
Stored at Haymarket 07/02/83.
Withdrawn 18/03/1985 E
It moved to Craigentinny by 06/85, then to Millerhill 07/85 and sold to Vic Berry, Leicester 12/86. It was moved from Millerhill to Thornton Junction 08/04/87 to be scrapped on site, and was broken up there by staff from Berrys on 13/06/87. The cabs were taken to Leicester and were still in Berry's yard on 02/11/87.

D5320
64H Leith Central 10/04/1959 E
Allocated new to Leith Central until the new diesel depot at Haymarket was ready.
64B Haymarket 05/1959 M
60A Inverness 06/1960 M
64B Haymarket 01/1969 M
Allocation recoded 64B to HA 05/1973 M
Renumbered 26028 04/1974 M
IS Inverness 11/1975 M
HA Haymarket 05/1982 M
Store 10/06/1982 E
Stored at Dundee 10/06/82, moved to Perth 17/06/82 and on to ZH Glasgow Works 24/06/82 for further storage.
HA Haymarket 06/06/1983 E
Returned to Service 06/06/1983 E
ED Eastfield 05/1987 M
Store 02/10/1991 E
Stored at Eastfield 02/10/91.
Withdrawn 02/1992 M
Moved to MC Metal Processing, Glasgow on 22/09/92 and was dismantled on 05/11/92.

D5321
64H Leith Central 17/04/1959 E
Allocated new to Leith Central until the new diesel depot at Haymarket was ready.
64B Haymarket 04/1959 M
60A Inverness 06/1960 M
64B Haymarket 05/1969 M
Allocation recoded 64B to HA 05/1973 M
Renumbered 26021 09/1974 M
IS Inverness 10/1975 M
HA Haymarket 11/1982 M
ED Eastfield 05/1987 M
Store 01/10/1991 E
Stored at Eastfield 01/10/91, then moved to Perth 07/92 for further storage.
Withdrawn 07/1993 M
Sold to MC Metal Processing, Glasgow 09/93 for scrap. Moved there from Perth 27-31/01/94 with cutting up taking place on 31/08/94.

D5322
64H Leith Central 24/04/1959 E
Allocated new to Leith Central until the new diesel depot at Haymarket was ready.
64B Haymarket 04/1959 M
60A Inverness 06/1960 M
64B Haymarket 05/1969 M
Allocation recoded 64B to HA 05/1973 M
Renumbered 26022 03/1974 M

Seemingly confined to the first ten Class 26s was the application of Coal Sector livery as seen here on 26003 at Markinch in June 1989. *(Colour-Rail.com*

D5322 contd.
IS Inverness 10/1975 M
Store 07/01/1981 E
Stored with collision damage and moved to ZH Glasgow Works 07/01/81.
Withdrawn 02/02/1981 E
Dismantled at ZH Glasgow Works by 14/01/82.

D5323
64B Haymarket 01/05/1959 E
60A Inverness 06/1960 M
64B Haymarket 04/1969 M
Allocation recoded 64B to HA 05/1973 M
Renumbered 26023 02/1974 M
IS Inverness 10/1975 M
HA Haymarket 10/1981 M
ED Eastfield 05/1987 M
Withdrawn 21/09/1990 E
Moved to BRML Glasgow Works in 10/90 and during 01/91 was moved next door to MC Metal Processing and very quickly broken up, being completed on 29/01/91.

D5324
64B Haymarket 08/05/1959 E
60A Inverness 06/1960 M
64B Haymarket 05/1969 M
Allocation recoded 64B to HA 05/1973 M
Renumbered 26024 04/1974 M

D5324 contd.
IS Inverness 10/1975 M
HA Haymarket 12/1984 M
IS Inverness 05/1985 M
HA Haymarket 09/1985 M
ED Eastfield 05/1987 M
Store 08/10/1991 E
ED Eastfield 12/10/1991 E
Returned to Service 12/10/1991 E
Store 14/10/1991 E
ED Eastfield 18/10/1991 E
Returned to Service 18/10/1991 E
Store 21/10/1991 E
ED Eastfield 26/10/1991 E
Returned to Service 26/10/1991 E
Store 28/10/1991 E
ED Eastfield 16/11/1991 E
Returned to Service 16/11/1991 E
Store 18/11/1991 E
ED Eastfield 22/11/1991 E
Returned to Service 22/11/1991 E
Store 25/11/1991 E
ED Eastfield 29/11/1991 E
Returned to Service 29/11/1991 E
Store 09/12/1991 E
ED Eastfield 14/12/1991 E
Returned to Service 14/12/1991 E
Store 16/12/1991 E

D5324 contd.
ED Eastfield 21/12/1991 E
Returned to Service 21/12/1991 E
Store 23/12/1991 E
ED Eastfield 11/01/1992 E
Returned to Service 11/01/1992 E
Store 13/01/1992 E
ED Eastfield 14/01/1992 E
Returned to Service 14/01/1992 E
Store 15/01/1992 E
ED Eastfield 17/01/1992 E
Returned to Service 17/01/1992 E
Store 20/01/1992 E
ED Eastfield 24/01/1992 E
Returned to Service 24/01/1992 E
IS Inverness 08/1992 M
Store 09/10/1992 E
Stored at Inverness 09/10/92
Withdrawn 04/1993 M

For preservation

Sold for preservation to the Bo'ness & Kinneil Railway 09/93. Arrived at MC Metal Processing, Glasgow for asbestos removal on 16/09/94 and upon completion went to Bo'ness, where it arrived on 30/11/94 for further use. Moved by road to the East

D5324 contd.

Lancashire Railway 02-04/06/06, returned to the Bo'ness & Kinneil Railway 05/12/07. Reregistered 09/01/09 to allow the locomotive to be moved to galas by rail.
BT Bo'ness 09/01/2009 E

D5325

64B Haymarket 14/05/1959 E
60A Inverness 06/1960 M
64B Haymarket 05/1969 M
Allocation recoded 64B to HA 05/1973 M
Renumbered 26025 04/1974 M
IS Inverness 10/1975 M
HA Haymarket 10/1981 M
IS Inverness 05/1985 M
HA Haymarket 05/1986 M
ED Eastfield 05/1987 M
Store 21/09/1987 E
Stored at Tinsley 21/09/87, moved to ZC Crewe Works 04/11/87.
ED Eastfield 13/11/1987 E
Returned to Service 13/11/1987 E
Store 29/07/1991 E
ED Eastfield 02/08/1991 E
Returned to Service 02/08/1991 E
Store 05/08/1991 E

The same batch of Class 26s later lost the sector livery in favour of the very drab, when dirty, Engineer's livery of grey with yellow on the top third of the bodyside. 26005 displays this style in March 1991 at Polmadie with the livery also appearing on some of the later class members.
(Colour-Rail.com

D5325 contd.
ED Eastfield 09/08/1991 E
Returned to Service 09/08/1991 E
Store 13/08/1991 E
ED Eastfield 16/08/1991 E
Returned to Service 16/08/1991 E
Store 19/08/1991 E
ED Eastfield 30/08/1991 E
Returned to Service 30/08/1991 E
Store 02/09/1991 E
ED Eastfield 06/06/1991 E
Returned to Service 06/09/1991 E
Store 09/09/1991 E
ED Eastfield 14/09/1991 E
Returned to Service 14/09/1991 E
Store 16/09/1991 E
ED Eastfield 20/09/1991 E
Returned to Service 20/09/1991 E
Store 23/09/1991 E
ED Eastfield 27/09/1991 E
Returned to Service 27/09/1991 E
Store 30/09/1991 E
ED Eastfield 01/10/1991 E
Returned to Service 01/10/1991 E
IS Inverness 08/1992 M
Store 26/04/1993 E
Withdrawn 04/10/1993 E
Moved to MC Metal Processing, Glasgow for scrap arriving there 24/01/95, but was used as yard shunter until 02/97.

For preservation

Sold for preservation to the Strathspey Railway. Asbestos was removed at MC Metal Processing, then it was moved to Aviemore, Strathspey Railway where it arrived by road on 26/03/97 for further use. Sold on to a private owner and moved to a private site at Port Elphinstone sidings, near Inverurie on 07/09/23.

D5326
64B Haymarket 22/05/1959 E
60A Inverness 11/1960 M
64B Haymarket 05/1969 M
Allocation recoded 64B to HA 05/1973 M
Renumbered 26026 02/1974 M
IS Inverness 10/1975 M
HA Haymarket 10/1981 M
IS Inverness 12/1984 M
HA Haymarket 05/1986 M
ED Eastfield 05/1987 M
IS Inverness 08/1992 M
Store 24/11/1992 E

D5326 contd.
Withdrawn 04/1993 M
Reported sold 09/93 to Pete Waterman for preservation at the Railway Age, Crewe, but the sale was cancelled, and the locomotive eventually arrived at MC Metal Processing, Glasgow 11/10/94 and was finally cut up 22/06/95.

D5327
64B Haymarket 05/06/1959 E
60A Inverness 05/1961 M
64B Haymarket 05/1969 M
Allocation recoded 64B to HA 05/1973 M
IS Inverness 05/1973 M
Renumbered 26027 07/1974 M
Store 14/11/1982 E
Stored at Inverness 14/11/82 , then moved to ZH Glasgow Works by 06/04/83 for further storage.
IS Inverness 06/1983 M
It was reallocated to Inverness in 06/83 but remained at Glasgow Works until working a test run from there on 11/10/83 when it suffered a main generator fire. It was returned to the works, was repaired, and on a test run, suffered a fire AGAIN and returned to the works where it was stored again 04/84.
Store 04/1984 M
HA Haymarket 10/1984 M
Returned to Service 10/1984 M
ED Eastfield 05/1987 M
Store 05/10/1987 E
Stored at Eastfield 05/10/87, then moved to ZC Crewe Works on 02/11/87 for further storage.
ED Eastfield 14/11/1987 E
Returned to Service 14/11/1987 E
Store 26/07/1991 E
Stored at Eastfield, then moved to Perth 07/92, and stabled at the back of the station.
Withdrawn 07/1993 M
Sold for preservation to the Bodmin & Wenford Railway, Cornwall 09/93, but the sale was cancelled and it remained at Perth until finally moved to MC Metal Processing, Glasgow where it arrived 24/01/95, with scrapping taking place on 29/01/95.

D5328
64B Haymarket 12/06/1959 E
60A Inverness 06/1960 M
Store 06/1968 M

D5328 contd.
Badly damaged in a freight derailment at Inverkeithing about 06/68 and stored.
64B Haymarket 05/1969 M
Store 05/1969 M
Reallocated to Haymarket but remained stored with accident damage, then moved to ZH Glasgow Works on 03/04/72.
Withdrawn 18/07/1972 E
Scrapped during 12/72 at ZH Glasgow Works.

D5329
64B Haymarket 12/06/1959 E
60A Inverness 11/1960 M
64B Haymarket 05/1969 M
65A Eastfield 05/1971 M
64B Haymarket 08/1971 M
60A Inverness 02/1973 M
Allocation recoded 60A to IS 05/1973 M
Renumbered 26029 07/1974 M
HA Haymarket 05/1982 M
ED Eastfield 05/1987 M
Involved in an accident at Grantshouse on 19/08/88 and fell onto its side. Rescued and taken to Haymarket 29/10/88, then to Eastfield about 04/11/88 for spares recovery.
Withdrawn 13/10/1988 E
Moved to BRML Glasgow Works and stored awaiting scrap. Moved next door to MC Metal Processing on 01/11/89 and was broken up during 11-12/89.

D5330
64B Haymarket 19/06/1959 E
34B Hornsey 07/1959 M
64H Leith Central 08/1959 M
64A St.Margarets 09/1959 M
Allocations to Leith Central and then St. Margarets unconfirmed, not shown in BR official returns. 09/1959 M
64B Haymarket 09/1959 M
60A Inverness 07/1960 M
Allocation recoded 60A to IS 05/1973 M
Renumbered 26030 07/1974 M
Store 12/07/1979 E
Stored at Polmadie 12/07/79
IS Inverness 04/1980 M
Returned to Service 10/1980 M
Store 10/1983 M
Stored at Polmadie 10/83, then moved to ZH Glasgow Works 02/85.
Withdrawn 18/03/1985 E
Sold to Vic Berry, Leicester in 12/86 and was

D5330 contd.
moved from ZH Glasgow Works to Thornton Junction on 28/01/87 for cutting up on site. Broken up by staff from Berry between 12-28/03/87, except the cabs that went to Berry's yard, and were noted there in 06/87.

D5331
64B Haymarket 26/06/1959 E
34B Hornsey 07/1959 M
64H Leith Central 08/1959 M
64A St.Margarets 09/1959 M
Allocations to Leith Central and then St. Margarets unconfirmed, not shown in BR official returns. 09/1959 M
64B Haymarket 09/1959 M
60A Inverness 07/1960 M
Allocation recoded 60A to IS 05/1973 M
Renumbered 26031 04/1974 M
HA Haymarket 05/1982 M
IS Inverness 12/1984 M
HA Haymarket 05/1986 M
ED Eastfield 05/1987 M
Withdrawn 04/10/1989 E
Moved to BRML Glasgow Works by 28/10/89 for component recovery and later scrapping. However, it remained until sold and was moved next door to MC Metal Processing in 07/90 and was cut up 06/09/90.

D5332
64B Haymarket 02/07/1959 E
34B Hornsey 07/1959 M
64B Haymarket 28/09/1959 E
60A Inverness 05/1961 M
Allocation recoded 60A to IS 05/1973 M
Renumbered 26032 04/1974 M
HA Haymarket 09/1986 M
ED Eastfield 05/1987 M
Store 29/07/1991 E
ED Eastfield 02/08/1991 E
Returned to Service 02/08/1991 E
Store 05/08/1991 E
ED Eastfield 09/08/1991 E
Returned to Service 09/08/1991 E
Store 12/08/1991 E
ED Eastfield 16/08/1991 E
Returned to Service 16/08/1991 E
Store 19/08/1991 E
ED Eastfield 30/08/1991 E
Returned to Service 30/08/1991 E
Store 02/09/1991 E
ED Eastfield 06/09/1991 E
Returned to Service 06/09/1991 E

D5332 contd.
Store 09/09/1991 E
ED Eastfield 14/09/1991 E
Returned to Service 14/09/1991 E
Store 16/09/1991 E
ED Eastfield 20/09/1991 E
Returned to Service 20/09/1991 E
Store 23/09/1991 E
ED Eastfield 27/09/1991 E
Returned to Service 27/09/1991 E
Store 30/09/1991 E
ED Eastfield 05/10/1991 E
Returned to Service 05/10/1991 E
Store 07/10/1991 E
ED Eastfield 09/10/1991 E
Returned to Service 09/10/1991 E
Store 14/10/1991 E
ED Eastfield 18/10/1991 E
Returned to Service 18/10/1991 E
Store 21/10/1991 E
ED Eastfield 26/10/1991 E
Returned to Service 26/10/1991 E
Store 28/10/1991 E
ED Eastfield 29/10/1991 E
Returned to Service 29/10/1991 E
Store 26/11/1991 E
ED Eastfield 27/11/1991 E
Returned to Service 27/11/1991 E
Store 05/12/1991 E
ED Eastfield 14/12/1991 E
Returned to Service 14/12/1991 E
Store 16/12/1991 E
ED Eastfield 21/12/1991 E
Returned to Service 21/12/1991 E
Store 23/12/1991 E
ED Eastfield 10/01/1992 E
Returned to Service 10/01/1992 E
Store 14/01/1992 E
ED Eastfield 17/01/1992 E
Returned to Service 17/01/1992 E
Store 20/01/1992 E
ED Eastfield 24/01/1992 E
Returned to Service 24/01/1992 E
IS Inverness 08/1992 M
Store 26/04/1993 E
IS Inverness 24/06/1993 E
Returned to Service 24/06/1993 E
Store 02/10/1993 E
Stored at Inverness 02/10/93.
Withdrawn 04/10/1993 E
Remained stored until it arrived at MC Metal Processing, Glasgow on 17/01/95 and was broken up 16/02/95.

D5333
64B Haymarket 10/07/1959 E
34B Hornsey 07/1959 M
64B Haymarket 28/09/1959 E
60A Inverness 06/1960 M
Allocation recoded 60A to IS 05/1973 M
Renumbered 26033 10/1973 M
HA Haymarket 05/1982 M
Store 17/10/1982 E
Stored at Polmadie 17/10/82, moved across the line to Shawfield Sidings by 27/11/83 for further storage but moved back to Polmadie by 20/10/84 and held awaiting scrapping. Moved to ZH Glasgow Works 02/85.
Withdrawn 18/03/1985 E
Sold to Vic Berry, Leicester 12/86 for scrap and was moved from ZH Glasgow Works to Thornton Junction on 28/01/87 for cutting up on site. Broken up by staff from Berry from 03-14/03/87, with the cabs going to Berry's yard and noted there in 06/87.

D5334
64B Haymarket 17/07/1959 E
34B Hornsey 07/1959 M
64H Leith Central 08/1959 M
64A St.Margarets 09/1959 M
Allocations to Leith Central and then St. Margarets unconfirmed, not shown in BR official returns. 09/1959 M
64B Haymarket 10/1959 M
60A Inverness 07/1960 M
Allocation recoded 60A to IS 05/1973 M
Renumbered 26034 07/1974 M
HA Haymarket 10/1985 M
ED Eastfield 05/1987 M
Sustained accident damage at Carlisle Kingmoor in 08/89.
Withdrawn 08/09/1989 E
Moved to Eastfield and noted being stripped on 17/09/89, remained there until shortly after 16/08/90 then sent to MC Metal Processing, Glasgow and was scrapped on 03/09/90.

D5335
64B Haymarket 24/07/1959 E
34B Hornsey 07/1959 M
64B Haymarket 10/1959 M
60A Inverness 06/1960 M
Allocation recoded 60A to IS 05/1973 M
Renumbered 26035 11/1973 M
Store 15/08/1983 E
Stored at Polmadie 15/08/83.

D5335 contd.
IS Inverness 10/1983 M
Returned to service 10/1983 M
HA Haymarket 09/1986 M
ED Eastfield 05/1987 M
IS Inverness 08/1992 M
Withdrawn 10/12/1992 E

For preservation

Stored at Inverness station yard until sold for preservation 09/93 for use at the South Yorkshire Railway Preservation Society, Meadowhall, Sheffield. Moved to MC Metal Processing, Glasgow for asbestos removal arriving there 07/09/94, and, upon completion, arrived at Meadowhall on 07/12/94. Sold to the Caledonian Railway, Brechin 10/95 and moved there in 01/96.

D5336
64B Haymarket 14/08/1959 E
60A Inverness 11/1960 M
Allocation recoded 60A to IS 05/1973 M
Renumbered 26036 10/1973 M
HA Haymarket 05/1982 M
IS Inverness 01/1984 M
HA Haymarket 01/1985 M
IS Inverness 05/1985 M
HA Haymarket 09/1986
ED Eastfield 05/1987 M

D5336 contd.
Store 03/10/1991 E
ED Eastfield 05/10/1991 E
Returned to Service 05/10/1991 E
Store 07/10/1991 E
ED Eastfield 09/10/1991 E
Returned to Service 09/10/1991 E
ED Eastfield 18/10/1991 E
Returned to Service 18/10/1991 E
Store 14/10/1991 E
ED Eastfield 26/10/1991 E
Returned to Service 26/10/1991 E
Store 28/10/1991 E
ED Eastfield 16/11/1991 E
Returned to Service 16/11/1991 E
Store 22/11/1991 E
ED Eastfield 23/11/1991 E
Returned to Service 23/11/1991 E
Store 25/11/1991 E
ED Eastfield 29/11/1991 E
Returned to Service 29/11/1991 E
Store 02/12/1991 E
ED Eastfield 07/12/1991 E
Returned to Service 07/12/1991 E
Store 16/12/1991 E
ED Eastfield 21/12/1991 E
Returned to Service 21/12/1991 E
Store 23/12/1991 E

D5325 was one of a number of Class 26s to be preserved in their native Scotland and was at Boat of Garten when carrying the original green livery on 3rd August 2001. It left the railway for a private site in 2023. *(Colour-Rail.com*

D5336 contd.
ED Eastfield 10/01/1992 E
Returned to service 10/01/1992 E
IS Inverness 08/1992 M
Store 26/04/1993 E
Stored at Inverness 26/04/93.
Withdrawn 04/10/1993 E
Moved to MC Metal Processing, Glasgow arriving on 24/01/95 and was dismantled on 19/02/95.

D5337
64B Haymarket 20/08/1959 E
60A Inverness 06/1960 M
Allocation recoded 60A to IS 05/1973 M
Renumbered 26037 09/1974 M
HA Haymarket 05/1982 M
IS Inverness 03/1985 M
HA Haymarket 10/1985 M
ED Eastfield 05/1987 M
Store 21/10/1991 E
ED Eastfield 26/10/1991 E
Returned to Service 26/10/1991 E
Store 28/10/1991 E
ED Eastfield 16/11/1991 E
Returned to Service 16/11/1991 E
Store 18/11/1991 E
ED Eastfield 22/11/1991 E
Returned to Service 22/11/1991 E
Store 25/11/1991 E
ED Eastfield 29/11/1991 E
Returned to Service 29/11/1991 E
Store 02/12/1991 E
ED Eastfield 07/12/1991 E
Returned to Service 07/12/1991 E
Store 10/12/1991 E
ED Eastfield 14/12/1991 E
Returned to Service 14/12/1991 E
Store 16/12/1991 E
ED Eastfield 21/12/1991 E
Returned to Service 21/12/1991 E
Store 23/12/1991 E
ED Eastfield 10/01/1992 E
Returned to Service 10/01/1992 E
Store 13/01/1992 E
ED Eastfield 17/01/1992 E
Returned to Service 17/01/1992 E
Store 20/01/1992 E
ED Eastfield 24/01/1992 E
Returned to Service 24/01/1992 E
IS Inverness 08/1992 M
Store 26/04/1993 E
Stored at Inverness 26/04/93.
Withdrawn 04/10/1993 E

D5337 contd.
Moved to MC Metal Processing, Glasgow arriving on 24/01/95 and was cut up on 08/02/95.

D5338
64B Haymarket 28/08/1959 E
60A Inverness 02/1960 M
Allocation recoded 60A to IS 05/1973 M
Renumbered 26038 07/1974 M
HA Haymarket 09/1986 M
ED Eastfield 05/1987 M
IS Inverness 08/1992 M
Store 19/10/1992 E
Failed due to a traction motor defect on 14/10/92, whilst working a Barassie-Glasgow train. Stored at Inverness 19/19/92.
Withdrawn 04/1993 M

For preservation

Sold for preservation 09/93 for use at the South Yorkshire Railway Preservation Society, Meadowhall, Sheffield. Moved from Inverness to MC Metal Processing, Glasgow for asbestos removal arriving on 06/09/94. When completed the locomotive was moved by road to Meadowhall on 20/12/94 but hadn't been used by 01/01.
Sold as a private purchase to Tom Clift, then the Managing Director of Cardiff Railway Company, and moved by road on 29-30/01/01 from Meadowhall to Cardiff Cathays workshops for restoration. With the closure of Cathays, the locomotive was due to be moved to Canton, but due to road access problems at that site, it was instead moved by road to DSDC, MoD Ashchurch in 06/05 and following removal of the problems at Canton, was moved there on 01/07/05 for restoration to continue.
HQ Headquarters Pool 03/2012 M
Reregistered in 03/12 to allow rail movement including attendance at galas. Moved from Pullman Rail, Cardiff to the Barry Tourist Railway on 28/03/12, then taken to the Bo'ness & Kinneil Railway on 11/07/12. Moved to The Keighley & Worth Valley Railway 24/04/13, and was named *Tom Clift 1954-2012* at Keighley on 27/04/13. Returned to Bo'ness and sold to the 6LDA Group in 12/13. Moved to the Spa Valley Railway 06/07/14, returned to the Bo'ness & Kinneil Railway 06/11/14
BT Bo'ness 15/05/2016 E

D5339

64B Haymarket 04/09/1959 E
60A Inverness 02/1960 M
Allocation recoded 60A to IS 05/1973 M
Renumbered 26039 08/1974 M
Store 04/1984 M
HA Haymarket 10/1984 M
Returned to Service 10/1984 M
ED Eastfield 05/1987 M
Store 05/10/1987 E
Stored at Eastfield 05/10/87, moved to ZC Crewe Works 20/10/87.
ED Eastfield 04/11/1987 E
Returned to Service 04/11/1987 E
Withdrawn 18/10/1990 E
Stored for the British Railways Board for inclusion in the National Collection, but the decision rescinded and it was sold for scrap 09/93. Moved to MC Metal Processing, Glasgow arriving on 14/10/93, and dispatched immediately, being cut up 20/10/93.

D5340

64B Haymarket 11/09/1959 E
60A Inverness 02/1960 M
61A Kittybrewster 04/1960 M
60A Inverness 06/1960 M
Allocation recoded 60A to IS 05/1973 M
Renumbered 26040 10/1973 M
HA Haymarket 05/1982 M
IS Inverness 05/1983 M
HA Haymarket 10/1984 M
IS Inverness 12/1984 M
HA Haymarket 10/1985 M
ED Eastfield 05/1987 M
IS Inverness 08/1992 M
Store 01/09/1992 E
IS Inverness 26/09/1992 E
Returned to Service 26/09/1992 E
Store 11/10/1992 E
Store 04/12/1992 E
Stored at Inverness 04/12/92
Withdrawn 04/1993 M

For preservation

Sold for preservation 09/93, initially for use on the Lochty Railway in Scotland but this idea was cancelled on closure of the Lochty Railway. Arrived at MC Metal Processing, Glasgow 01/11/94 for asbestos removal. Departed 19/12/94 upon completion, by road to Methil Power Station for storage.
By 2004 the locomotive was located at

D5340 contd.

Barclay Brown Yard, Methil under restoration and, following completion of most work, was moved from Methil to the new Kingdom of Fife Railway at Kirkland Yard, Leven late in 2004. Stored at Barclay Brothers yard, Methil West in 2013. Moved to Whitrope Heritage Centre 07-10/03/16.

D5341

64B Haymarket 18/09/1959 E
60A Inverness 02/1960 M
61A Kittybrewster 04/1960 M
60A Inverness 06/1960 M
Allocation recoded 60A to IS 05/1973 M
Renumbered 26041 06/1974 M
HA Haymarket 10/1985 M
ED Eastfield 05/1987 M
IS Inverness 08/1992 M
Store 24/11/1992 E
Withdrawn 04/1993 M
Sold for preservation in 09/93 to the Mid Norfolk Railway but the sale was later cancelled. Moved to MC Metal Processing, Glasgow for scrap on 15/03/95 and was cut on the following day.

D5342

64B Haymarket 25/09/1959 E
60A Inverness 02/1960 M
62B Dundee Tay Bridge 04/1960 M
60A Inverness 06/1960 M
Allocation recoded 60A to IS 05/1973 M
Renumbered 26042 04/1974 M
HA Haymarket 12/1984 M
ED Eastfield 05/1987 M
Store 01/10/1991 E
ED Eastfield 04/10/1991 E
Returned to Service 04/10/1991 E
Store 08/10/1991 E
ED Eastfield 12/10/1991 E
Returned to Service 12/10/1991 E
Store 14/10/1991 E
ED Eastfield 18/10/1991 E
Returned to Service 18/10/1991 E
Store 21/10/1991 E
ED Eastfield 26/10/1991 E
Returned to Service 26/10/1991 E
Store 28/10/1991 E
ED Eastfield 16/11/1991 E
Returned to Service 16/11/1991 E
Store 18/11/1991 E
ED Eastfield 23/11/1991 E
Returned to Service 23/11/1991 E
Store 25/11/1991 E

A trend in recent years has been to restore locomotives in the once detested Rail Blue with 26007 being an example seen at Barrow Hill in August 2008. With this number it hides that fact that it was first of class as D5300 back in 1958. *(Ray Reed/RCTS Photo Archive*

D5342 contd.
ED Eastfield 29/11/1991 E
Returned to Service 29/11/1991 E
Store 04/12/1991 E
ED Eastfield 07/12/1991 E
Returned to Service 07/12/1991 E
Store 09/12/1991 E
ED Eastfield 14/12/1991 E
Returned to Service 14/12/1991 E
Store 19/12/1991 E
ED Eastfield 21/12/1991 E
Returned to Service 21/12/1991 E
Store 13/12/1991 E
ED Eastfield 10/01/1992 E
Returned to Service 10/01/1992 E
IS Inverness 08/1992 M
Store 09/10/1992 E
Stored at Inverness 09/10/92.
Withdrawn 04/1993 M
Sold for preservation to the Weardale Railway 09/93 but the sale cancelled. The locomotive arrived at MC Metal Processing, Glasgow for scrap on 03/04/95 and was broken up 13/06/95.

D5343
64B Haymarket 02/10/1959 E
60A Inverness 02/1960 M
62B Dundee Tay Bridge 04/1960 M
60A Inverness 06/1960 M

D5343 contd.
Allocation recoded 60A to IS 05/1973 M
Renumbered 26043 01/1974 M
HA Haymarket 05/1985 M
IS Inverness 06/1985 M
HA Haymarket 05/1986 M
ED Eastfield 05/1987 M
IS Inverness 08/1992 M
Store 24/11/1992 E
Stored at Perth 24/11/92.
Withdrawn 04/1993 M
For preservation
Sold for preservation to the Cotswold Group 09/93 for use on the Gloucestershire Warwickshire Railway. Arrived at MC Metal Processing, Glasgow for asbestos removal on 08/11/94 and upon completion was moved by road to Toddington on 12-15/12/94. Repainted in 07/13 in BR small logo blue as D5343 with the logo unusually on cab doors at one end. Repainted again in blue as 26043 but no logo in 06/25. Makes appearances at galas at other heritage railways.

D5344
64B Haymarket 09/10/1959 E
60A Inverness 02/1960 M
64B Haymarket 04/1960 M

D5344 contd.
60A Inverness 05/1960 M
65B St. Rollox 06/1960 M
60A Inverness 02/1961 M
Allocation recoded 60A to IS 05/1973 M
Renumbered 26044 05/1974 M
Withdrawn 17/01/1984 E
Burnt out in a snowdrift between Blair Atholl and Dalwhinnie on 17/01/84, whilst working in multiple on snowplough duty, 26040 was undamaged.
Moved to Dunfermline Townhill for store, then to Thornton Junction about 12/84 for further storage. Sold to Vic Berry, Leicester 12/86 for scrap; the decision was taken to break it up on site, which was completed by staff from Berry by 03/02/87.

D5345
64B Haymarket 23/10/1959 E
60A Inverness 02/1960 M
64B Haymarket 04/1960 M
60A Inverness 06/1960 M
Allocation recoded 60A to IS 05/1973 M
Renumbered 26045 04/1974 M
Caught fire on 23/09/82 on an Inverness-Glasgow train.
Stored at Inverness 26/09/82, moved to Dundee 10/82 and then ZH Glasgow Works 12/82, both for further storage.

D5345 contd.
Store 10/1982 M
Withdrawn 04/07/1983 E
Moved to Polmadie by 15/08/83, then moved across the main line to Shawfield Sidings in the middle of 1986 for further storage. Sold to Vic Berry, Leicester 12/86, but still remained at Polmadie until 01/07/87 when it moved to Carlisle, to Workington 03/07/87, to Crewe Basford Hall 09/07/87, and to Leicester Humberstone Road on 10/07/87, remaining there until shunted into Berry's yard on 28/07/87. It was partly cut up by 10/08/87, and completed by 01/09/87, except the cabs still there on 02/11/87.

D5346
64B Haymarket 30/10/1959 E
60A Inverness 02/1960 M
Allocation recoded 60A to IS 05/1973 M
Renumbered 26046 01/1974 M
HA Haymarket 10/1984 M
ED Eastfield 05/1987 M
Withdrawn 19/04/1991 E
Stored at Eastfield then moved to BRML Glasgow Works by 03/93 for further storage. Sold for scrap to next door MC Metal Processing in 09/93, moved there on 23/09/93 and was scrapped on 01/10/93.

Another of the many Class 26s to be preserved was 26043 seen at the Glos.-Warks. Railway on 15th November 1995 in tired-looking Engineers' livery. *(D. Pye/Colour-Rail.com*

CLASS 27

Following the pattern seen with a number of designs it was decided that a more powerful version of the Class 26s was required so, a follow on order from D5346 was placed with BRCW which extended to 69 units which under TOPS were designated as Class 27. As with the Class 24/25 design the 27s received the Sulzer 6LDA28B engine of 1,250 hp paired with GEC WT459 traction motors instead of the Crompton type used on Class 26. The class was however instantly recognisable from the 26s as the locomotives were fitted with four character headcode boxes. D5347-69 were new to the Scottish region and spent most of their working lives allocated to either Eastfield or Haymarket although having duties taking them to the Highlands every day. D5370-78 were new to Thornaby for freight duties but after a possible flirtation with life in the Midlands moved to Scotland in 1970 whilst D5379-D5415 were all new to Cricklewood depot working duties out of and around St. Pancras. They also moved to Scotland via the Midlands and hence forward all of the class were based there until very near the end when one locomotive escaped to Tyseley!

As well as their association with the Highland line some 24 of the class were fitted with push-pull control equipment as well as dual braking to enable them to work the gruelling Glasgow-Edinburgh service, being renumbered in the 271xx series. Subsequently some also had electric heating capability fitted replacing their steam heat boilers thus becoming 272xx locomotives. A number from both series later reverted to 270xx numbers making it difficult to identify original numbering. A table is provided at the end of the book detailing that renumbering.

The demanding work on the push-pull duties took its toll on the class and it was found that Class 26 was more reliable than Class 27 leading to the decision to withdraw the 27s as Class 47s took over the Glasgow-Edinburgh duties and Class 26 became available for freight duties following their replacement in the Highlands by Class 37s. The end for the class came in 1987 so not completing 30 years in service. Most were broken up in Scotland although eight survived to pass to preservationists.

Class 27 liveries mirrored those of the Class 26 but ended with the Rail Blue era. However, at least one Class 27 received a white bodyside stripe on blue late in its career.

The final Class 27 to be delivered was D5415 which is seen here at Doncaster Works. It was new in October 1962 and possibly carried yellow warning panels from the outset, these being applied to both Class 26 and 27, starting around that time. *(Colour-Rail.com*

D5347
62A Thornton Junction 30/06/1961 E
65A Eastfield 07/1961 M
64B Haymarket 02/1970 M
65A Eastfield 01/1972 M
64B Haymarket 03/1972 M
Allocation recoded 64B to HA 05/1973 M
ED Eastfield 05/1973 M
Renumbered 27001 04/1974 M
Store 09/1982 M
Stored at Dundee 09/82, moved to Perth 10/82 the back to Dundee 11/10/82, both for further storage.
ED Eastfield 06/06/1983 E
Returned to Service 06/06/1983 E
Store 19/02/1987 E
ED Eastfield 03/1987 M
Returned to Service 03/1987 M
Withdrawn 08/07/1987 E
Stored at Eastfield, then moved to ZH Glasgow Works by 07/11/87.
For preservation
Sold for preservation to the Caledonian Railway, Brechin and moved there on 27/02/88 for further use. Moved to the Bo'ness & Kinneil Railway in 12/91. Having previously been reregistered as 89247 to allow movement to galas by rail, it was officially renumbered back to 27001 in 02/09.
BT Bo'ness 18/06/2009 E

D5348
62A Thornton Junction 17/07/1961 E
65A Eastfield 07/1961 M
64B Haymarket 02/1970 M
65A Eastfield 01/1972 M
64B Haymarket 03/1972 M
65A Eastfield 07/1972 M
Allocation recoded 65A to ED 05/1973 M
Renumbered 27002 04/1974 M
IS Inverness 10/1981 M
Store 02/1984 M
Moved to ZL Swindon Works for refurbishing on 27/04/84, it was reinstated to Inverness in 05/84 and reallocated to Haymarket in 06/84 while still at Swindon Works, returned to Scotland 03/01/85.
IS Inverness 05/1984 M
Returned to service 05/1984 M
HA Haymarket 06/1984 M
ED Eastfield 07/1985 M
HA Haymarket 09/1985 M

D5348 contd.
Withdrawn 06/01/1986 E
Stored at Millerhill and still there when sold for scrap to Vic Berry, Leicester in 12/86. It was going to be broken up on site at Millerhill, but decision rescinded and loco eventually moved to Polmadie in 06/87, to Carlisle 01/07/87, to Workington 03/07/87, to Crewe Basford Hall 09/07/87, then to Leicester Humberstone Road on 10/07/87 and final movement into Berry's Yard on 28/07/87. However, scrapping was only completed by 04/03/88, except for one cab that was still in evidence on 06/05/90, but was disposed of by the end of the month.

D5349
65A Eastfield 28/07/1961 E
64B Haymarket 07/1972 M
Allocation recoded 64B to HA 05/1973 M
ED Eastfield 05/1973 M
Renumbered 27003 11/1973 M
IS Inverness 03/1980 M
ED Eastfield 05/1986 M
Withdrawn 16/01/1987 E
Stored at Eastfield until moved to BRML Glasgow Works by 07/11/87. Sold and moved next door to MC Metal Processing on 06/12/87 and was cut up 21/12/87.

D5350
65A Eastfield 23/08/1961 E
Allocation recoded 65A to ED 05/1973 M
Renumbered 27004 04/1974 M
IS Inverness 10/1984 M
HA Haymarket 11/1984 M
Withdrawn 11/05/1986 E
Stored at Ayr depot, then moved to Falkland Junction Yard by 03/87. Sold to Vic Berry, Leicester for scrap and moved to Carlisle on 03/07/87, to Crewe Basford Hall 06/07/87, and to Leicester Humberstone Road Yard on 07/07/87 and into Berry's Yard, on 08/07/87. Cutting started about 10/08/87 and just the frame and cabs were left by 19/09/87, just the cabs by 23/09/87, and they were still there on 02/11/87.

D5351
65A Eastfield 30/08/1961 E
Allocation recoded 65A to ED 05/1973 M
Renumbered 27005 10/1974 M
IS Inverness 03/1980 M
ED Eastfield 05/1986 M

D5351 contd.
Withdrawn 10/07/1987 E
Stored at Eastfield, then sent to ZH Glasgow Works by 07/11/87 for further storage.
For preservation
Sold for preservation to the Scottish Railway Preservation Society at the Bo'ness & Kinneil Railway about 12/87. Moved to Falkirk by rail 14/02/88, then by road to Bo'ness for further use. It was named *Dr. R. A. Reid* at Bo'ness on 02/09/89 for one day only, and now runs as D5351. Previously reregistered to allow movement to galas by rail, it was reallocated in 2009 when the Bo'ness & Kinneil Railway got its own depot code and later its own pool code.
BT Bo'ness 09/01/2009 E

D5352
65A Eastfield 06/09/1961 E
Allocation recoded 65A to ED 05/1973 M
Renumbered 27006 09/1974 M
ED Eastfield 01/1976 M
Withdrawn 21/01/1976 E
Withdrawn due to fire damage. Stored at Eastfield, then moved to ZH Glasgow Works by 07/08/76 and scrapped there in 01/77.

D5353
65A Eastfield 13/09/1961 E
Allocation recoded 65A to ED 05/1973 M
Renumbered 27007 04/1974 M
IS Inverness 03/1980 M
Withdrawn 21/01/1985 E
For preservation
Sold for preservation to the Mid-Hants Railway. Having been stored at Mossend Yard, departed on 24/10/85 and arrived at ZL Swindon Works on 31/10/85. Moved to the Mid-Hants Railway on 26/11/85 where it was repainted as D5353. Damaged by fire at Ropley shed on 10/07/86, stored and covered with tarpaulins. Repair work started in 06/90, it had trial runs on 09/12/91 and all work was completed on 11/09/92, and finally put into service.
Moved to Caledonian Railway, Brechin 21-27/01/18.

D5354
65A Eastfield 20/09/1961 E
Allocation recoded 65A to ED 05/1973 M
Renumbered 27008 12/1973 M

D5354 contd.
IS Inverness 03/1980 M
ED Eastfield 05/1985 M
Withdrawn 18/08/1987 E
Stored at Eastfield until moved into BRML Glasgow Works by 07/11/87 awaiting scrap, but sold almost immediately to MC Metal Processing next door and broken up on 26/11/87. This was the first locomotive scrapped there.

D5355
65A Eastfield 28/09/1961 E
Allocation Recoded 65A to ED 05/1973 M
Renumbered 27009 04/1974 M
Withdrawn 27/07/1980 E
Withdrawn due to fire damage. Moved to ZH Glasgow Works by 27/06/81 where it was broken up by 15/01/82, but some parts remained on 30/03/82. Disposed of early 04/82.

D5356
65A Eastfield 11/10/1961 E
Allocation Recoded 65A to ED 05/1973 M
Renumbered 27010 11/1973 M
HA Haymarket 05/1982 M
ED Eastfield 07/1985 M
HA Haymarket 09/1985 M
Withdrawn 19/04/1986 E
Stored at Ayr depot, then moved to Falkland Junction Yard by 14/03/87. Sold to Vic Berry, Leicester for scrap. Moved to Carlisle 03/07/87, to Basford Hall 06/07/87, then to Leicester Humberstone Road Yard 07/07/87 and into Berry's Yard next day. Put into the 'pyramid', where it remained until removed and noted being cut up 23/10/87, with just the cabs left by 02/11/87. These were scrapped by 13/11/87.

D5357
65A Eastfield 18/10/1961 E
Allocation Recoded 65A to ED 05/1973 M
Renumbered 27011 04/1974 M
Withdrawn 30/03/1981 E
Moved to Polmadie 06/81 for further storage, then to ZE Derby Works 22/03/82 and broken up on 04/09/82.

D5358
65A Eastfield 25/10/1961 E
Allocation recoded 65A to ED 05/1973 M
Renumbered 27012 05/1974 M
Store 07/1975 M

D5358 contd.
ED Eastfield 08/09/1975 E
Returned to Service 08/09/1975 E
HA Haymarket 05/1982 M
Store 05/1986 M
Withdrawn 12/05/1986 E
Stored at Ayr depot, then moved to Falkland Junction, Ayr about 03/87. Sold to Vic Berry, Leicester for scrap. Moved to Carlisle 03/07/87, to Crewe Basford Hall 06/07/87, to Leicester Humberstone Road 07/07/87 and into Berry's Yard next day. It was noted still intact on 24/12/87, but was completely cut up by 22/01/88.

D5359
65A Eastfield 01/11/1961 E
Allocation recoded 65A to ED 05/1973 M
Renumbered 27013 04/1974 M
Withdrawn 13/07/1976 E
Withdrawn after it ran away out of control at Eastfield depot on 01/07/76 and was derailed at the head shunt. Moved to ZH Glasgow Works and broken up 07/77, with cabs only remaining by 06/08/77, these were still there on 26/05/84. Believed disposed of about 07/84.

D5360
65A Eastfield 18/11/1961 E
Allocation recoded 65A to ED 05/1973 M
Renumbered 27014 02/1974 M
Store 10/10/1981 E
Caught fire near Eastfield 09/10/81, stored the next day and moved to ZH Glasgow Works by 30/11/81 for repair.
Moved to ZE Derby Works for further repairs, noted en route there on 12/08/82. Displayed at works open day 04/09/82. Officially reinstated to Eastfield in 09/82 while at the works. After repairs were completed it was displayed at Coalville open day 05/06/83, then returned to Scotland.
ED Eastfield 09/1982 M
Returned to Service 06/1983 M
IS Inverness 10/1984 M
ED Eastfield 07/1985 M
HA Haymarket 05/1986 M
Withdrawn 08/09/1986 E
Moved to Smithy Lye sidings, Glasgow in 12/86, then to Polmadie by 15/08/87. Moved to Carlisle 04/09/87, Crewe Basford Hall 07/09/87, then Leicester Humberstone Road on 18/09/87, and to Vic Berry, Leicester 21/09/87. It was cut up by 04/10/87, except the cabs were still there on 02/11/87.

It is believed that D5382 was the only class member to receive two-tone green with yellow panels and it does not seem to have survived long in that guise. It is here at Ayr in 1968. This is possibly the only known image of this style that we can find. *(W. Hamilton/Colour-Rail.com*

D5361
65A Eastfield 22/11/1961 E
Allocation recoded 65A to ED 05/1973 M
Renumbered 27015 05/1974 M
Store 17/01/1977 E
Withdrawn 27/01/1977 E
Withdrawn due to fire damage. Moved to ZH Glasgow Works 24/02/77 and was broken up by 21/04/77.

D5362
65A Eastfield 30/11/1961 E
Allocation recoded 65A to ED 05/1973 M
Renumbered 27016 04/1974 M
Caught fire 24/03/83 and was dumped at Eastfield 26/03/83, moved to ZH Glasgow Works by 06/04/83 and stored there 11/04/83.
Store 11/04/1983 E
Withdrawn 09/04/1984 E
Remained stored at ZH Glasgow Works until sold to Vic Berry, Leicester for scrap 12/86. Moved to Thornton Junction 29/01/87 to be broken up on site, but decision changed and it was moved to Mossend 10/06/87, to Carlisle 13/06/87, to Basford Hall 22/06/87, then Leicester Humberstone Road 23/06/87, and into Berry's yard 30/06/87. Cutting up was in progress 04/07/87 and completed by 10/07/87, except for the cabs.

D5363
65A Eastfield 07/12/1961 E
Allocation recoded 65A to ED 05/1973 M
Renumbered 27017 04/1974 M
HA Haymarket 05/1982 M
Withdrawn 11/05/1986 E
Stored at Ayr depot, then moved to Falkland Junction by 03/87. Moved to Carlisle 27/07/87, to Basford Hall 29/07/87, Leicester Humberstone Road 30/07/87, and to Vic Berry, Leicester 03/08/87, where it was noted being scrapped on 09/04/88, and completed by 15/05/88.

D5364
65A Eastfield 13/12/1961 E
Allocation recoded 65A to ED 05/1973 M
Renumbered 27018 04/1974 M
HA Haymarket 05/1982 M
Withdrawn 11/05/1986 E
Stored at Perth until 07/88, moved to Motherwell on 20/07/88 and then to ZH Glasgow Works to 11/88 for further storage. Sent to Eastfield 03/89 then back to Glasgow

D5364 contd.
Works 05/89, to MC Metal Processing next door in 06/89, and cut up on 13/07/89.

D5365
65A Eastfield 30/12/1961 E
Allocation recoded 65A to ED 05/1973 M
Renumbered 27019 04/1974 M
Store 01/1982 M
ED Eastfield 01/1982 M
Returned to Service 01/1982 M
Store 06/1983 M
Stored at Polmadie 06/83, then stored at Haymarket 08/83.
ED Eastfield 11/1983 M
Returned to Service 11/1983 M
Store 02/1984 M
Stored in 02/84, then moved to ZL Swindon Works 27/04/84.
Withdrawn 28/05/1984 E
Broken up at Swindon Works by 21/05/85.

D5366
65A Eastfield 04/01/1962 E
Allocation recoded 65A to ED 05/1973 M
Renumbered 27020 05/1974 M
HA Haymarket 05/1982 M
ED Eastfield 05/1983 M
IS Inverness 10/1984 M
HA Haymarket 09/1985 M
ED Eastfield 02/1986 M
Store 04/1986 M
Withdrawn 11/04/1986 E
Stored at Haymarket until sold to Vic Berry, Leicester 12/86 for scrap. Moved to Thornton Junction on 21/01/87 for breaking up on site. Noted being dismantled on site by Berry staff on 03/02/87, with remains only by 13/02/87.

D5367
65A Eastfield 04/01/1962 E
Allocation recoded 65A to ED 05/1973 M
Renumbered 27021 04/1974 M
IS Inverness 04/1980 M
Withdrawn 03/06/1985 E
Withdrawn due to fire damage. Stored at Perth until sold to Vic Berry, Leicester 12/86. Decision was taken to break the locomotive on site at Thornton Junction. It was moved there on 22/01/87 and scrapped during 04/87. The cabs were noted at Berry's yard, Leicester in 06/87.

D5368

65A Eastfield 11/01/1962 E
Allocation recoded 65A to ED 05/1973 M
Renumbered 27022 11/1973 M
Caught fire at Eastfield depot on 05/01/85.
Withdrawn 21/01/1985 E
Stored at Eastfield then sold to Vic Berry, Leicester for scrap and moved to Smithy Lye sidings, Glasgow in 12/86. Remained there until 08/87 when it went to Polmadie. Moved to Carlisle 04/09/87, to Crewe Basford Hall 07/09/87, then to Leicester Humberstone Road 18/09/87, and into Berry's yard on 21/09/87, where it was cut up by 04/10/87.

D5369

65A Eastfield 17/01/1962 E
Allocation recoded 65A to ED 05/1973 M
Renumbered 27023 02/1974 M
HA Haymarket 03/1985 M
Withdrawn 12/05/1986 E
Moved to Smithy Lye sidings, Glasgow in 12/86 and sold for scrap to Vic Berry, Leicester. Moved to Polmadie about 06/87, then to Carlisle 12/08/87, to Crewe Basford Hall 14/08/87 and onto Leicester Humberstone Road 19/08/87. Shunted into Berry's yard on 20/08/87 and remained intact until noted off its bogies on 25/03/89; was cut up completely by 07/04/89.

D5370

51L Thornaby 17/01/1962 E
D15 Leicester Division 12/1965 M
51L Thornaby 12/1965 M
Thought to have remained at 51L on loan rather than moving to D15 in 12/65, in which case both the above changes were 'paper transfers' and didn't happen.
D15 Leicester Division 01/1966 M
D16 Nottingham Division 08/1967 M
65A Eastfield 11/1969 M
Allocation recoded 65A to ED 05/1973 M
Renumbered 27024 04/1974 M
Withdrawn 02/07/1987 E
Stored at Eastfield
Renumbered ADB968028 08/87 M
Taken into Departmental stock as a training loco and renumbered ADB968028.
Noted at Eastfield and marked condemned on 07/05/88 and, although it had ceased working, it wasn't withdrawn until September 1989

D5370 contd.

Withdrawn 15/09/1989 E
Moved to MC Metal Processing, Glasgow by 17/07/90 for asbestos removal.
For preservation
Sold for preservation to the Northampton & Lamport Railway in 1990. Moved to Eastfield TMD for safekeeping 12/90, then to ZH Glasgow Works 02/91 and moved by road to Pitsford, on the Northampton & Lamport Railway, also known as the Northampton Steam Railway, where it arrived on 05/02/91. However, its stay was short and it was moved to the Caledonian Railway, Brechin in 1992 and later painted back to 27024.
Moved to the Lakeside & Haverthwaite Railway in 2011 and repainted back to D5370 while there. Returned to the Caledonian Railway 30-31/07/14.

D5371

51L Thornaby 19/01/1962 E
D15 Leicester Division 12/1965 M
51L Thornaby 12/1965 M
Thought to have remained at 51L on loan rather than moving to D15 in 12/65, in which case both the above changes were 'paper transfers' and didn't happen.
D15 Leicester Division 01/1966 M
D16 Nottingham Division 08/1967 M
65A Eastfield 02/1970 M
Allocation recoded 65A to ED 05/1973 M
Renumbered 27025 09/1974 M
IS Inverness 07/1985 M
ED Eastfield 05/1986 M
Store 10/06/1987 E
Withdrawn 19/06/1987 E
Moved to Thornton Junction 12/03/87 for cutting up on site, but decision rescinded and moved from there to Polmadie in 07/87, then to Carlisle on 13/08/87, to Basford Hall next day and Leicester Humberstone Road on 19/08/87, then to Vic Berry, Leicester on 20/08/87 and was still intact on 04/03/89, then completely cut up by 25/03/89.

D5372

51L Thornaby 24/01/1962 E
D15 Leicester Division 12/1965 M
51L Thornaby 12/1965 M
Thought to have remained at 51L on loan

The authorities seemed loathed to apply full yellow ends to its Class 26s and Class 27s but, 5347 (minus the 'D' prefix), was one of the few to be so adorned and is at St. Rollox in the 1960s.
(David Swale/Colour-Rail.com

D5372 contd.
rather than moving to D15 in 12/65, in which case both the above changes were 'paper transfers' and didn't happen.
D15 Leicester Division 01/1966 M
D16 Nottingham Division 08/1967 M
65A Eastfield 10/1969 M
Allocation recoded 65A to ED 05/1973 M
Renumbered 27026 09/1974 M
IS Inverness 07/1985 M
ED Eastfield 05/1986 M
Withdrawn 06/07/1987 E
Sold immediately to Vic Berry, Leicester and moved from Motherwell to Carlisle 09/07/87, Crewe Basford Hall on 10/07/87, Bescot 14/07/87, Toton and onto Leicester Humberstone Road on 15/07/87, then into Berry's Yard on 05/08/87. Placed in the 'pyramid' until broken up by 04/03/88. Both cabs were still in the yard on 06/05/90, but were quickly got rid of.

D5373
51L Thornaby 31/01/1962 E
D15 Leicester Division 12/1965 M
51L Thornaby 12/1965 M

D5373 contd.
Thought to have remained at 51L on loan rather than moving to D15 in 12/65, in which case both the above changes were 'paper transfers' and didn't happen.
D15 Leicester Division 01/1966 M
D16 Nottingham Division 08/1967 M
65A Eastfield 11/1969 M
Allocation recoded 65A to ED 05/1973 M
Renumbered 27027 04/1974 M
Store 30/07/1981 E
Stored at Inverness 30/07/81 due to fire damage.
IS Inverness 06/09/1982 E
Allocation to Inverness while stored unconfirmed, not shown in BR official returns. 06/09/1982 E
Store 06/09/1982 E
Withdrawn 13/06/1983 E
Moved to ZH Glasgow Works by 06/04/83 for further storage until sold for scrap to Vic Berry, Leicester. Moved to Thornton Junction on 28/01/87 for scrapping on site. It was still intact on 14/03/87, but had been dismantled by Berry staff by 13/06/87. The cabs were moved to Berry's yard.

D5374
51L Thornaby 07/02/1962 E
D15 Leicester Division 12/1965 M
51L Thornaby 12/1965 M
Thought to have remained at 51L on loan rather than moving to D15 in 12/65, in which case both the above changes were 'paper transfers' and didn't happen.
D15 Leicester Division 01/1966 M
D16 Nottingham Division 08/1967 M
65A Eastfield 10/1969 M
Allocation recoded 65A to ED 05/1973 M
HA Haymarket 12/1973 M
Renumbered 27101 04/1974 M
ED Eastfield 01/1980 M
Renumbered 27045 09/1984 M
Withdrawn 12/05/1986 E
Stored at Haymarket, then sold to Vic Berry, Leicester about 03/87. Moved to Humberstone Road, Leicester on 27/07/87, and into Berry's yard 30/07/87. Put in the 'pyramid' 10/87 and still intact 03/01/89, but was cut up by 28/01/89, except for some bits that were still about on site 04/03/89.

D5375
51L Thornaby 14/02/1962 E
D15 Leicester Division 12/1965 M
51L Thornaby 12/1965 M
Thought to have remained at 51L on loan rather than moving to D15 in 12/65, in which case both the above changes were 'paper transfers' and didn't happen.
D15 Leicester Division 01/1966 M
D16 Nottingham Division 08/1967 M
65A Eastfield 10/1969 M
Allocation recoded 65A to ED 05/1973 M
Renumbered 27028 12/1973 M
Store 13/03/1983 E
Stored, then moved to Polmadie 14/08/83 for further storage.
ED Eastfield 07/1984 M
Returned to Service 07/1984 M
Withdrawn 19/08/1984 E
Withdrawn due to collision damage and moved to ZH Glasgow Works, then to ZL Swindon Works 18/09/84 arriving there 28/09/84; finally broken up by 07/08/85.

D5376
51L Thornaby 21/02/1962 E
D15 Leicester Division 12/1965 M
51L Thornaby 12/1965 M

D5376 contd.
Thought to have remained at 51L on loan rather than moving to D15 in 12/65, in which case both the above changes were 'paper transfers' and didn't happen.
D16 Nottingham Division 01/1966 M
65A Eastfield 02/1970 M
Allocation recoded 65A to ED 05/1973 M
Renumbered 27029 04/1974 M
IS Inverness 11/1984 M
Store 01/1985 M
IS Inverness 01/1985 M
Returned to Service 01/1985 M
ED Eastfield 07/1985 M
Withdrawn 13/01/1986 E
Moved to ZH Glasgow Works for store. Sold to Vic Berry, Leicester 12/86 for scrap and moved to Thornton Junction 28/01/87 for cutting up on site. Broken up there by Berry staff by 20/04/87. The cabs were moved to Berry's yard and were still there 02/11/87.

D5377
51L Thornaby 28/02/1962 E
D15 Leicester Division 12/1965 M
51L Thornaby 12/1965 M
Thought to have remained at 51L on loan rather than moving to D15 in 12/65, in which case both the above changes were 'paper transfers' and didn't happen.
D16 Nottingham Division 01/1966 M
65A Eastfield 03/1970 M
Allocation recoded 65A to ED 05/1973 M
Renumbered 27030 09/1974 M
Store 10/1984 M
ED Eastfield 10/1984 M
Returned to Service 10/1984 M
Withdrawn 20/04/1986 E
Withdrawn due to fire damage at Uphall on 09/04/86. Stored at Motherwell until sold to Vic Berry, Leicester. Moved to Mossend Yard, then to Carlisle 24/09/87, to Crewe Basford Hall 25/09/87, then Humberstone Road 28/09/87 and into Berry's Yard 30/09/87. Scrapping started immediately, noted part cut on 04/10/87 and was gone completely by 17/10/87.

D5378
51L Thornaby 07/03/1962 E
D15 Leicester Division 12/1965 M
51L Thornaby 12/1965 M
Thought to have remained at 51L on loan

D5378 contd.

rather than moving to D15 in 12/65, in which case both the above changes were 'paper transfers' and didn't happen.

D16 Nottingham Division 01/1966 M

65A Eastfield 11/1969 M

Allocation recoded 65A to ED 05/1973 M

Renumbered 27031 04/1974 M

Withdrawn 06/05/1978 E

Withdrawn due to fire damage. Moved to ZH Glasgow Works 05/78 and cut up 09/78, leaving only the cabs by 10/78, which were cut up later.

D5379

14A Cricklewood 31/03/1962 E

14E Bedford 08/1963 M

Allocation recoded 14E to 14C 09/09/1963 E

14B Cricklewood West 02/1964 M

LMML LM Midland Lines 16/01/1965 E

D16 Nottingham Division 01/1966 M

65A Eastfield 11/1969 M

Allocation recoded 65A to ED 05/1973 M

Renumbered 27032 04/1974 M

IS Inverness 10/1984 M

Withdrawn 27/05/1985 E

Withdrawn due to fire damage. Taken to ZH Glasgow Works, then sold to Vic Berry, Leicester 12/86 for scrap. Moved to

D5379 contd.

Thornton Junction on 17/02/87 to be broken up on site. Noted being chopped up there by Berry staff 13/03/87 and completed by 21/03/87.

D5380

14A Cricklewood 07/04/1962 E

14E Bedford 08/1963 M

Allocation recoded 14E to 14C 09/09/1963 E

14B Cricklewood West 03/1964 M

LMML LM Midland Lines 16/01/1965 E

D16 Nottingham Division 17/06/1968 E

65A Eastfield 11/1969 M

64B Haymarket 01/1972 M

65A Eastfield 03/1972 M

Allocation recoded 65A to ED 05/1973 M

Renumbered 27102 10/1973 M

Renumbered 27046 09/04/1983 E

Withdrawn 06/07/1987 E

Stored at Eastfield until moved to ZH Glasgow Works on 07/11/87 and held awaiting scrap. However, it was sold to MC Metal Processing next door and moved into its yard 05/88 and scrapped on 17/05/88.

D5381

14A Cricklewood 07/04/1962 E

14E Bedford 08/1963 M

The application of standard BR blue commenced quite early on the class and D5357 is at Oban in blue with full yellow ends with the double arrow placed centrally on the bodyside. Note that at this time the yellow did not extend to the side cab window surrounds.

(Ray Reed/RCTS Photo Archive

D5381 contd.
Allocation recoded 14E to 14C 09/09/1963 E
14B Cricklewood West 02/1964 M
LMML LM Midland Lines 16/01/1965 E
D14 London (Midland) Division 06/1966 M
LMML LM Midland Lines 09/1967 M
D16 Nottingham Division 17/06/1968 E
65A Eastfield 02/1970 M
Allocation recoded 65A to ED 05/1973 M
Renumbered 27033 09/1974 M
Store 04/1979 M
ED Eastfield 11/1979 M
Returned to Service 11/1979 M
HA Haymarket 10/1984 M
Withdrawn 24/02/1986 E
Sold to Vic Berry, Leicester 12/86. Moved from Haymarket to Thornton Junction 21/01/87 and was broken up on site 03/02/87 by Berry staff.

D5382
14A Cricklewood 21/04/1962 E
14E Bedford 08/1963 M
Allocation recoded 14E to 14C 09/09/1963 E
14B Cricklewood West 03/1964 M
LMML LM Midland Lines 16/01/1965 E
D16 Nottingham Division 17/06/1968 E
65A Eastfield 07/1968 M
Allocation recoded 65A to ED 05/1973 M
Renumbered 27034 04/1974 M
Withdrawn 22/07/1984 E
Withdrawn due to severe fire damage at Perth on 24/06/84. Stored at ZH Glasgow Works, then sent to ZL Swindon Works on 18/09/84, arriving there on 28/09/84. Finally dismantled by 18/12/85.

D5383
14A Cricklewood 28/04/1962 E
14E Bedford 08/1963 M
Allocation recoded 14E to 14C 09/09/1963 E
14B Cricklewood West 03/1964 M
D14 London (Midland) Division 16/01/1965 E
LMML LM Midland Lines 03/1965 M
Withdrawn 15/01/1966 E
Withdrawn due to accident damage at East Langton on 20/08/65. Moved to ZE Derby Works by 28/11/65, then to J. Cashmore, Great Bridge 26/06/67 and broken up 07/67. However, the move to J. Cashmore has been disputed so the actual location of cutting up therefore cannot be confirmed.

D5384
14A Cricklewood 05/05/1962 E
14B Cricklewood West 09/09/1963 E
Allocation recoded 14A to 14B and renamed Cricklewood West 09/09/1963 E
15A Leicester (Midland) 10/1963 M
14B Cricklewood West 07/1964 M
D14 London (Midland) Division 16/01/1965 E
LMML LM Midland Lines 06/1965 M
D16 Nottingham Division 17/06/1968 E
65A Eastfield 02/1970 M
Allocation recoded 65A to ED 05/1973 M
Renumbered 27035 04/1974 M
Withdrawn 29/09/1976 E
Moved to ZH Glasgow Works by 02/10/76 and cut up 03/77.

D5385
14A Cricklewood 12/05/1962 E
14B Cricklewood West 09/09/1963 E
Allocation recoded 14A to 14B and renamed Cricklewood West 09/09/1963 E
D14 London (Midland) Division 16/01/1965 E
LMML LM Midland Lines 06/1965 M
D14 London (Midland) Division 06/1966 M
D16 Nottingham Division 09/1967 M
LMML LM Midland Lines 02/1968 M
D16 Nottingham Division 17/06/1968 E
65A Eastfield 02/1970 M
Allocation recoded 65A to ED 05/1973 M
Renumbered 27036 11/1973 M
HA Haymarket 10/1982 M
Store 11/1983 M
Stored at ZH Glasgow Works 11/83, moved to Millerhill Yard 03/84 and then to ZL Swindon Works 27/04/84 for refurbishing. Officially reinstated to Haymarket 05/84 while still at Swindon Works, and still there 16/08/84, subsequently returned to Scotland.
HA Haymarket 05/1984 M
Store 05/1984 M
HA Haymarket 09/1984 M
Returned to Service 09/1984 M
Store 03/04/1986 E
Stored at Haymarket 03/04/86
Withdrawn 21/04/1986 E
Remained stored at Haymarket until sold to Vic Berry, Leicester 12/86. Moved to Thornton Junction 21/01/87 for cutting on site by Berry's staff. Noted partly cut up 15/02/87, with remains only noted on 14/03/87. The cabs went to Berry's yard and were still there 02/11/87.

D5386

14A Cricklewood 19/05/1962 E
14B Cricklewood West 09/09/1963 E
Allocation recoded 14A to 14B and renamed Cricklewood West 09/09/1963 E
15A Leicester (Midland) 10/1963 M
14B Cricklewood West 06/1964 M
15A Leicester (Midland) 07/1964 M
D15 Leicester Division 16/01/1965 E
LMML LM Midland Lines 08/1965 M
D16 Nottingham Division 17/06/1968 E
65A Eastfield 10/1969 M
Allocation recoded 65A to ED 05/1973 M
Renumbered 27103 04/1974 M
Renumbered 27212 15/03/1975 E
Store 01/1982 M
ED Eastfield 01/1982 M
Returned to Service 01/1982 M
Renumbered 27066 11/1982 M
Withdrawn 29/07/1987 E
Stored at Eastfield then to Motherwell 08/87. Sold to Vic Berry, Leicester and moved to Carlisle 02/09/87, Basford Hall, Crewe on 03/09/87, to Humberstone Road, Leicester 04/09/87; shunted into Berry's Yard 07/09/87.

For preservation

Sold for preservation to the North Norfolk Railway and moved to Sheringham on 14/03/88. Returned to use by 05/90 when it had been repainted in original livery; BR logo, horizontal white band and number D5386 applied soon after. It was named *The Holt Pioneer* at Sheringham on 18/10/95.
Reported as sold to the Keith & Dufftown Railway about 03/02 but this appears to have fallen through. Repainted in BR small logo blue as 5386 by 06/03. Sold to the Dean Forest Railway, but was moved to the East Lancs. Railway, Bury by road 09/03, for restoration, however, due to existing workshop commitments there and the work expected to take at least a year, it was moved to the Dean Forest Railway, Lydney, by road on 19/02/04. Bodyside number 5386 replaced by 27066 and Eastfield 'Scottie Dog' reapplied by 2006. Visited the Nene Valley Railway in 2006 and 2008 and the Gloucestershire-Warwickshire Railway in 2008. Sold privately and moved to Barrow Hill 18/02/15.

D5387

14A Cricklewood 26/05/1962 E
14B Cricklewood West 09/09/1963 E
Allocation recoded 14A to 14B and renamed Cricklewood West 09/09/1963 E
2E Saltley 09/1963 M
14B Cricklewood West 10/1963 M
15A Leicester (Midland) 10/1963 M
LMML LM Midland Lines 16/01/1965 E
D14 London (Midland) Division 06/1966 M
D16 Nottingham Division 09/1967 M
LMML LM Midland Lines 02/1968 M
D16 Nottingham Division 17/06/1968 E
65A Eastfield 11/1969 M
Allocation recoded 65A to ED 05/1973 M
Renumbered 27104 04/1974 M
Store 08/1981 M
Moved to ZH Glasgow Works with fire damage 08/81, sent to ZE Derby Works for repair, being noted en route on 12/08/82 and was on display at the works open day on 04/09/82. Renumbered while at Derby Works.
Renumbered 27048 09/1983 M
ED Eastfield 10/1983 M
Returned to Service 10/1983 M
IS Inverness 10/1985 M
Withdrawn 12/05/1986 E
Stored at Motherwell, then moved to Polmadie in 05/87 for further storage. Sold for scrap to Vic Berry, Leicester. Moved to Carlisle 13/08/87, to Basford Hall 14/08/87, then to Humberstone Road, Leicester 19/08/87, and into Berry's Yard 20/08/87. Cutting up started 19/09/87 and was completed by 02/10/87.

D5388

14A Cricklewood 02/06/1962 E
14B Cricklewood West 09/09/1963 E
Allocation recoded 14A to 14B and renamed Cricklewood West 09/09/1963 E
15A Leicester (Midland) 10/1963 M
D15 Leicester Division 16/01/1965 E
D16 Nottingham Division 08/1967 M
LMML LM Midland Lines 02/1968 M
D16 Nottingham Division 17/06/1968 E
65A Eastfield 03/1970 M
Allocation recoded 65A to ED 05/1973 M
Renumbered 27105 04/1974 M
IS Inverness 01/1981 M
Renumbered 27049 17/08/1983 E

D5388 contd.
ED Eastfield 02/1986 M
IS Inverness 04/1986 M
HA Haymarket 05/1986 M
ED Eastfield 09/1986 M
Withdrawn 27/04/1987 E
Withdrawn due to collision damage. Stored at Motherwell, then sold for scrap to Vic Berry, Leicester. Moved to Carlisle 02/09/87, Crewe Basford Hall 03/09/87, to Humberstone Road, Leicester 04/09/87 and into Berry's Yard on 07/09/87 where it was placed in the 'pyramid' by 10/87 and removed from it in 02/88. It was still intact on 04/03/88, but had been broken up by 13/03/88.

D5389
14A Cricklewood 02/06/1962 E
14B Cricklewood West 09/09/1963 E
Allocation recoded 14A to 14B and renamed Cricklewood West 09/09/1963 E
D14 London (Midland) Division 16/01/1965 E
LMML LM Midland Lines 10/1965 M
D16 Nottingham Division 06/1966 M
LMML LM Midland Lines 02/1968 M
D16 Nottingham Division 17/06/1968 E
65A Eastfield 11/1969 M
Allocation recoded 65A to ED 05/1973 M
Renumbered 27037 10/1973 M
HA Haymarket 05/1982 M
IS Inverness 10/1984 M
ED Eastfield 07/1985 M
HA Haymarket 09/1985 M
ED Eastfield 02/1986 M
Withdrawn 23/03/1986 E
Stored at Eastfield, then moved to Smithy Lye Sidings, Glasgow 12/86 and later to Polmadie for further storage. Sold to Vic Berry, Leicester and moved to Carlisle 12/08/87, to Basford Hall 14/08/87, to Humberstone Road, Leicester 19/08/87 and into Berry's Yard next day. Put in the 'pyramid' by 10/87, where it remained until 26/03/89 when cutting started and was completed by 07/04/89.

D5390
14A Cricklewood 09/06/1962 E
14B Cricklewood West 09/09/1963 E
Allocation recoded 14A to 14B and renamed Cricklewood West 09/09/1963 E
2E Saltley 09/1963 M
14B Cricklewood West 11/1963 M

D5390 contd.
15A Leicester (Midland) 11/1963 M
D15 Leicester Division 16/01/1965 E
LMML LM Midland Lines 08/1965 M
D15 Leicester Division 09/1965 M
D16 Nottingham Division 08/1967 M
LMML LM Midland Lines 02/1968 M
D16 Nottingham Division 17/06/1968 E
65A Eastfield 11/1969 M
Allocation recoded 65A to ED 05/1973 M
Renumbered 27038 04/1974 M
Withdrawn 10/02/1987 E
Stored at Polmadie, then moved to Mossend Yard about 18/08/87, to Carlisle 20/08/87, to Basford Hall 21/08/87, then Humberstone Road, Leicester on 27/08/87 and to Vic Berry, Leicester next day. Recorded as officially cut up in 09/87, actual details of scrapping are not available. Cabs still there 02/11/87.

D5391
14A Cricklewood 09/06/1962 E
14B Cricklewood West 09/09/1963 E
Allocation recoded 14A to 14B and renamed Cricklewood West 09/09/1963 E
15A Leicester (Midland) 11/1963 M
D15 Leicester Division 16/01/1965 E
D16 Nottingham Division 08/1967 M
66A Polmadie 07/1969 M
65A Eastfield 07/1969 M
64B Haymarket 03/1971 M
Allocation recoded 64B to HA 05/1973 M
Renumbered 27119 07/1973 M
The locomotive was erroneously repainted as 27201 at ZE Derby Works on 02/06/73, but on 06/06/73 it had correctly changed to 27119 although it was only officially renumbered in 07/73.
Renumbered 27201 11/05/1974 E
Withdrawn 22/01/1979 E
Withdrawn due to fire damage. Stored at Polmadie in 04/79, then moved to ZH Glasgow Works 22/05/79 and cut up with only the cabs remaining 10/09/79. These were still on site at the works 26/05/84.

D5392
14A Cricklewood 16/06/1962 E
14B Cricklewood West 09/09/1963 E
Allocation recoded 14A to 14B and renamed Cricklewood West 09/09/1963 E
15A Leicester (Midland) 10/1963 M

The Class 27s had one of the most complex set of loco renumberings of any class as some were modified to enable them to work in push-pull mode on Edinburgh to Glasgow duties. One such was D5393 which became 27121 in July 1974 but was renumbered again just four months later as 27203. It is at Edinburgh Waverley on 27th August 1977. *(Ray Reed/RCTS Photo Archive*

D5392 contd.
D15 Leicester Division 16/01/1965 E
D16 Nottingham Division 08/1967 M
65A Eastfield 06/1969 M
64B Haymarket 03/1971 M
Allocation recoded 64B to HA 05/1973 M
Renumbered 27120 04/1974 M
Renumbered 27202 31/08/1974 E
ED Eastfield 01/1980 M
Withdrawn 10/08/1980 E
Withdrawn due to fire damage. Moved to ZH Glasgow Works 15/08/80 and broken up between 09/81 and 01/82, with some parts still remaining on 02/04/82.

D5393
14A Cricklewood 16/06/1962 E
14B Cricklewood West 09/09/1963 E
Allocation recoded 14A to 14B and renamed Cricklewood West 09/09/1963 E
15A Leicester (Midland) 10/1963 M
D15 Leicester Division 16/01/1965 E
D16 Nottingham Division 08/1967 M
65A Eastfield 06/1969 M
Allocation recoded 64B to HA 05/1973 M
HA Haymarket 05/1973 M
Renumbered 27121 07/1974 M

D5393 contd.
Renumbered 27203 09/11/1974 E
ED Eastfield 01/1980 M
Store 01/1981 M
Stored at ZC Crewe Works 01/81. Officially reinstated to Eastfield 05/81 but had been moved to ZE Derby Works that month, appearing at the works open day on 06/06/81, returned to Scotland 03/82.
ED Eastfield 05/1981 M
Returned to Service 03/1982 M
Collided with EMU 303018 on 14/09/82 and suffered severe damage and was stored in Glasgow. Left on 21/12/82 for Derby Works but didn't arrive there until 17/01/83.
Withdrawn 04/05/1983 E
Had been allocated the number 27057 but was withdrawn before the renumbering could take place.
Remained at Derby Works in derelict condition until towed round to Etches Park and cut up by staff from Vic Berry, Leicester on 02/03/86.

D5394
14A Cricklewood 23/06/1962 E
14B Cricklewood West 09/09/1963 E

D5394 contd.
Allocation recoded 14A to 14B and renamed Cricklewood West 09/09/1963 E
15A Leicester (Midland) 10/1963 M
D15 Leicester Division 16/01/1965 E
D16 Nottingham Division 08/1967 M
65A Eastfield 07/1968 M
Allocation recoded 65A to ED 05/1973 M
Renumbered 27106 04/1974 M
IS Inverness 10/1981 M
Renumbered 27050 11/1982 M
HA Haymarket 05/1986 M
ED Eastfield 09/1986 M
Unofficially named *Meld* sometime in 1986.
Withdrawn 06/07/1987 E
Stored at Eastfield, then moved to BRML Glasgow Works on 07/11/87, where it remained until sold for preservation.

For preservation

Sold to M. G. Green of Rugby for use on the Strathspey Railway, moved there arriving about 02/09/09. Later painted as D5394.

D5395
14A Cricklewood 23/06/1962 E
14B Cricklewood West 09/09/1963 E
Allocation recoded 14A to 14B and renamed Cricklewood West 09/09/1963 E
15A Leicester (Midland) 11/1963 M
D15 Leicester Division 16/01/1965 E
D16 Nottingham Division 08/1967 M

D5395 contd.
65A Eastfield 06/1969 M
Allocation recoded 65A to ED 05/1973 M
Renumbered 27107 04/1974 M
IS Inverness 01/1981 M
Renumbered 27051 09/1982 M
HA Haymarket 07/1985 M
ED Eastfield 09/1986 M
Withdrawn 06/07/1987 E
It was taken out of use and moved to Thornton Junction 12/03/87 for scrap although not withdrawn until 06/07/87. Moved to Ayr 08/87, then to Falkland Junction, Ayr both for further storage. Sold to Vic Berry, Leicester. Moved to Carlisle 14/09/87, then to Workington and on to Warrington 16/09/87, to Basford Hall 25/09/87, then on to Humberstone Road, Leicester on 28/09/87, into Berry's yard 30/08/87. It was cut up from 07/10/87 and was completed by 17/10/87, but with cabs still extant on 02/11/87.

D5396
14A Cricklewood 30/06/1962 E
14B Cricklewood West 09/09/1963 E
Allocation recoded 14A to 14B and renamed Cricklewood West 09/09/1963 E
D14 London (Midland) Division 16/01/1965 E
LMML LM Midland Lines 10/1965 M
D16 Nottingham Division 05/1968 M

A rare and possibly unique livery was applied to 27056 with it gaining a white bodyside stripe. Whether it denoted a modification to the locomotive is unknown. (Colour-Rail.com

D5396 contd.
65A Eastfield 07/1968 M
Allocation recoded 65A to ED 05/1973 M
Renumbered 27108 04/1974 M
IS Inverness 02/1980 M
Renumbered 27052 12/1984 M
HA Haymarket 07/1985 M
ED Eastfield 09/1986 M
Withdrawn 06/07/1987 E
Stored at Motherwell, then sold to Vic Berry, Leicester. Moved to Carlisle 09/07/87, Basford Hall 10/07/87, Bescot 14/07/87, then Toton and on to Humberstone Road, Leicester on 15/07/87, finally into Berry's Yard on 05/08/87. Cutting started about 10/09/87, with only the body left 19/09/87, and this was broken up by 22/09/87, leaving the cabs that were still there on 02/11/87.

D5397
14A Cricklewood 11/08/1962 E
14B Cricklewood West 09/09/1963 E
Allocation recoded 14A to 14B and renamed Cricklewood West 09/09/1963 E
15A Leicester (Midland) 11/1963 M
D15 Leicester Division 16/01/1965 E
D16 Nottingham Division 08/1967 M
65A Eastfield 07/1969 M
Allocation recoded 65A to ED 05/1973 M
Renumbered 27109 05/1974 M
IS Inverness 02/1980 M
ED Eastfield 02/1981 M
IS Inverness 10/1981 M
Renumbered 27053 15/06/1983 E
HA Haymarket 07/1985 M
ED Eastfield 09/1986 M
Store 05/1987 M
Stored at Polmadie 05/87.
Withdrawn 19/05/1987 E
Sold for scrap to Vic Berry, Leicester. Moved to Mossend Yard, then to Carlisle 20/08/87, Crewe Basford Hall 21/08/87, then Humberstone Road, Leicester on 27/08/87 and into Berry's Yard next day. Placed in the 'pyramid' by 10/87 and remained there until 26/03/89, when it was removed and broken up by 07/04/89.

D5398
14A Cricklewood 07/07/1962 E
14B Cricklewood West 09/09/1963 E
Allocation recoded 14A to 14B and renamed Cricklewood West 09/09/1963 E
D14 London (Midland) Division 16/01/1965 E

D5398 contd.
D16 Nottingham Division 09/1967 M
65A Eastfield 06/1969 M
Allocation recoded 65A to ED 05/1973 M
Renumbered 27039 12/1973 M
Store 09/1975 M
Withdrawn 05/10/1975 E
Stored at Carstairs, then moved to Eastfield 11/75 for further storage. Sent to ZH Glasgow Works 05/06/76 and dismantled during 04/77.

D5399
14A Cricklewood 07/07/1962 E
14B Cricklewood West 09/09/1963 E
Allocation recoded 14A to 14B and renamed Cricklewood West 09/09/1963 E
D14 London (Midland) Division 16/01/1965 E
D16 Nottingham Division 09/1967 M
65A Eastfield 06/1969 M
Allocation recoded 65A to ED 05/1973 M
Renumbered 27110 04/1974 M
IS Inverness 02/1980 M
ED Eastfield 04/1980 M
Store 01/1982 M
ED Eastfield 01/1982 M
Returned to Service 01/1982 M
Renumbered 27054 07/03/1983 E
HA Haymarket 07/1985 M
ED Eastfield 09/1986 M
Withdrawn 06/07/1987 E
ED Eastfield 07/1987 M
Reinstated 07/1987 M
Withdrawn 14/07/1987 E
Moved to BRML Glasgow Works 07/11/87 and held for scrapping, but instead sold to MC Metal Processing next door and moved into its yard in 06/88 where it was dismantled on 17/06/88.

D5400
14A Cricklewood 14/07/1962 E
14B Cricklewood West 09/09/1963 E
Allocation recoded 14A to 14B and renamed Cricklewood West 09/09/1963 E
D14 London (Midland) Division 16/01/1965 E
D01 London Division 17/06/1968 E
D16 Nottingham Division 07/1968 M
65A Eastfield 06/1969 M
Allocation recoded 65A to ED 05/1973 M
Renumbered 27111 04/1974 M
Renumbered 27055 24/05/1983 E
HA Haymarket 07/1985 M
ED Eastfield 09/1986 M
Withdrawn 06/07/1987 E

D5400 contd.

Stored at Motherwell and sold immediately to Vic Berry, Leicester. Moved to Carlisle 09/07/87, Basford Hall 10/07/87, Bescot 14/07/87, Toton and on to Humberstone Road, Leicester 15/07/87. It was shunted into Berry's Yard on 05/08/87, put in the 'pyramid' 10/87, and was removed about 03/88. Noted being cut up 09/04/88 and completed by 15/05/88.

D5401

14A Cricklewood 14/07/1962 E
14B Cricklewood West 09/09/1963 E
Allocation recoded 14A to 14B and renamed Cricklewood West 09/09/1963 E
D14 London (Midland) Division 16/01/1965 E
D01 London Division 17/06/1968 E
D16 Nottingham Division 07/1968 M
65A Eastfield 06/1969 M
64B Haymarket 01/1972 M
65A Eastfield 03/1972 M
Allocation recoded 65A to ED 05/1973 M
Renumbered 27112 02/74 M
Renumbered 27056 10/08/1982 E
Withdrawn 10/02/1987 E

Stored at Eastfield, then moved to Motherwell for further storage until sold to Vic Berry, Leicester for scrap. Moved to Carlisle 02/09/87, Basford Hall 03/09/87, then Humberstone Road, Leicester 04/09/87 and into Berry's Yard 07/09/87, where it remained intact until sold for preservation.

For preservation

Moved to the Northampton & Lamport Railway, Pitsford, also known as the Northampton Steam Railway, on 27/02/88. Whilst continuing to be based at the Northampton & Lamport Railway it has made several visits to the Great Central Railway on loan and is currently to be found there carrying the number 27056; it has also carried D5401 in preservation.

D5402

14A Cricklewood 14/07/1962 E
14B Cricklewood West 09/09/1963 E
Allocation recoded 14A to 14B and renamed Cricklewood West 09/09/1963 E
D14 London (Midland) Division 16/01/1965 E
D01 London Division 17/06/1968 E
65A Eastfield 07/1968 M

The allocation to Eastfield in 06/68 was officially a loan, this being made permanent the following month. 07/1968 M

D5402 contd.

Allocation recoded 65A to ED 05/1973 M
Renumbered 27040 04/1974 M
HA Haymarket 05/1982 M
Withdrawn 27/01/1986 E

Taken to ZH Glasgow Works 01/86, then sold for scrap to Vic Berry, Leicester 12/86. Decision made to cut it up on site at Thornton Junction, so moved there 28/01/87. It was still intact 30/03/87, but was cut up by Berry staff by 11/04/87.

D5403

14A Cricklewood 21/07/1962 E
31B March 08/1963 M
14B Cricklewood West 11/1963 M
D14 London (Midland) Division 16/01/1965 E
D01 London Division 17/06/1968 E
D16 Nottingham Division 07/1968 M
65A Eastfield 02/1969 M
64B Haymarket 12/1970 M
Allocation recoded 64B to HA 05/1973 M
Renumbered 27122 04/1974 M
Renumbered 27204 19/04/1975 E
ED Eastfield 01/1980 M
Renumbered 27058 03/1986 M
Withdrawn 12/05/1986 E

Stored at Grangemouth. Sold for scrap to Vic Berry, Leicester and moved to Mossend yard 03/08/87, to Carlisle 05/08/87, to Basford Hall 07/08/87, then Humberstone Road, Leicester 12/08/87, and shunted into Berry's Yard 17/08/87. Cutting was started immediately, well underway on 23/08/87 and was completed by 04/09/87, except for the cabs which were still there on 02/11/87.

D5404

14A Cricklewood 21/07/1962 E
14B Cricklewood West 09/09/1963 E
Allocation recoded 14A to 14B and renamed Cricklewood West 09/09/1963 E
16C Derby 10/1963 M
14B Cricklewood West 11/1963 M
15A Leicester (Midland) 11/1963 M
D15 Leicester Division 16/01/1965 E
LMML LM Midland Lines 04/1965 M
D16 Nottingham Division 06/1966 M
D14 London (Midland) Division 10/1966 M
D01 London Division 17/06/1968 E
D16 Nottingham Division 07/1968 M
65A Eastfield 02/1969 M
64B Haymarket 03/1971 M
Allocation recoded 64B to HA 05/1973 M

Some Class 27s had an unusual path to the scrap yard in as much as they were sold to Vic Berry of Leicester but were cut up at Thornton Junction. One such was 27027. It was stored in 1982 and withdrawn in June 1983. It then languished at St. Rollox Works until January 1987 when it moved to Thornton Junction but it was another six months before if finally met its end. It is here at St. Rollox in 1983. (*Colour-Rail.com*

D5404 contd.
Renumbered 27113 02/1974 M
Renumbered 27207 25/10/1975 E
ED Eastfield 03/1981 M
Store 02/08/1981 E
Withdrawn 12/05/1986 E
Had been allocated the number 27061 but was withdrawn before the renumbering could take place.
Stored at Eastfield 11/86 and was then taken into Departmental stock as ADB968025.
Renumbered ADB968025 11/86 M
Taken into stock as a training locomotive based at Eastfield and renumbered from 27207 as ADB968025, but erroneously painted as ADB68025, in 11/86.
Withdrawn 08/1987 M
It was moved the short distance from Eastfield to BRML Glasgow Works and was noted being cut up on site by staff working for MC Metal Processing on 05/03/88, the work was completed by 11/03/88.

D5405
14A Cricklewood 28/07/1962 E
14B Cricklewood West 09/09/1963 E
Allocation recoded 14A to 14B and renamed Cricklewood West 09/09/1963 E

D5405 contd.
15A Leicester (Midland) 10/1963 M
D15 Leicester Division 16/01/1965 E
LMML LM Midland Lines 04/1965 M
D16 Nottingham Division 02/1966 M
D14 London (Midland) Division 11/1966 M
D01 London Division 17/06/1968 E
D16 Nottingham Division 07/1968 M
65A Eastfield 03/1969 M
Allocation recoded 65A to ED 05/1973 M
Renumbered 27041 04/1974 M
Store 20/01/1983 E
ED Eastfield 21/04/1983 E
Returned to Service 21/04/1983 E
Withdrawn 12/05/1986 E
Stored at Haymarket until sold to Vic Berry, Leicester. Moved to Humberstone Road, Leicester on 27/07/87 and into Berry's Yard on 03/08/87. Placed in the 'pyramid' by 10/87, remained there until removed 27/03/89; completely broken up by 07/04/89.

D5406
14A Cricklewood 04/08/1962 E
14B Cricklewood West 09/09/1963 E
Allocation recoded 14A to 14B and renamed Cricklewood West 09/09/1963 E
15A Leicester (Midland) 10/1963 M

D5406 contd.
D15 Leicester Division 16/01/1965 E
LMML LM Midland Lines 04/1965 M
D16 Nottingham Division 02/1966 M
D14 London (Midland) Division 06/1968 M
D01 London Division 17/06/1968 E
D16 Nottingham Division 07/1968 M
65A Eastfield 03/1969 M
Allocation recoded 65A to ED 05/1973 M
Renumbered 27042 01/1974 M
HA Haymarket 10/1982 M
IS Inverness 10/1984 M
ED Eastfield 05/1986 M
Store 29/06/1987 E
Withdrawn 06/07/1987 E
Out of use 29/06/87. Stored at Haymarket and sold straight away to Vic Berry, Leicester. Moved to Humberstone Road, Leicester on 27/07/87, into Berry's Yard on 17/08/87 and was being cut up 23/08/87, with completion by 10/11/87.

D5407
14A Cricklewood 04/08/1962 E
14B Cricklewood West 09/09/1963 E
Allocation recoded 14A to 14B and renamed Cricklewood West 09/09/1963 E
15A Leicester (Midland) 11/1963 M
14B Cricklewood West 08/1964 M
D14 London (Midland) Division 16/01/1965 E
LMML LM Midland Lines 02/1968 M
D14 London (Midland) Division 05/1968 M
D01 London Division 17/06/1968 E
65A Eastfield 07/1968 M
64B Haymarket 03/1971 M
Allocation recoded 64B to HA 05/1973 M
Renumbered 27114 01/1974 M
Renumbered 27208 19/12/1975 E
ED Eastfield 01/1980 M
Withdrawn 24/02/1986 E
Had been allocated the number 27062 but was withdrawn before the renumbering could take place.
Withdrawn due to fire damage. Stored at Polmadie. Sold to Vic Berry, Leicester 12/86 for scrap. Remained at Polmadie until moved to Carlisle 01/7/87, to Workington 03/07/87, to Basford Hall 09/07/87 and Humberstone Road, Leicester next day. Taken into Berry's Yard 28/7/87 and was put in the 'pyramid' 10/87, and remained until 04/01/89, when cutting began and was completed by 28/01/89, except for some bits noted 15/03/89.

D5408
14A Cricklewood 18/08/1962 E
14B Cricklewood West 09/09/1963 E
Allocation recoded 14A to 14B and renamed Cricklewood West 09/09/1963 E
D14 London (Midland) Division 16/01/1965 E
LMML LM Midland Lines 02/1968 M
D14 London (Midland) Division 05/1968 M
D01 London Division 17/06/1968 E
D16 Nottingham Division 07/1968 M
65A Eastfield 02/1969 M
64B Haymarket 03/1971 M
Allocation recoded 64B to HA 05/1973 M
Renumbered 27115 09/1974 M
Renumbered 27209 15/02/1975 E
ED Eastfield 01/1980 M
Renumbered 27063 01/09/1982 E
HA Haymarket 10/1982 M
IS Inverness 10/1984 M
ED Eastfield 09/1985 M
Withdrawn 06/07/1987 E
Stored at Motherwell. Sold to Vic Berry, Leicester and moved to Carlisle 09/07/87, Basford Hall 10/07/87, Bescot 14/07/87, Toton, on to Humberstone Road, Leicester on 15/07/87, and into Berry's 05/08/87. Placed in the 'pyramid' 10/87 and remained until taken off 02/89, last noted intact on 04/03/89, but had disappeared completely by 25/03/89. One cab was still intact on 07/05/89, but disposed of shortly afterwards.

D5409
14A Cricklewood 11/08/1962 E
14B Cricklewood West 09/09/1963 E
Allocation recoded 14A to 14B and renamed Cricklewood West 09/09/1963 E
15A Leicester (Midland) 10/1963 M
14B Cricklewood West 06/1964 M
D14 London (Midland) Division 16/01/1965 E
D16 Nottingham Division 01/1968 M
D01 London Division 07/1968 M
D16 Nottingham Division 07/1968 M
65A Eastfield 03/1969 M
64B Haymarket 03/1971 M
Allocation recoded 64B to HA 05/1973 M
Renumbered 27116 03/1973 M
Carried the number 27116 but Scottish Region reported officially renumbered from 5409 to 27210 in 06/74.
Renumbered 27210 06/1974 M
ED Eastfield 01/1980 M
HA Haymarket 10/1982 M

Relatively few Class 27s survived into preservation but 27001 was one of the lucky ones and is at Bo'ness in July 1992. Its original preservation home was the Caledonian Railway at Brechin moving to Bo'ness in 1991. (Colour-Rail.com

D5409 contd.
Renumbered 27064 07/1984 M
ED Eastfield 08/1984 M
IS Inverness 10/1984 M
Withdrawn 12/05/1986 E
Stored at Grangemouth. Sold for scrap to Vic Berry, Leicester, then moved to Mossend yard 03/08/87, on to Carlisle on 05/08/87, to Basford Hall 07/08/87, to Humberstone Road, Leicester 12/08/87, and shunted into Berry's Yard on 17/08/87. Noted being cut up 23/08/87 and completed by 05/09/87, except for the cabs still there 02/11/87.

D5410
14A Cricklewood 01/09/1962 E
14B Cricklewood West 09/09/1963 E
Allocation recoded 14A to 14B and renamed Cricklewood West 09/09/1963 E
D14 London (Midland) Division 16/01/1965 E
D16 Nottingham Division 01/1968 M
65A Eastfield 02/1969 M
64B Haymarket 03/1971 M
65A Eastfield 03/1972 M
Allocation recoded 65A to ED 05/1973 M
Renumbered 27123 01/1974 M

D5410 contd.
Renumbered 27205 14/12/1974 E
Renumbered 27059 25/02/1983 E
Withdrawn 06/07/1987 E
ED Eastfield 07/1987 M
Returned to Service 07/1987 M
Withdrawn 14/07/1987 E
Stored at Eastfield. Moved to Carlisle and on to Basford Hall 21/08/87, then to Crewe DMD and on to Tyseley 27/08/87.
TS Tyseley 09/1987 M
Reinstated 09/1987 M
Withdrawn 19/10/1987 E

For preservation
Stored at Tyseley until sold for preservation to Sandwell District Council. It was moved to Leicester 15/06/88, and to Vic Berry, Leicester the next day for asbestos removal. Upon completion it moved from Berry's Yard to Humberstone Road, Leicester and on to Toton 25/10/88, to Bescot 26/10/88, and then to Birmingham Railway Museum, Tyseley the same afternoon for safekeeping. Moved to the Severn Valley Railway about 06/91 and is painted as D5410.
HQ Headquarters Pool 12/11/2015 E

D5410 contd.

Reregistered 12/11/15 to allow for movement to galas by rail.

Moved to East Somerset Railway for repairs 22/02/16, left there 22/03/18 arriving at Tyseley 03/04/18. After an intermediate stop at Goodman's Yard, Wishaw, awaiting for space at Leicester depot, moved by road to Knighton Sidings, Leicester 08/05/18 and then by rail to Leicester depot 05/08/18 where it is being restored, photographed looking externally complete and in undercoat in 07/23.

D5411

14A Cricklewood 08/09/1962 E
14B Cricklewood West 09/09/1963 E
Allocation recoded 14A to 14B and renamed Cricklewood West 09/09/1963 E
15A Leicester (Midland) 10/1963 M
D15 Leicester Division 16/01/1965 E
LMML LM Midland Lines 04/1965 M
D16 Nottingham Division 02/1966 M
65A Eastfield 02/1969 M
64B Haymarket 12/1970 M
Allocation recoded 64B to HA 05/1973 M
Renumbered 27117 03/1974 M
Renumbered 27211 16/03/1976 E
ED Eastfield 01/1980 M
Store 01/1982 M
ED Eastfield 01/1982 M
Returned to Service 01/1982 M
HA Haymarket 10/1982 M
IS Inverness 10/1984 M
Renumbered 27065 02/1985 M
ED Eastfield 02/1985 M
Withdrawn 12/05/1986 E

Stored at Ayr depot, then to Falkland Junction, Ayr 03/87 for further storage. Sold for scrap to Vic Berry, Leicester and moved to Carlisle 27/07/87, Basford Hall 29/07/87, then to Humberstone Road, Leicester on 30/07/87 and moved into Berry's Yard 03/08/87. Was in process of scrapping on 23/08/87 and completed by 08/09/87.

D5412

14A Cricklewood 08/09/1962 E
14B Cricklewood West 09/09/1963 E
Allocation recoded 14A to 14B and renamed Cricklewood West 09/09/1963 E
15A Leicester (Midland) 10/1963 M
D15 Leicester Division 16/01/1965 E
LMML LM Midland Lines 04/1965 M

D5412 contd.

D16 Nottingham Division 02/1966 M
D14 London (Midland) Division 11/1966 M
LMML LM Midland Lines 11/1967 M
D16 Nottingham Division 05/1968 M
65A Eastfield 02/1969 M
64B Haymarket 03/1971 M
65A Eastfield 03/1972 M
Allocation recoded 65A to ED 05/1973 M
HA Haymarket 08/1973 M
ED Eastfield 12/1973 M
Renumbered 27124 04/1974 M
Renumbered 27206 20/07/1974 E
Store 03/1986 M
Withdrawn 23/03/1986 E

Had been allocated the number 27060 but was withdrawn before the renumbering could take place.

Withdrawn due to fire damage. Stored at ZH Glasgow Works, then moved to Smithy Lye sidings, Glasgow 12/86 for further storage. Sold to Vic Berry, Leicester for scrap about 04/87. Moved to Polmadie 08/87, then to Carlisle 04/09/87, Basford Hall 07/09/87, Humberstone Road, Leicester 17/09/87 and into Berry's Yard 21/09/87. It was broken up by 04/10/87, except the cabs still extant on 02/11/87.

D5413

14A Cricklewood 15/09/1962 E
14B Cricklewood West 09/09/1963 E
Allocation recoded 14A to 14B and renamed Cricklewood West 09/09/1963 E
15A Leicester (Midland) 11/1963 M
D15 Leicester Division 16/01/1965 E
LMML LM Midland Lines 04/1965 M
D16 Nottingham Division 17/06/1968 E
65A Eastfield 03/1969 M
64B Haymarket 10/1970 M
Allocation recoded 64B to HA 05/1973 M
Renumbered 27118 11/1973 M
Renumbered 27103 19/04/1975 E
ED Eastfield 04/1975 M
HA Haymarket 11/1975 M
ED Eastfield 01/1980 M

Moved to Glasgow Works with fire damage 10/83 but not officially stored, returned to service 07/84.

Renumbered 27047 08/1985 M
IS Inverness 10/1985 M
Store 28/04/1986 E

D5413 contd.
Stored 28/04/86 having failed at Plumpton, near Penrith.
Withdrawn 12/05/1986 E
Stored at Ayr depot, then moved to Falkland Junction, Ayr by 03/87 for further storage. Sold to Vic Berry, Leicester 04/87, moved to Carlisle 27/07/87, then Crewe Basford Hall 29/07/87, Humberstone Road, Leicester 30/07/87 and into Berry's Yard 03/08/87. Cutting commenced 22/09/87 and was completed by 25/09/87.

D5414
14A Cricklewood 22/09/1962 E
14B Cricklewood West 09/09/1963 E
Allocation recoded 14A to 14B and renamed Cricklewood West 09/09/1963 E
15A Leicester (Midland) 11/1963 M
D15 Leicester Division 16/01/1965 E
12A Kingmoor 02/1965 M
D15 Leicester Division 06/1965 M
LMML LM Midland Lines 01/1966 M
D16 Nottingham Division 17/06/1968 E
65A Eastfield 08/1968 M
Allocation recoded 65A to ED 05/1973 M
Renumbered 27043 04/1974 M
Withdrawn 21/04/1980 E
Withdrawn due to fire damage. Moved to ZH Glasgow Works 05/80 for store, then to Eastfield 11/80 for further storage where it

D5414 contd.
was used infrequently for rerailing exercises. It was lifted off its bogies in late 08/85 and placed on the ground.
On 12/11/85 the shell was collected by road transport and taken to Patterson's Tip, near Mount Vernon, Glasgow and tipped into a big pit, after being covered in a big 'plastic bag' due to contamination with blue asbestos. It was not cut up.

D5415
14A Cricklewood 06/10/1962 E
14B Cricklewood West 09/09/1963 E
Allocation recoded 14A to 14B and renamed Cricklewood West 09/09/1963 E
D14 London (Midland) Division 16/01/1965 E
LMML LM Midland Lines 01/1966 M
D16 Nottingham Division 17/06/1968 E
65A Eastfield 07/1968 M
64B Haymarket 02/1971 M
65A Eastfield 09/1971 M
Allocation recoded 65A to ED 05/1973 M
Renumbered 27044 04/1974 M
Store 07/1980 M
Withdrawn 14/07/1980 E
Withdrawn due to fire damage. Stored at Eastfield 07/80, then moved to ZH Glasgow Works by 27/06/81 and was dismantled by 03/82. The cabs were still at Glasgow Works in 10/86, they were later moved to Vic Berry, Leicester and noted there 02/11/87.

D5401's first home was the Northampton & Lamport Railway but subsequently moved to the Great Central Railway. Like many of the preserved diesels it has been loaned to various lines for gala appearances and in May 2011 was at the Severn Valley Railway. (*Paul Chancellor/Colour-Rail.com*

NAMES CARRIED WHILST IN British Railways use (SUMMARY) For details see Individual Locomotive Records.

Class 24

(D5061, 24061, RDB968007, TDB968007)

97201	*Experiment* 06/80 to date unknown.

Class 25

(D5184) 25034	*Castell Aberystwyth/Aberystwyth Castle* sometime between mid-1985 and the end of 1986.
(D5185) 25035	*Castell Dinas Bran* - date unknown but post 01/81.
(D5208) 25058	*Castell Criccieth/Criccieth Castle*, date unknown but probably in late 1985 or early 1986.
(D5259) 25109	*Castell Trefaldwyn/Montgomery Castle* -date not recorded but post 1982.
(D7507) 25157	*City of Stoke-on-Trent*, date unknown but thought to be between 07/80 and 10/82.
(D7551) 25201	*Castell-y-Bere* date unknown but probably in mid-1986.
(D7615) 25265	*Castell Harlech/Harlech Castle* date unknown but possibly in 1985.
(D7628) 25278	*Castell Powys/Powis Castle*, date u/k but probably after 03/86.
(D7655, 25305) 97251	*ETHEL 2.*
(D7660, 25310, ADB97250) 97250	*ETHEL 1.*
(D7663) 25313	*Chirk Castle/ Castell - y - Waun* in 1986.
(D7664, 25314) 97252	*ETHEL 3.*
(D7672) 25322, 25912	*Tamworth Castle* 12/05/84.

Class 26

(D5301) 26001	*Eastfield* 26/07/91

Class 27

(5394, 27106) 27050	*Meld*, 1986, exact date unknown.

Speed restriction and weight as painted on the cabside of 97252.
(D. Stocker/Colour-Rail.com

The data panel applied to Class 27 27045.
(D. Stocker/Colour-Rail.com

RENUMBERING SUMMARY

Class 24

24001-24004 previously D5001-D5004
24005 - D5000 (D5005 having been withdrawn before TOPS numbers were allocated).
24006-24150 — previously D5006-D5150
Note: Not all locomotives were renumbered into the TOPS series.
24054 also carried TDB968008.
24061 also carried TDB968007, RDB 968007 and 97201.
24142 also carried TDB968009.

Class 25

25001-25149 previously D5151-D5299
25200-25327 previously D7500-D7677
Later renumbering:
(25131) 97202
(25262) 25901
(25268) 25902
(25276) 25903
(25283) 25904
(25286) 25905
(25296) 25906
(25297) 25907
(25307) 25908
(25309) 25909
(25315) 25910
(25316) 25911
(25322) 25912

(25305) 97251
(25310) ADB97250, 97250
(25314) 97252

Class 26

D5300 became 26007
D5301-D5306 to 26001-26006
D5307 became 26020
D5308-D5319 to 26008-26019
D5320 became 26028
D5321-D5327 to 26021-26027
D5328 did not receive a TOPS number
D5329-D5346 to 26029-26046.

Class 27

D5347-D5373 to 27001 27027*
*(D5370 then 27024) ADB968028
(D5374) 27101, then 27045
(D5375) 27028
(D5376) 27029
(D5377) 27030
(D5378) 27031
(D5379) 27032
(D5380) 27102, then 27046
(D5381) 27033
(D5382) 27034
D5383 did not receive a TOPS number
(D5384) 27035
(D5385) 27036
(D5386) 27103, then 27212, then 27066
(D5387) 27104, then 27048
(D5388) 27105, then 27049
(D5389) 27037
(D5390) 27038
(D5391) 27119, then 27201
(D5392) 27120, then 27202
(D5393) 27121, then 27203
(D5394) 27106, then 27050
(D5395) 27107, then 27051
(D5396) 27108, then 27052
(D5397) 27109, then 27053
(D5398) 27039
(D5399) 27110, then 27054
(D5400) 27111, then 27055
(D5401) 27112, then 27056
(D5402) 27040
(D5403) 27122, then 27204 then 27058
(D5404) 27113, then 27207 then ADB968025
(D5405) 27041
(D5406) 27042
(D5407) 27114, then 27208
(D5408) 27115, then 27209, then 27063
(D5409) 27116, then 27210, then 27064
(D5410) 27123, then 27205, then 27059
(D5411) 27117, then 27211, then 27065
(D5412) 27124, then 27206
(D5413) 27118, then 27103, then 27047.
(D5414) 27043
(D5415) 27044.

SPECIMEN ALLOCATIONS

Class 24

January 1965

Camden	D5004/7/9/15/6/8-23/6, D5140/1
Crewe North	D5008/9/12/7/82/3, D5133/44/5
Cricklewood West	D5084-6/8
Finsbury Park	D5050-72/94/5
Gateshead	D5097, D5101-13/47-50
Ipswich	D5036-49
Inverness	D5114-32
London Midland Lines	D5084-6/8
Longsight	D5014, D5135-9/42/6
Rugby	D5002/3/5/6/9-13, D5134/44/5
Willesden	D5000/1/4/7/20/1/3-5/7-35/73-81/7/9-93, D5143
York	D5096/8/9, D5100

January 1975

Crewe Diesel	24026/9-42/4-50/2-64/74-87/9/91/2, 24133-7/40-6
Eastfield	24001-7/9-19/73/90/6-9, 24100/1/5-10/47/8/50
Haymarket	24065/6/9-72/94/5
Inverness	24102-4/11-3/5-21/23-30/2
Longsight	24001/4/5/20-7/9
Store	24008

Class 25

January 1965

Note: this month coincided with the start of 'Division' allocations on the LMR so many locomotives appear twice in this listing.

Burton	D7500-5
Coalville	D5249
Cricklewood Division	D5214-22/42/6/81/4-8/90-3
Cricklewood West	D5184/5, D5204/6/8-23/7-30/42/6/81/4-8/90/1-3, D7568/9/72-5
Derby	D5188-90/3/6, D5201/5/7/56/9/60/5/6/8/80, D7571/6-8/81/3/5/94/6
Gateshead	D5177-82
Leicester	D5186/91/2/4/8, D5225/49/89, D7579/84/8/9/92-5
Leicester Division	D5289
LM Main Line	D5184-94/8/9, D5200/1/3-13/23-31/5/43-5/8/51/4, D7568/9/72-6/80/4/9-93/5/7
Nottingham	D5187/95/9, D5201-3/24/31/5/7/52/3/8/82/3/94-8, D7511/80/90/1/7
Nottingham Division	D5195/6, D5202/37-41/7/50/2/3/5-73/80/2/3/94-8, D7500-27/71/7/8/81/3/5/6/94/6
Saltley	D5183/97, D5226/32/3/4/6, D7570/82/7
Thornaby	D5151-75
Toton	D5238-41/3-5/7/8/50/1/4/5/7/61-4/7/9-73, D7506-10/2-22
Trafford Park	D5274-9, D7586
York	D5176

January 1975

Bath Road	25052/9/63/77/80, 25152/3/5/6, 25220/7
Bescot	25038-40/96, 25105-7/42/3/5/87/825206/7/51-3/6/9-63/71-3/6/7/80/1, 25302/5/25
Cardiff Canton	25029-32, 25154/7-72
Cricklewood East	25065-7/70, 25243/50/95, 25313/4/6

Eastfield	25001
Haymarket	25006-8/11/28, 25215-7/26/8-34/7/40/1/6
Kingmoor	25041/2, 25146/9/84/90/1/6-9, 25200-4/49, 25320-2
Laira	25219/23-5/38/74/5, 25306/7/26/7
Longsight	25027/43/7-51/3-6/8/60-2/82/6/8/97, 25119/41/4/7/8/89/94/5, 25208/9/35/9/42/4/57/90, 25303/4
Springs Branch	25036/44/5/56-8/93/4, 25103/9-14/38-40/86/92/3/7, 25205/32-4/47-9/66/78/9/82-94/6/8, 25300/1/8/17-9/23
Tinsley	25002-5/9/10/2-26/33-5/64/78/9/83-5/9-92, 25101/4-8/50/1, 25213, 25302
Toton	25037/46/65/73-6/81/7/95/8/9, 25100/2/15-8/20-7/9-37/85, 25210-2/4/8/45/54/8/64/7-70/99
Willesden	25068-72, 25173-83, 25221/2/36/65, 25309-12/5/24

January 1985

Bescot	25034/48/51/8/95, 25145/54, 25205/9/11/69/76/82, 25313/22/5
Crewe Diesel	25032/5/7/42/54/9/60/4/72/8/80/9, 25119/73/5/6/8/81/2/9/90/2/4/5, 25206/10/2/24/6/9-31/4/5/7/44/5/9/51/4/6/7/9/65/6/8/79/83-8/96-8, 25300/2/3/6/23/6
Kingmoor	25044, 25191/6/8/9, 25200-3/62/78, 25307/9/11/5
Longsight	25057, 25316/21/4

Class 26

January 1965

Haymarket	D5300-17
Inverness	D5318-46

January 1975

Haymarket	26001-26/8
Inverness	26027/9-46

January 1985

Haymarket	26001-8/10/1/4/5/20/1/3-5/7/9/36/7/9/46
Inverness	26008/26/9/31/2/4-6/8/40-3

Class 27

January 1965

Cricklewood West	D5389/91/2/6/8/9, D5400-3/7-10/5
Eastfield	D5347-69
Leicester Midland	D5386-8/90/2-7, D5404-6/11-4
Leicester Division	D5386/8/90-5/7, D5404-6/11-4
LM (Midland Division)	D5389/96-9, D5400-3/7-10/5
Midland Main Line	D5387
Thornaby	D5370-8

January 1975

Eastfield	27001-32/9-44, 27106-12, 27205/6
Haymarket	27101/13/4/7/8/22, 27201-3/10

January 1985

Eastfield	27001/2/22-6/30/8/41/5/6/8/54-6/9/66, 27103, 27204/6/8
Haymarket	27004/10/2/7/8/33/6/40
Inverness	27003/5/7/8/14/20/1/9/32/7/42/9-53/63/4, 27211.

THE DIGITAL ARCHIVE

The Railway Correspondence & Travel Society (RCTS) has been publishing definitive locomotive histories, stock books and the like since 1935. As most of them are out-of-print, the Society has decided to reimagine them for the digital age.

The RCTS Digital Archive seeks to republish the content to suit different types of users, wherever they may be and whatever digital device they may use. It is possible to buy some of the material in traditional book form but the archive is mainly designed to support online reading and downloading. All items are also available as a download subject to a fee in some cases.

The RCTS Digital Archive is available to registered users. Registration is free.
Please sign in each time to view the collections.

Visit rcts.org.uk to view and register

SCOPE OF ARCHIVE

The archive was launched in September 2022. The initial scope was:

Locomotives of the LNER – Originally a 19-part series printed in 1963-94. Now available as eight digital book-style versions

The Railway Observer – The Society's monthly magazine, 1,004 editions continuous from 1928 to 2011.

All copies are available as single items, or can be purchased by a year's volumes or by decades.

Added in September 2023 were:

Locomotives of the GWR – Originally in 14-parts published during 1951-93. Now available as three digital book style versions.

Locomotives of the SR/L&SWR/LB&SCR – 11 parts published during 1965-76. Now available as four digital book style versions.

Locomotive stock books – Printed at intervals from 1934 to 1983.

Coaching stock books – Bi-annual publication from 1974-82.

October 2024 saw the addition of the remaining back catalogue, including:

Locomotives of the LMS – These are digital scans of hardback books that are currently out-of-print.

Locomotives of the Great Northern – Four Volumes published from1986 to 1992.

There are also digital copies of individual locomotive histories, locality reports and traffic surveys available for online reading or to download.

Visit rcts.org.uk

RCTS
THE RAILWAY CORRESPONDENCE AND TRAVEL SOCIETY

Founded in 1928 the RCTS is Britain's largest Railway Society, still, after more than 90 years, taking a leading role for all those interested in all aspects of the railways past, present and future.

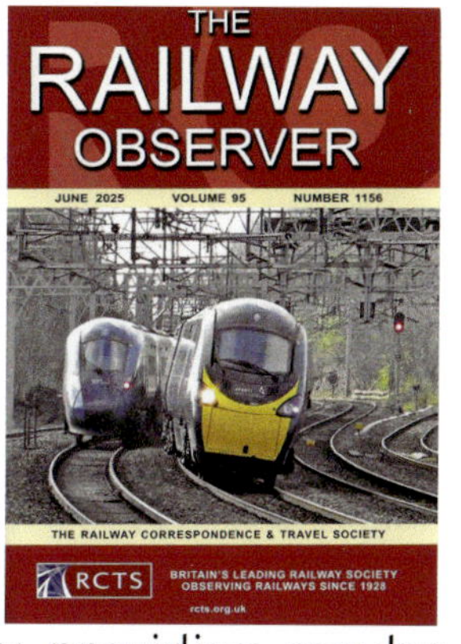

The monthly magazine *The Railway Observer*, published continuously since 1928, is available to all members, either in print or electronic format. Now with a larger page size, larger pictures and an increased text size the *RO* retains 72 pages of the latest news and photographs, balanced with a mix of nostalgia.

The Society has 28 branches throughout the country providing regular meetings, where speakers, many railway professionals, offer quality presentations on a host of railway subjects, both current and historic. These gatherings also provide an opportunity to meet like-minded people, chat, and share experiences. Many branches sell new and secondhand books and photographs.

A RAILWAY JOURNEY ACROSS SOUTH WALES DURING THE LATE 1950s and 1960s

By MICHAEL CLEMENS

RCTS PUBLICATIONS

The Society publishes books on various railway themes and these are available to members at a discounted rate. An Archive and Library in the former station master's house at Leatherhead station in Surrey, provides facilities packed with an extensive range of books, magazines, working timetables and much more of railway interest. The Society has an extensive photographic archive containing many thousands of images, available to purchase as downloads or prints.

The Society has also developed a Digital Archive that contains mainly historical items and reports, including those of the back catalogue of all RCTS publications and all editions of the society magazine plus many items from the Society Library archive. All these are available to read and to carry out research. Discounts are available to members at some UK Railway Heritage sites.

These are some of the benefits of becoming a member of the RCTS.
Visit rcts.org.uk

CURRENT TITLES IN OUR CATALOGUE AS AT AUGUST 2025

Locomotives of the LMS		
Raising Steam on the LMS	978-0-901115-85-0	6.50
L&NWR Locomotive Names	978-0-901115-90-4	8.00
The Stanier Class Five 4-6-0s Volume 1	978-0-901115-98-0	20.00
The Stanier Class Five 4-6-0s Volume 2	978-0-901115-99-7	20.00
Both Vol.1 and Vol.2 available as a bundle		30.00
The Stanier Pacifics (reprint)	978-0-9934908-0-4	22.50
The Patriot 4-6-0s	978-0-9934908-1-1	20.00
Both Patriot and Pacific books as a bundle		30.00
The Royal Scot 4-6-0s	978-0-9934908-7-3	29.50
Non Series Books		
Plymouth's Railways	978-0-901115-91-1	5.00
THE JOURNEY	978-0-9934908-2-8	10.00
Brush Diesel & Electric Locomotives 1980-2020	978-0-9934908-3-5	20.00
Michael Mensing – Railway Photographer Vol.1	978-0-9934908-4-2	17.50
A Photographic Journey from 1980 to 2020	978-0-9934908-8-0	19.95
An Illustrated History of first generation DMUs	978-1-7391324-0-8	25.00
Michael Mensing – Railway Photographer Vol.2	978-1-7391324-4-6	25.00
Both Mensing 1 and Mensing 2 books as a bundle		30.00
The GWR King Class 4-6-0s	978-1-7391324-3-9	25.00
Observing the Railway in 2022	978-0-9934908-9-7	25.00
Observing the Railway in 2023	978-1-7391324-1-5	25.00
Both OTR 22 and OTR 23 books as a bundle		30.00
LNER Investment during the Inter-War Years	978-1-7391324-2-2	20.00
A Railway Journey around the Cotswold and Malvern Hills	978-1-7391324-5-3	25.00
Modern Traction Loco Data — Brush Type 2s	978-1-7391324-6-0	15.00
A Railway Journey across South Wales during the late 1950s and 1960s	978-1-7391324-7-7	25.00
Observing the Railway in 2024	978-1-7391324-9-1	20.00
The Railways of Northern England and Scotland	978-1-0683883-0-9	25.00
BR Diesel and Gas Turbine Prototypes	978-1-7391324-8-4	25.00

Purchase via our website rcts.org.uk or alternatively by post from
RCTS Sales, 16 Welby Close, Maidenhead SL6 3PY
Cheques payable to RAILWAY CORRESPONDENCE & TRAVEL SOCIETY
For all orders please add £4.00 P/P.

Join our mailing list to hear about each new title when it is published - just e-mail publications at rcts.org.uk to be added to our list.